# Naval Le.......
# the Atlantic World:
# The Age of Reform and
# Revolution, 1700–1850

Edited by
Richard Harding and Agustín Guimerá

UNIVERSITY OF WESTMINSTER PRESS

Published by
University of Westminster Press
101 Cavendish Street
London W1W 6XH
www.uwestminsterpress.co.uk

First published 2017

Cover design by Diana Jarvis
Cover image *Anne S.K. Brown Military Collection,
Brown University Library, USA*

Printed in the UK by Lightning Source Ltd.
Print and digital versions typeset by Siliconchips Services Ltd.

ISBN (Hardback): 978-1-911534-08-2
ISBN (Paperback): 978-1-911534-76-1
ISBN (PDF): 978-1-911534-09-9
ISBN (EPUB): 978-1-911534-10-5
ISBN (Mobi/Kindle): 978-1-911534-11-2
DOI: https://doi.org/10.16997/book2

The full text of this book has been peer-reviewed to ensure high academic standards. For full review policies, see http://www.uwestminsterpress.co.uk/site/publish/

Suggested citation:
Harding, R. and Guimerá, A. 2017. *Naval Leadership in the Atlantic World: The Age of Reform and Revolution, 1700–1850*. London: University of Westminster Press. DOI: https://doi.org/10.16997/book2. License: CC-BY 4.0

To read the free, open access version of this book online, visit https://doi.org/10.16997/book2 or scan this QR code with your mobile device:

*Dedicated to the memory of Professor Colin White (1951–2008),*
*Director of the Royal Navy Museum Portsmouth (2006–08):*
*a scholar and great enthusiast in the study of naval leadership*

# Naval Leadership in the Atlantic World: The Age of Revolution and Reform, 1700–1850

Richard Harding and Agustín Guimerá (editors)

# Contents

# Foreword

## Vice-Admiral Sir Adrian Johns KCB CBE DL

Second Sea Lord and Commander-in-Chief Naval Home Command (2005–8)
Governor and Commander-in-Chief Gibraltar (2009–13)
President of the Navy Records Society

I recall only too well the impact of the Practical Leadership Tests we suffered as young officers at Dartmouth. We thought then that leadership was all about self-projection, generating a sense of urgency and taking care of the team. But we soon learned that real leadership came into play when things went wrong. How many times do we hear today that failure is the result of a lack of leadership? Often perhaps, but that may be a simplistic conclusion and there are two truisms worth bearing in mind: no plan survives first contact with the enemy; and everything in war is simple but the simplest things are often the most difficult to achieve.

This collection of essays sprang out of a conference held at the National Museum of the Royal Navy in 2011 and provides an illuminating insight into naval leadership during a period of significant historical turbulence. Those in command at sea at that time enjoyed very limited communications and intelligence that often extended not much further than the visual horizon. Leaders had to rely on their own raw initiative and judgement in a very different way from today's commanders in this globally networked world.

But while in practical terms leadership may be exercised rather differently today, the insights offered in these essays point to enduring themes and a better understanding of a complex subject.

I am delighted that this collection is dedicated to the memory of Professor Colin White, sadly departed but an old friend and an inspiring naval historian. He would have approved!

# Contributors

**Dr Carlos Alfaro Zaforteza** (King's College, London) is a visiting research fellow at the Department of War Studies. He completed his PhD thesis there in 2011, on Sea Power, State and Society in Liberal Spain, 1833–1868. He has published on Spanish naval history in American, British and Spanish scholarly journals and edited books. He is also co-author of the book *European Navies and the Conduct of War* (Routledge, forthcoming).

**Professor Olivier Chaline** (Université de Sorbonne, Paris IV) is a French modernist historian. He has held professorships at the University of Rennes II (1999–2001) and the University of Paris IV (Paris-Sorbonne), a post he has held since 2001. He is Director of the Centre for Maritime Archaeology and Historical Research and Head of the international research program about Admiral de Grasse's fleet.

**Dr Michael Duffy** (University of Exeter) has retired from his positions as Head of History and Director of the Centre for Maritime Studies at Exeter University but remains a University Fellow and is presently Vice-President of the Navy Records Society. He was the Editor of *The Mariner's Mirror: The Journal of the Society for Nautical Research* throughout the 1990s. His books on naval subjects include *The Military Revolution and the State 1500–1800* (1980), *Soldiers, Sugar and Seapower* (1987), *Parameters of British Naval Power 1650–1850* (1992), *The New Maritime History of Devon* (1992, 1994) edited with S. Fisher, B. Greenhill, D. Starkey and J. Youings, *The Glorious First of June: A Naval Battle and its*

*Aftermath* (2003) edited with R. Morriss, *Touch and Take: The Battle of Trafalgar* (2005) and, with R. Mackay, *Hawke, Nelson and British Naval Leadership in the Age of Sail 1747–1805* (2009).

**Dr Agustín Guimerá** (Instituto de Historia, Consejo Superior de Investigaciones Científicas, Madrid) is the author of numerous studies of comparative naval leadership, including: 'Métodos de liderazgo naval en una época revolucionaria: Mazarredo y Jervis (1779–1808)', in Manuel Reyes García-Hurtado, Domingo L. González-Lopo and Enrique Martínez-Rodríguez, eds., *El mar en los siglos modernos* (Santiago de Compostela: Xunta de Galicia, 2009), vol. 2, 221–33; Agustín Guimerá and José María Blanco Núñez, eds., *Guerra naval en la Revolución y el Imperio* (Madrid: Marcial Pons Historia, 2008); Agustín Guimerá and Víctor Peralta, *El Equilibrio de los Imperios: de Utrecht a Trafalgar* (Madrid: FEHM, 2005).

**Professor Richard Harding** (University of Westminster) is Professor of Organisational History and Head of the Department of Leadership and Professional Development at the University of Westminster. His recent works include *Modern Naval History: Debates and Prospects* (London: Bloomsbury Press, 2015); *The Emergence of Britain's Global Naval Supremacy: The War of 1739–1748* (Woodbridge: Boydell Press, 2010), *Naval Leadership and Management, 1650–1950* (Boydell Press, 2012) (edited with Helen Doe), *A Great and Glorious Victory: New Perspectives on the Battle of Trafalgar* (Barnsley: Seaforth Publishing, 2008).

**Professor Andrew Lambert** (King's College, London) is Laughton Professor of Naval History in the Department of War Studies at King's College, London, and Director of the Laughton Naval History unit housed in the department. His work focuses on the naval and strategic history of the British Empire between the Napoleonic Wars and the First World War. His books include: *The Crimean War: British Grand Strategy against Russia 1853–1856* (Manchester: 1990), *'The Foundations of Naval History': Sir John Laughton, the Royal Navy and the Historical Profession* (London: 1997), *Nelson: Britannia's God of War* (London: 2004), *Admirals* (London: 2008), *Franklin: Tragic Hero of Polar Navigation* (London: 2009) and *The Challenge: Britain versus America in the Naval War of 1812* (London: 2012), which won the Anderson Medal of the Society for Nautical Research for the best maritime history book of that year.

**Contre-Amiral Rémi Monaque** (Marine française) is a rear Admiral (retired) of the French navy. Since 1992, he has devoted all his time to naval history research. His main books are: *Latouche-Tréville, l'amiral qui défiait Nelson*, *Trafalgar*, *Suffren, un destin inachevé* and, recently published, *Une histoire de la marine de guerre française*. He published several articles in *The Mariner's*

*Mirror* and was a co-author of *The Trafalgar Companion* published by Alexander Stilwell in 2005.

**Dr. Agustín Ramón Rodríguez González** is a member of the Real Academia de la Historia, Madrid,  Spain. His works on the eighteenth-century Spanish navy include 'Los españoles en Trafalgar: Navíos, cañones, hombres y una alianza problemática', in Agustín Guimerá, Alberto Ramos and Gonzalo Butrón, eds., *Trafalgar y el mundo atlántico* (Madrid: Marcial Pons Historia, 2004); *Trafalgar y el conflicto naval anglo-español del siglo XVIII* (San Sebastián de los Reyes: Actas, 2005); 'Las innovaciones artilleras y tácticas españolas en la campaña de Trafalgar,' in *XXXI Congreso Internacional de Historia Militar (Madrid, 21–27 Agosto 2005)* (Madrid: Ministerio de Defensa, 2006); *Victorias por mar de los españoles* (Madrid: Grafite Ediciones, 2006); 'Cádiz en la estrategia naval de la Guerra de la Independencia, 1808–1814', in Agustín Guimerá and José M. Blanco (coords.), *Guerra naval en la Revolución y el Imperio: Bloqueos y operaciones anfibias, 1793–1815* (Madrid: Marcial Pons Historia, 2008); 'La Marina Ilustrada: Reflexiones sobre su eficacia combativa', in Manuel R. García-Hurtado, ed., *La Armada española en el siglo XVIII. Ciencia, hombres y barcos* (Madrid: Sílex, 2012); 'Les objectifs de la marine espagnole,' in Olivier Chaline, Philippe Bonnichon and Charles-Philippe de Vergennes (dir.), *Les marines de la Guerre d'Independance américaine (1763–1783). I. L'instrument naval* (Paris: PUF, 2013).

**Dr Catherine Scheybeler** worked at the travel and exploration department of Bernard Quaritch, Antiquarian Booksellers, Ltd., from 2005 to 2009. For two of these years she studied for an MA in the History of Warfare at the War Studies Department of King's College, London, passing with a distinction before continuing on to complete a full-time PhD in War Studies in 2014. Her thesis was on Spanish naval policy during the reign of Ferdinand VI (1746–59). Since her PhD, Catherine has written *Africana: A Distant Journey into Unknown Lands. The Paolo Bianchi Collection of Works on the Exploration of Africa up to the Year 1900* (Shapero, 2014).

**Professor Simon Surreaux** (Centre Roland Mousnier), *agrégé de l'Université*, PhD in History, researcher associated with the Centre Roland Mousnier (Paris-Sorbonne University), has taught in Paris IV-Sorbonne University and Charles De Gaulle-Lille 3. Since September 2014, he has been Professor in preparatory classes to business schools in France, in Lyon and Saint-Etienne. Besides many articles on the place and role of the marshals of France of the Enlightenment in the cultural, political, diplomatic and military domains, he participated, supervised by Professor Lucien Bély, in the *Dictionary Louis XIV* (Paris: Robert Laffont, 2015). He published in particular: *Les maréchaux de France des  Lumières. Histoire et dictionnaire d'une élite militaire sous l'Ancien*

*Régime* (Paris: SPM-L'Harmattan, 2013). *'Aimez-moi autant que je vous aime'.* *Correspondance de la duchesse de Fitz-James 1757–1771* (Paris: Vendémiaire, 2013). His PhD thesis, defended at Paris-Sorbonne University in 2011 on *Les maréchaux de France au XVIIIe siècle. Histoire sociale, politique et culturelle d'une élite militaire,* received the Daniel and Michel Dezés of the Fondation de France prize in March 2012. His research interests are political and institutional, military and naval, diplomatic and cultural history in the seventeenth and eighteenth centuries.

PART ONE

# Naval Leadership:
# A Voyage of Discovery

# Naval Leadership in the Age of Reform and Revolution, 1700–1850

Richard Harding* and Agustín Guimerá[†]

*University of Westminster

[†]Instituto de Historia, Consejo Superior de Investigaciones Científicas, Madrid

In 1995 Rear Admiral James Goldrick called for historians of modern navies to analyse 'much more comprehensively the multitude of technological, financial and operational issues involved in decision-making for naval development'. In doing so he called for these historians to replicate the technical mastery of the subject that he felt 'has hitherto largely been confined to students of the age of sail'.[1] While this reflected the relative interest in the context of naval decision-making displayed by historians of different periods, there was one aspect in which the level of mastery was possibly reversed – that of naval leadership.

Today, leadership is one of the most contested aspects of organisational behaviour and analysis. It is a subject of intense study for psychologists, sociologists, anthropologists, political scientists and, to a lesser degree, historians. The academic discussions concerning definitions, sources of leadership power, its distribution and its meaning resonate far beyond these disciplines into cultural studies, other social discourses and the wider public domains of policy, politics, business and entertainment.[2]

---

**How to cite this book chapter:**
Harding, R and Guimerá, A. 2017. Introduction: Naval Leadership in the Age of Reform and Revolution, 1700–1850. In: Harding, R and Guimerá, A (eds.). *Naval Leadership in the Atlantic World*. Pp. 3–7. London: University of Westminster Press. DOI: https://doi.org/10.16997/book2.a. License: CC-BY-NC-ND 4.0

Whether it is ethics, organisational efficiency and effectiveness, international relations or general social relations, the word 'leadership' is seldom far from the centre of the debate. Better, more effective, more authentic leadership is almost always presented as at least part of the answer to the problems posed. For individuals, personal development often has the sub-text of becoming leaders in one shape or another. Lack of leadership is presented as the contemporary problem, becoming a leader is the driving ambition for right-minded people and good leadership is the panacea. The process by which this term has become so embedded in Western social relations is far from being understood. Even the first steps towards this understanding are faltering in as much as the definition of leadership mutates in different contexts and societies. Like so many other terms that underpin modern social discourses, the meaning of leadership and its practice runs a gamut of interpretation, from those who insist it is a special form of activity that can only be understood by highly trained or encultured specialists to those who see its performance as little more than everyday activity in particular circumstances.[3]

Military organisations are far from immune from this contemporary concern. Indeed, the reverse might be true – they are particularly enthralled with understanding the concept. The quality of leadership lies at the heart of their perceptions of success and failure, organisational design and the real, lived experience of the members of those forces. Challenges from the battlefield to the budget settlements have implications for the practice and theory of leadership. Thus, for the general public and military organisations there is no lack of advice or publications on the theme.

Historians have contributed their share to the outpouring of work on leadership, and naval historians have never lagged behind. In 2005, the bicentenary of the Battle of Trafalgar was commemorated in Britain in a public manner which no individual battle (except, perhaps, the Battle of Britain in 1940) has known in the last fifty years. Central to this was the figure of Horatio Lord Nelson (1758–1805), the great hero-leader who died at the moment of his greatest victory, which, in the public's imagination at least, saved Britain from imminent invasion by the French Emperor Napoleon. The bicentenary provided the occasion to burst many myths, including that of imminent invasion. Equally important was the chance to review the leadership of the nations and fleets that were involved in the battle. The essays, books and conference proceedings that emerged from that commemoration did a great deal to cause historians to rethink the idea of leadership in the early nineteenth-century navies. What became obvious was that far from the last word having been said on naval leadership, there were many aspects of the phenomenon that had been glossed over, encrusted with nationalist myth or lost in the passage of time.

One result of this was the convening of an international conference at the National Museum of the Royal Navy, Portsmouth, in December 2011. It brought together speakers from Spain, France and Britain to discuss naval leadership in the period from 1700 to 1850. They explored the subject from the level of national policy to tactical command. This collection of essays emerged from that first exchange of views. They are not the proceedings of the conference. Some essays have been modified as a result of discussions and subsequent research, and another has been added as a result of lacunae that were identified at the conference. However, they do represent the balance of views, writing and interests that were evident at that gathering. They provide insights into how navies operated in a period of long-term, high-intensity global conflict. They show how important it was for navies to be integrated into the political context of their host societies. The reputation of naval officers, their contacts with political elites and how navies are deployed are subjects covered by Surreaux, Chaline, Harding and Scheybeler. At sea the admirals were usually isolated from these domestic pressures (although as the study of d'Orvilliers shows, traditional social relations were not left behind at the shoreline). These officers commanded great power in the form of the fleets they led. Their decisions could have huge consequences for the societies to which they owed allegiance. Their performances were judged by contemporaries and became part of the historical narrative of nations. The essays on Mazarredo, Suffren, Barceló, Salazar and Napier all pose different questions as to how this behaviour has been interpreted and integrated into the traditional national narratives. Here we see very different approaches to command in relation to subordinates, relations with the political masters and, crucially, in the face of the enemy.

Taken as a whole, what do these essays tell us? The essays focus on a period of major change. During the eighteenth century, navies became one of the main vehicles of geopolitical and economic strategy for European states extending their influence on a global scale. The range, robustness and impact of navies across the world expanded tremendously. Navies were very much at the forefront of the technological and organisational shifts that accompanied this phase of European expansionism. In July 1789 one of the defining events of European history occurred with the outbreak of the French Revolution. By 1792 the French naval officer corps had all but crumbled in the wake of the revolutionary upheavals and Europe was plunged into 23 years of intense, almost non-stop warfare. During this time the impact of the revolution was felt not just in Europe but in South America and the Caribbean as well. The independence and reform movements led to bloody civil wars in which navies played important, even decisive, parts. Some of these essays shed light on how states reacted to the demands of maritime and naval power before 1789. Others look at how naval commanders performed in the long wars that succeeded 1792. What they all show is that although there was a common understanding of how wars at sea should be fought, there were distinct differences between states and commanders as they had to respond to different conditions. There are clear comparisons at one level, but the contrasts are just as informative.

What they also confirm is that the concern for leadership has been with us for centuries. The twenty-first century is not breaking new ground. The practice of leadership may be different and some of the reasons for this emerge from the essays, but the problems faced by societies and nations have a great deal in common and navies as tools for solving those problems are also much the same. The 'modern' naval problem of inter-state rivalry, which is again raising its head across the world, dominated the state decision-making processes for navies in the eighteenth century. The 'post-modern' naval problems of our world, from economic security, piracy and smuggling, to maintaining good order on the maritime commons and managing alliances, had their counterparts in those eighteenth- and early nineteenth-century navies in an age of mercantilism.[4] These essays take us away from the well-known world of the great sea battles of annihilation that are the culmination of great power rivalry to the death, and which dominated naval thinking from the 1880s to the end of the Cold War, to the variety of naval duties and operations that occur in those long periods of naval confrontation, which range from diplomatic flag or sabre waving to police actions, and upwards to low-intensity, regional conflict. There are many more dimensions to the problem of naval leadership which need to be explored. History never repeats itself and leadership is not a universal technique or method of social control. The world is constantly changing, and as Western navies face growing regional and global challenges with fewer platforms and a greater need to work in partnership, they have, at the same time, to respond to national public perceptions of what navies do and how they do it. An understanding of how leaders behaved and how leadership was exercised is an important step in forming a better understanding of the role leadership plays in the life of navies.

This collection started as a response to the questions and debates that had been stimulated during the bicentenary commemorations of Trafalgar. Central to that year of activities was Professor Colin White. Colin dedicated much of his life to the study of Nelson and he became a great enthusiast for spreading the word about Nelson and the naval history of his times to the wider public. Apart from the energy he displayed in organising and being part of a whole range of commemorative events, he produced a new edition of Nelson's correspondence and a monograph reflecting on Nelson as an admiral.[5] Although a great admirer of Nelson, he did not neglect the contributions of others to the great war at sea during these years. From the common seaman to the problems faced by other navies, Colin was quick to point out they all needed to be understood. One of his characteristics was the welcome he gave to scholars of all nations to discuss and debate naval leadership of the period. His early death after becoming Director of the Royal Navy Museum Portsmouth (the precursor of the National Museum of the Royal Navy) was a sad loss to the subject. He would have been an enthusiastic contributor to these essays had he lived and it seems fitting that these essays are dedicated to his memory.

A number of debts of gratitude have been incurred during this project. First, the sponsors of the original conference made it possible. These are the National Museum of the Royal Navy, the Society for Nautical Research, the 1805 Club, La Sorbonne et Musée national de la Marine, Paris, the Ministerio de Ciencia e Innovación, Madrid, the Consejo Superior de Investigacionnes Cienificas, Madrid, and the Gunroom, HMSSurprise.org. We are also grateful to all the contributors for developing their papers. Finally, we are very grateful for the patience of Andrew Lockett of the University of Westminster Press, who helped us bring it all together.

CHAPTER ONE

# The Royal Navy, History and the Study of Leadership

Richard Harding
University of Westminster

Given the apparent ubiquity of interest in leadership today it is curious that the study of leadership has not featured more strongly as an explicit feature in naval history. This is not to suggest that it is entirely absent. In fact, we know a remarkable amount both about leaders and what leadership was expected to be. Throughout the ages, history has provided examples for emulation or warnings to avoid. Indeed, modern naval history emerged from a determination to teach naval officers and statesmen the information and the principles it was thought would guide them as they assumed leadership roles. History was the discipline for the aspirant leader – and this explicit function is one factor that has led to the greater focus on leadership in modern navies than their sailing predecessors. After the First World War, other disciplines, such as psychology, economics and political science, with their ambitions, or claims, to provide scientific predictability, began to assume the dominant role in leadership development, and historians, more acutely aware of the dangers of teleology and sensibly unwilling to delve into 'psycho-history', were generally disinclined to compete with their social science colleagues on this ground.[6] Nevertheless, history remained an essential part of the cultural capital of naval officers and the biographical or autobiographical publications of senior officers provided

**How to cite this book chapter:**
Harding, R. 2017. The Royal Navy, History and the Study of Leadership. In: Harding, R and Guimerá, A (eds.). *Naval Leadership in the Atlantic World*. Pp. 9–17. London: University of Westminster Press. DOI: https://doi.org/10.16997/book2.b. License: CC-BY-NC-ND 4.0

a constant institutional link to the past. Operational history from the point of view of the commander is a standard narrative approach. Similarly, institutional and political histories delineated by the reigns of monarchs, or the spans of particular office-holders, are also standard narrative tropes. In many ways, 'history from the top' is a history of leadership.

Naval history is hugely popular and there are many implicit lessons for leadership in the stream of operational histories, memoirs and social studies that emerge every year. Leadership can be studied from many directions. 'Who are the leaders?' is a relatively well-researched question that is yielding excellent results. Naval history has benefited from the development of social and ethnographic approaches to organisations. We now have a better understanding of the social and political contexts, demographics and career trajectories of various naval officer corps.[7] We still need to know much more, across chronological spans and, particularly, we need to know about the officers of other navies. If the assumption is that leaders make a difference to organisations, we need to know how those leaders differed in different navies and at different times.

One of the significant contributions of the 'new naval history' of the second half of the twentieth century is that it has deepened our appreciation of the complex administrative, logistical systems needed for successful operations at sea. We also now have a better view of the totality of navies as institutions – how they have evolved to exercise an expanding sea power with ever more complex, interlinked and expensive weaponry. This has helped us appreciate the diffusion of leadership throughout systems that enable effective operations. Thus, what leaders do and what defines successful leadership has evolved. The social and institutional norms for recognising high-performing naval leaders in the eighteenth century were intimately tied up with successful action at sea. Administrative leadership was seen as important, but entirely secondary to the officer at sea. These norms seem to have continued largely unaltered over two centuries, despite the growing bureaucratic and industrial contribution to operational success.[8] There are good reasons for this, as the concept of the 'heroic' leader was simultaneously blossoming with the growth of popular culture and media.[9] Nevertheless, the processes involved in assessing this evolving organisational leadership requirement and the popular understanding of the leader in the Royal Navy and other navies remain to be fully investigated.

While historians have done a great deal to explore the complexity of naval organisations and establish the social structure of officers corps, there has been less sustained engagement with the idea of leadership as an historical phenomenon. In some ways, naval historians, whose discipline emerged out of the demands for instructing leaders, are now less able to articulate an understanding of naval leadership than their social science colleagues. From the middle of the nineteenth century until midway through the twentieth, civilian organisations learned a great deal about leadership from military organisations. Today, the reverse is more likely to be true. Given the huge changes in the challenges faced by navies and the advances in leadership research, it is curious that leadership has not commanded more attention within navies and among naval historians. For example, we can now look at the late eighteenth-century Royal Navy as an institution that was qualitatively distinct from its rivals in terms of tactical proficiency, administrative capability, depth of supporting infrastructure and the strength of its linkage to domestic political culture. We can suppose that these made an operational difference, but we have not given the social function of leadership that much attention. Leadership seems to be an uncontentious phenomenon. After the resolution of the seventeenth-century friction between the relative merits of 'gentlemen' or 'tarpaulin' commanders, there seems to be a view that the naval officer corps evolved organically and incrementally, learning to adapt to growing tasks and burdens under the pressures of frequent wars until it reached its apogee in Nelson and his 'Band of Brothers'.[10] The years of peace and the decades of limited challenge to the Royal Navy left it in a weakened state. Reward, promotion, routines and procedures were no longer mediated by operational fleet action and the performance of the navy in the First World War reflected this.[11] Within the navy there was a clear discomfort about the perceived inadequacy in its performance during the war. Very soon, attention was paid to the higher education of the senior officer corps, but it took until the early 1930s for significant changes in initial leadership development to take place.[12] The Second World War did not throw up naval leaders with the profile of a Beatty in an earlier generation, or of military commanders like Montgomery. After the war, the experience of operations was integrated into the corporate memory of the officer corps, and the capability of the corps rose in conjunction with more scientific approaches to selection and promotion. Since 1990, in the absence of cold or hot war pressures, these scientific approaches, rigorous training and education (including some historical studies) are now the baseline for understanding the capability of the navy's officer corps. Overall, naval leadership has not produced the historical interest that has developed for army leadership, whether it is the revisionist conclusions about military command in the First World War or the relative performance of senior officers in the Second.[13]

This leaves a number of important questions open. For example, when so much of the material and operational context of the Royal Navy changed between 1689 and 1914, was naval leadership unchanging? Has naval leadership changed in response to the social changes of the twentieth century and if so, how and why, and what impact has it had on the navy? How did contemporaries understand leadership and what attributes did they ascribe to successful leaders? If operational experience in war is such an important determinant of the capability of the officer corps, why did the Royal Navy not excel in the American War of Independence, when the officers in command during this war learned their trade during the most decisive and successful naval war of the century, under the eye of senior officers who had many years of operational experience?[14] In which aspects of leadership did the navy excel and which were an Achilles heel? Does naval leadership differ from other types of leadership, particularly the leading of armies or other government organisations? Probably most important, was the leadership of the Royal Navy different from that in other navies at any point; if so, did it have an impact on the outcome of operations and why?

These are big questions, requiring a systematic approach to analysis and cannot be answered in the space of a single essay. However, I hope that looking at one aspect of leadership may make a useful contribution in linking the navy to the nation. As has been outlined above, leadership can be examined in terms of what leaders did, how they were expected to behave, what success or failure they experienced or what characteristics they are supposed to have possessed. Most studies of naval leaders are viewed from the perspective of the leader, through the medium of biographical or operational studies. Less common are studies that examine a leader in the social context of leadership. Yet all leadership is a social process that occurs within a complex environment that includes individuals who are leaders, followers, opponents and bystanders, all of whom are influenced by a wide range of stimuli. While the naval command decisions are in the hands of the leader, the interpretation and subsequent action are in the hands of the followers and the results are determined by the interaction between those actions and a wide range of variables in the environment. Furthermore, the evaluation of the quality of naval leadership is determined not by the leader but by others: the crew of a ship, the Admiralty, the monarch, Parliament, the public and even the wider global audience. Each of these may differ from the commander in their judgement of the action and there is no certainty that those judgements will be consistent. From the middle of the seventeenth century at the very latest, English (and then British) society was connected to the leadership of the navy. National support for the navy, and thus its naval leadership, expressed through Parliament, press and entertainments, was essential to its financial and social existence. This leads us to an important question that needs some sort of answer: given that British society changed so much over the period 1680–2000, and the importance of external social and political judgements of naval performance, why have naval historians paid so little attention to the changes in thinking about leadership over the past half century? Only the sketchiest of answers can be suggested here, but the following is offered as a starting point.

At one level the answer is fairly obvious. The success of the Royal Navy over nearly 300 years suggests that whoever was leading that force was doing a good job. It was failure that prompted reflection on leadership performance, not success, and there was no need for theory development by contemporaries. For subsequent historians there was such a plethora of evidence showing how the Royal Navy materially and operationally outstripped its competitors that seeking additional causality in leadership – unless it was obviously exceptional (such as with Hawke or Nelson) – was unnecessary. There was a seemingly natural, virtuous symbiosis in which quality of leadership was something that emerged from the successful application of seapower, which was, in turn, reinforced by the quality of the leaders it bred.

However, beneath this there was another assumption: that leadership capability was an innate personal attribute that could be developed by imitating the great and good, but it was essentially God-given and, increasingly in the nineteenth century, the product of a gentlemanly upbringing. Christian concepts of providential interventions in response to human moral behaviours provided a strong philosophical basis for believing that failure was the result of moral weakness just as success reflected a virtuous character.[15] The Enlightenment and Romantic focus on the human rather than the divine did not weaken this relationship between individual morality and success. Science contributed to a better understanding of the natural environment and thus better design and operations in maritime affairs.[16] However, the individual's efforts were still the major determinant of good fortune. The virtues of hard work and thrift mixed with evangelical ethics provided the basis for explaining the rise of humankind and more particularly the British. It was no part of the naval training and education process to explore this linkage in depth, but to provide the opportunities for officers to demonstrate these virtues in leadership tasks. Even when the search for the underlying principles of naval war was embedded in naval higher education, the quest did not extend to leadership.[17] Higher education focused on expanding the rational capability of the mind rather than moral development. Strategic judgement could be inculcated through the scientific study of history and war, allied to more technical disciplines to aid decision-making.[18] By the end of the nineteenth century, intellectual strength and knowledge developed by formal naval education, allied with moral strength fostered by an initial gentlemanly education, the professional example of past naval heroes and the practical experience of leading men in battle, provided the ideal environment for developing successful naval leadership. It was a formula that seemed intuitively right to a generation of naval officers who served in one or both of the world wars and it has barely been seriously questioned in historical studies.[19] The assumptions could easily be read back into the eighteenth century.[20] There is, therefore, a long tradition of consensus that naval leadership is a personal attribute and is highly developed by the organisational culture, its education, systems and practices so that the best get through to the higher leadership of the force. It is an institutional belief that is shared by other navies.[21]

While this consensus holds firm, there have been developments in other academic fields. Historians have always plundered the intellectual fruits of other disciplines in order to help them develop insights into their own subjects. With leadership studies the plundering has generally been in the reverse. The two world wars provided plenty of examples for those studying leadership to populate their case studies. Military case studies continue to provide a selling point for the more popular end of the market. The result is not always satisfactory – a misunderstood situation applied to an irrelevant theory does no one any good. Nevertheless, there has been a substantial amount of theory development within leadership studies over the last 50 years which might enrich our historical understanding. For example, motivation theories have produced some interesting reflections on prize taking in the eighteenth-century Royal Navy.[22]

Where the lack of attention to leadership is most apparent is in the analyses of comparative naval power. In many histories, the differences in leadership are taken for granted, indeed embedded in a founding ideology. For over 250 years, a national myth of British difference, based on Britons' relationship with the sea, was slowly created and entrenched in British thinking.[23] The idea that Britain bred natural seamen and sea officers became a standard element in explaining the rise of British naval power.[24] The difference between seamen such as Hawkins, Frobisher and Drake and their Spanish adversaries, who were primarily soldiers, forms an important part in the story of the Spanish Armada of 1588. Similarly, the contrast between the experience of officers in the Royal Navy and those of the more obviously aristocratic-led navies of Bourbon France and Spain is important to the traditional story of the British rise to naval hegemony by 1815. The fact that these differences existed has been well established, and there is an intuitive sense that such social differences could have been significant, but the impact of these differences on the performance of navies over spans of time has not been extensively studied. Individual situations in which the impact of the quality of leadership is clear can be found, most obviously after the collapse of the French naval officer corps in 1790, but there are very few such clear-cut examples. Furthermore, there are other occasions when any assumption of superior leadership is less tenable. The leadership differences between the Dutch and British naval officer corps in the seventeenth century are less clear. United States and British officer corps have been extensively studied, but the operational impact of differences over 200 years are not transparent. The different trajectories of leadership development for the officer corps of most European navies over the nineteenth century are still seriously under-researched. Historically, the leadership assumptions in the Japanese and Chinese navies have not received much scholarly attention.

Long-term success, an intuitively coherent ideology of seapower and the entrenched belief in the moral foundations of leadership, therefore, may be three reasons why naval leadership has not been of much interest to historians of the British public. Another factor might be the nature of networks that support the Royal Navy. The navy, like any military force, exists within a network of contexts which impinge on its operational performance and the choices made by the leaders of this organisation. Broadly, one can see two immediate and two deeper, long-term elements of this network. The most immediate is the operational environment. Navies exist to fight or deter conflict. The operational context is usually explicit and immediate with platforms, weapons and training directed to defeating the expected enemy. The second immediate element is the contemporary, domestic, political context. How the political system interprets naval power, what value it places on the costs and benefits produced by navies will have a direct impact on tangible factors, such as budgets and rewards, as well as intangible factors like definitions of success.

However, beneath these two immediate elements, there are others: the institutional and social. All organisations, including navies, are the product of accumulated experience. The Royal Navy is very aware of this experience and is aware of the experiences of other navies, both contemporary and historical. This creates an institutional environment within which the daily operational capability evolves. It produces the norms of behaviour, the structure within which doctrine is created and the deeper assumptions regarding the use of navies and naval power.

The Royal Navy is one of the best-researched organisations in British history. This reflects not just the extent of the sources that are available to historians, but the strength of the navy as an institution in British society. It has been consciously involved in research for over a century and the fruits of that research have an enthusiastic audience. By writing the history, or dominating its writing, the navy contributes powerfully to what is considered to be good leadership. Naval history from a naval officer's point of view was an important feature of early twentieth-century historiography. The result of this is that the navy has an important role in determining where leadership success and failure lie. A good example of history being written from a naval perspective is the work of Sir Herbert Richmond, a fine scholar with a strong and clear operational viewpoint that enabled him to discriminate between good and bad naval leaders, but distorted his judgement with regard to the civilian role in leadership decisions.[25] One of the important features of new naval history has been to put the navy into the wider social framework to explain the logistical, political and economic dimensions of naval operations, but the systematic exploration of naval leadership has yet to be undertaken.

Beyond this, there is the influence of wider society. The operational, institutional and political systems interact within society. The wider social and cultural norms help shape them, place parameters around decision-making and provide priorities or stimuli for trajectories of action. The new naval history is a manifestation of a wider public, in this case academic, participation in naval history. However, the public are not just the producers of naval history, they are a principal consumer. Naval history is written for the public more than it is for professionals. In the public mind the leader as hero is still the dominant model of naval leadership. While twenty-first-century navies are fully aware of the complexity of leadership in defence organisations, they are also aware of the role heroes play in public perceptions of the force and the need to present history and the navy in a heroic mould remains important.[26]

Together, the operational, political, institutional and social contexts are constantly evolving, providing the background for public interest in the navy, naval history and leadership. Throughout the last 120 years, naval history has become richer and more varied, but has not led to a major focus upon naval leadership. Instead, leadership tends to emerge in relation to other features of naval history.

The rapid operational changes after 1914 have attracted more attention than others. One of the truisms that emerges from this differential change process is that military organisations are always preparing to fight the last war. Leaders are the product of their experiences and training, and when the experience or training proves to be inappropriate for new operational situations catastrophe can result – the step change in technology or operational arts is one of the stock features of military history from the invention of gunpowder to Blitzkrieg. Consequently, the leaders of the Royal Navy and the decisions they made, facing steam power in the second half of the nineteenth century, long-range gunnery, new realities of competition, the submarine and air warfare in the next 50 years, have attracted a good deal of historical attention.[27] From these studies there are good examples of both individuals and the naval institutional systems that have influenced leadership and decision-making. Much less attention has been paid to the years after 1945. It does not offer the drama of change, or operational stress. Yet the whole period from 1918 to the present day is a particularly important field of study as it is marked by the rise of the profession of leadership development in Western society. Navies have not been immune from its influence, and understanding how institutions such as the Royal Navy have adapted and developed their understanding of leadership practice is a vital element in understanding their operational assumptions.

The lack of interest in naval leadership in the twentieth century is in marked contrast to that related to the British army. Perhaps, despite all the changes between 1890 and 1939, the navy was able to deal with the challenges it faced with its institutional framework and philosophy undamaged. The same was not true for the British army, which had barely recovered from the experience of the Russian War (1854–6) when the shock of the Boer Wars (1880–1 and 1899–1902), the First World War and the adjustments to a peace in which its purpose was unclear, raised a succession of leadership questions to which the answers were ambiguous at the time and remain contested to the present day.[28] It was also a period when the very nature of leadership and management in modern British society was being questioned and debated.[29] During the whole period, the Royal Navy remained a powerful institution. It had not won another Trafalgar, but it had won the war at sea and there were few existential doubters. Nevertheless, there remains a need to explore the leadership assumptions of the Royal Navy against the debates and changes that were going on elsewhere.

The lack of analysis is even more true for earlier centuries. The period 1815 to 1890 was a time of major technological changes that entailed social and institutional adjustment against a background of extensive operational activity but little military threat. The navy has been placed firmly in the context of the administrative changes of the time. It was a period in which the 'expert' – technical or bureaucratic – became far more influential in the decision-making processes of governmental bodies. So far not much attention has been paid to this and a thorough modern, comprehensive analysis of the leadership assumptions, values, training and rewards of officer corps has still to be written.[30]

The period between 1739 and 1815 was one of major operational and military threat. The Royal Navy emerged victorious and without parallel in the world. Our understanding of the logistical and administrative effort that underpinned this naval triumph is now quite extensive and the diffuse nature of the leadership required for this massive, complex exercise of naval power is better understood. However, there has been far less critical attention paid to the exercise of operational leadership. Possibly the dominance of Nelson as leader and personification of an ideal has done much to shape assumptions about leadership and leaders. It was a period in which the Royal Navy was consolidating as an institution – not just an organisation. By 1815 it was an institution with a political presence in the wider social environment, a culture of its own, respected internally and externally, on a journey of centralised control through which leaders and leadership could be controlled and shaped. It was not always like this and the process by which this happened, particularly in the first half of the century, is still in need of substantial research. What impact the changing intellectual environment, commonly known as the Enlightenment, had on the leadership of the navy is currently unknown. Once again, we know rather more about how this influenced armies than we do about the Royal Navy.[31]

The purpose of this paper has been to lay out some possibilities for the future study of naval leadership – primarily in the national context of the Royal Navy. Leadership has always been an implicit element in naval histories and there is now much excellent work about the social and intellectual origins of the officer corps and the performance of individual officers. However, given the chronological opportunities and importance of leadership as a variable in operational success or failure, there is a need for a more systematic study. The assumptions about virtuous symbiosis of naval leadership and seapower, between combat experience and leadership or between national connections and naval leadership all need to be explored in more detail – all the more so as the exercise of seapower becomes more tenuous, the opportunities for operational experience diminish and the national connection with the navy becomes more opaque.

It is a subject that is in need of serious attention and a vital element of this is to understand comparative naval leadership. Although this paper has focused on the nation and the navy, we will only really begin to understand how naval leadership works when we can see it operating across nations and time spans. It is an exciting agenda.

# PART TWO

# Naval Leadership in the
# Ancien Régime

# CHAPTER TWO

# Leadership Networks and the Effectiveness of the British Royal Navy in the Mid-Eighteenth Century

Richard Harding
University of Westminster

It is difficult to conceive of the history of naval warfare being researched, discussed or taught without the idea of leadership emerging at some point in the process. Surviving on the sea, let alone fighting in ships, demands consistent collaborative action among those who undertake it. For a ship to move and fight, it requires individuals to apply their efforts in precise conjunction with their colleagues, and for this to happen the effort has to be coordinated and directed by someone recognised in that role. The importance of the leadership role or roles in this confined and hazardous environment has been enshrined in the rules conferring legal status and responsibilities since the Middle Ages.[32] These laws recognised the limits of authority, the need to consult others and the consequences of negligence or incompetence as well as defining the power of the master. They were distinct from the rules concerning the command of soldiers on the ships. However, in the 200 years between the 1490s and 1700, as the ship at war transformed from what was essentially a transport for soldiers into a formidable gun platform to be fought with in its own right, the separate leadership roles of the 'master' (commanding the seamen and navigation) and

**How to cite this book chapter:**
Harding, R. 2017. Leadership Networks and the Effectiveness of the British Royal Navy in the Mid-Eighteenth Century. In: Harding, R and Guimerá, A (eds.). *Naval Leadership in the Atlantic World*. Pp. 21–34. London: University of Westminster Press. DOI: https://doi.org/10.16997/book2.c. License: CC-BY-NC-ND 4.0

the 'captain' (commanding the soldiers and the fighting function) had to merge and, in the process, became a matter of serious concern. Although the primacy of the combat role and thus the captain has been recognised since the Middle Ages, ensuring land officers had adequate navigational and ship-handling skills was beset by operational, social and cultural obstacles which were never entirely resolved in Europe during the eighteenth century.[33]

The evolution of this professional competence of naval officers is a complex story and this paper only concerns itself with one aspect of this – the leadership exercised by flag officers in the Royal Navy before 1789. Much of our understanding of naval leadership has been shaped by the popular and professional naval histories that were published between 1890 and 1914. In these years, naval history was written with an explicit didactic purpose of educating the public, servicemen and statesmen about the importance of naval power and the means to exercise it. It was particularly the history of the naval wars against France, from 1793 to 1815, that formed the core of this history. These wars brought about the oceanic *Pax Britannica* of the next 70 years. During the nineteenth century navies changed dramatically, but the ideal of leadership that was abstracted from the campaigns of the French wars remained the model. The ideal naval officer for navies everywhere was Horatio Nelson (1758–1805). Nelson was a remarkable, outstanding leader and commander. His dedication to duty, his bravery and success in battle left little to be desired or explained. 'The Nelson Touch' was a semi-mystical sensitivity to what it was possible to achieve with one's own squadron against the enemy that succeeding generations of officers were expected to emulate. Nelson encapsulated leadership of the heroic kind that became the frame of reference for naval officers and the measure against which historians would judge them.

The consequence of this is that in most naval histories, the question of leadership is unproblematic. The benchmark is clear and the officers under examination are at some point on a continuum between good and bad that could be determined by their operational performance compared to Nelson or the way in which their command reflected the Nelsonic attributes. In more recent naval histories the nature and context of that leadership is more nuanced. Historians are more sensitive to the demands of leading naval forces in the complex, changing, multi-dimensional battle spaces of the period post-1939. While this sensitivity to near-contemporary environmental complexity is considered important, the same cannot be said of the naval history that precedes the wars of 1793–1815. There is the temptation to infer that before the demands of industrialised warfare, there was a golden age of naval leadership in which everything was clearly defined. Nelson and his contemporaries eventually produced a dominance at sea that was unprecedented, but they did not live in a world of certainty in which command and leadership were uncomplicated. However, their tremendous success, and particularly the clarity with which Nelsonic attributes were subsequently distilled and presented by historians as causal factors of that naval dominance, has deflected from serious consideration of how leadership worked in the period before the French Revolution.

There are a number of questions concerning leadership that have not yet been fully absorbed into the realm of historical analysis. Scholars in other disciplines have been trying to understand leadership for decades. Leadership has been seen as a set of tasks or functions that are carried out more or less effectively. It has also been seen as a set of personal attributes which leaders possess in different proportions and quantities. It is not possible to construct experiments in which the absence or presence of a leader (with known attributes and functional capability) is the only variable, and attempts to establish historically the precise contribution of either the leadership functions or qualities to the outcome of any specific operational activity have proved impossible. Similarly, attempts to identify a successful outcome and then infer the leader's contribution to this success are plagued by distortions of reporting, lack of information and a multiplicity of other variables. For example, it is commonly understood that it is the followers who achieve the result for the leader, but they are not passive automata responding to the leader's will. What the followers inject into any operation is unpredictable and often neglected. The immediate operational context will influence the leader and the willingness of the followers to be led, but this is often relegated to a factor that is assumed to be under the control of the leader. This post-facto attribution of leadership qualities to the victorious commander makes the quality of leadership dependent upon the outcome rather than vice versa.

With these debates surrounding the study of leaders and leadership, and the centrality of the subject to naval history, it is surprising how little attention naval historians have paid to the question of leadership at all levels.[34] This paper aims to lay out a few thoughts for bringing a closer study of leadership into the study of command in the eighteenth century. Informing this discussion is another set of debates underutilised in the realm of naval history, that of network analysis and decision theory. Since the 1960s, historians of technology and international relations have been working on influencing networks in decision-making. From developing nuclear weaponry to managing international crises, analysing the different role of influencers has informed historical judgements.[35] These works hold additional interest for historians of naval leadership. As Spinadi's study of the development of the Polaris missile suggests, Admiral Arleigh Burke's ability to convince the networks of decision-makers about his definition of success for the project was as important to the eventual development of the family of Fleet Ballistic Missiles as the engineering achievement itself. While network analysis is established in the study of post-1945 naval history, it is not commonly applied to earlier history. There seems to be no reason why this should be so, and the following is an attempt to shed some light on the historical context facing British admirals in the eighteenth century.

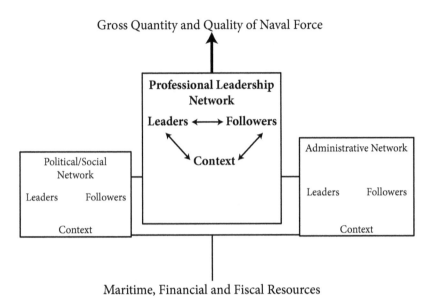

**Fig.1:** A simple network of influence on naval power.

A very simple network of influence on naval power is set out below.[36] A network consists of a connected group of people. They exist within a context that unites or distinguishes them from others, and many networks may overlay one another in the social environment under investigation. We are interested in the exercise of naval power and for our purposes it is possible to identify at least three significant networks that are critical to its generation in Britain during the eighteenth century. It is assumed that naval power rests on the ability to convert maritime, financial and fiscal resources into naval assets. These resources may exist in a society, but their conversion to naval assets is a social and political process that requires at least these three primary networks to be working effectively – the political/social network, the professional naval network and the administrative network. Individuals overlap by being in all three of these networks, but it is the concerted action of the networks as a whole that enables the effective channelling of resources into naval power. Just from this very crude framework, one can imagine the possible channels and potential blockages. The political/social network that linked Court, Parliament and the wider political community was the context in which the political battle for the financial and fiscal resources was fought and generally won. The administrative network provided the direction and structures within which ships, stores and manpower were brought together. They also had to link to the political/social network of contractors for all kinds of stores, manpower and even the building of the ships themselves for much of the period. The professional naval network had to take these weapons and employ them to effect in battle or on campaign. Together they generate the quantity and quality of fighting ships

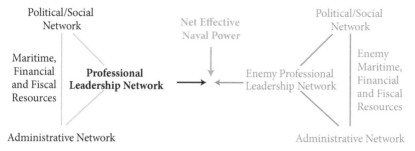

**Fig. 2:** Net effective naval power.

that are available at any given time and place (the gross quantity and quality of naval force).

However, this is, at best, only half of the situation. Similar networks were at work generating the enemy's naval forces and its gross naval force. Relative, or net, seapower can be said to emerge from the opposition of these naval powers. Warfare is a dynamic environment in which the networks are in a state of flux, stimulated by and stimulating the progress of a campaign. Seen in this way, it becomes clearer how complex the issue of leadership and followership can be. Leaders and followers interact constantly at different levels within their own networks and they influence other networks. Their effectiveness alters relatively and absolutely as a result of these interactions.

The idea of the single controlling will bringing about victory or causing defeat becomes less compelling when viewed from this perspective. Only very rarely would an individual be so dominant across all the contributing networks as to become the sole author of the result. However, to conclude that the leader is irrelevant is equally unconvincing when one looks at these networks in operation. Below is a simple leadership network within which Nelson operated during his years of greatest triumph, 1798–1805.

In this illustration the squadron commander, Nelson, sits at the centre of a series of networks, all of which he influenced and had influence on him. In 1805 he was strongly connected and supported by his professional community, represented here by Lord St Vincent. Similarly, he was well connected to the civil administration of the navy, represented by Lord Barham, the First Lord of the Admiralty. Nelson was also connected (and supported by his professional standing) with his captains and the crews of his ships in his squadron. By 1805 Nelson was also strongly connected to the social and political networks (represented here by the Prime Minister William Pitt). However, these networks were not static: they varied and the strength of the ties between them varied continuously as a result of changes within them (new leaders, new priorities, new tasks etc.) and as a result of other networks of factors that influenced the connections. For example, the connections that bound Nelson to his professional community and the civil administration were strongly influenced by traditions of command,

**Fig. 3:** Leadership network: squadron 1805.

control, communication and intelligence. These were relatively stable during 1804–5. However, in 1798–9, Nelson's behaviour in the Mediterranean, possibly as a result of the wound he received at the Battle of the Nile, caused changes in the supporting networks that fed back into the political and social network as well. Over his lifetime, Nelson's relations with this network were more volatile, but Nelson himself did a great deal to influence opinion positively. The actors within these networks not only formed opinions of people, but also of the operational problems and how they could be resolved (the perceived operational problem). Sometimes perceptions might be shared, but on other occasions they could vary widely. Furthermore, depending on the quality of intelligence and communications, the real operational problem might have been entirely different, presenting serious disconnection between the leadership expectations of the actors in various networks and the leadership actions of the commander. Nelson played a crucial role in shaping these perceptions. He was closest to the immediate operational problem and the way he articulated it to others fed back into their perceptions of his operational problems. Part of Nelson's public appeal was his aggression and certainty, which played into shaping how other actors expected a commander in Nelson's position to behave.

This very simple network is enough to illustrate how important networks are in perceptions of leadership. If Nelson is replaced by Sir Robert Calder, the dynamics of the networks immediately change. Calder met the Franco-Spanish

Combined Squadron in foggy weather about 100 miles west of Cape Finisterre on 22 July 1805. Calder met them with an inferior force, captured two of their ships and forced the Combined Fleet away from Brest, to Vigo and then to Ferrol, where the fateful decision to head south to Cádiz was made. Yet the political expectations were for a decisive victory and, judging from Calder's subsequent reprimand at a court martial, the professional service expectations were the same. Calder's action was a major factor in finally thwarting Napoleon's invasion plans, but by not clinging to the Combined Fleet after the first day of action, he did not precisely answer expectations in London and his career never recovered.[37] Calder's leadership was found wanting within the critical networks, despite the tactical and strategic success he achieved.

Calder's experience illustrates how judgements about leadership are heavily influenced by the networks that exist at any given point. In earlier years, with different actors in key positions, the response to Calder's action would probably have been different. It also highlights how leadership has to be judged within the context of its own networks and times. This being so, how then are we to assess the leadership of British admirals before 1789?

First, it is clear that we cannot treat the leadership of these admirals as an undifferentiated whole. Over the eighteenth century, the networks that supported them, and through which contemporary definitions of successful leadership emerged, were constantly changing. Perceptions of problems changed over time as the actors in the networks changed, or changed their relationships with other actors. Of the three networks we have discussed, the political, with the influence of public opinion, was probably the most volatile. The social concept of leadership changed more slowly, but over the century there was a distinct shift. In the second half of the century, the general Enlightenment shift of focus from Mankind's relationship with Providence to the study of Man as the main mover of events was important. By the last quarter of the century, there was a rising public interest in biography and autobiography, and particularly an interest in the heroic. Nelson and his contemporaries were serving in an environment that was looking for heroes/heroic leaders and, because of the revolutionary threat, believed it needed them.

Thus, if the social, cultural and political context of Nelson's predecessors was rather different, we must suppose that contemporary definitions of success and good leadership might also have been different and we need to establish what these were. Admirals were not trying to meet the standards imposed by later generations of historians, or even consciously struggling to create what was later to be a Nelsonic ideal, but to meet the expectations of their own contemporaries. While victory is an obvious and relatively stable concept, what constitutes victory is more ambiguous. Despite a generalised feeling that the Royal Navy should be able to achieve whatever was desired, expectations of operations as diverse as the expeditions to the Baltic (1715–9 and 1726), the Mediterranean and the Atlantic coast of Spain (1718–9), the West Indies (1726) and Lisbon (1736) were not universal among the decision-makers and other actors at the time. The disjunction between expectations, or between expectations and reality, was a core element in the political disputes of the century, which appear most obviously during the major wars. The rest of this paper seeks to illustrate just one of these points – the dynamic nature of the leadership networks – by reference to a short period in the eighteenth century, 1740–6.

The early 1740s was a period of intense public expectation and crushing disappointment. In 1739 Britain had entered a war with Spain confidently expecting that the Royal Navy would rapidly force Spain to a humiliating peace.[38] This would be done by severing the trans-oceanic trade link to Spain's American empire, along which the vital supplies of silver flowed from Mexico and Peru into the treasuries of the Spanish crown. Furthermore, the Royal Navy would devastate Spanish trade in Europe and the Americas and even land an expeditionary force to take and hold some part of the Spanish empire to be held as a perpetual threat to Spanish trade in the future. Seven years later Spanish trade had been severely mauled, but this had not forced Spain to come to terms. Britain was at war with France and Spain by this time. The navy had failed to deliver conquests in the Caribbean. It had failed to win a decisive victory over the Franco-Spanish fleets. It had failed to maintain control of the Channel, as a French squadron penetrated as far as Dungeness in support of an invasion force in Flanders, before being forced to retreat in the face of winter storms. To contemporaries and to later generations the cause of this failure was clear and simple – bad leadership within the civil administration, the political leadership and within the naval officers corps. The First Lord of the Admiralty between 1741 and 1744, the Earl of Winchelsea, has borne much of the blame, but the naval officers and the administrators within the Admiralty have not escaped censure.

That the results were bad is unquestionable. However, the role of leadership in the failure has received little real analysis. For contemporaries and historians, the centrality of leadership failure was demonstrated by a change of fortunes that began in 1747 and reached a glorious climax in 1762. By this latter date the Royal Navy had effectively destroyed the French and Spanish navies, stifled their trade and conquered vast parts of their overseas empires. The reason was the new leadership that Admiral George Anson brought to the service after his return from his remarkable circumnavigation in 1744. He entered the Admiralty in 1746 and retained a sea-going command. Guided and inspired by his professionalism the navy regained its edge. Two battles (First and Second Finisterre) were fought and won in May and October 1747. By the time the peace was finally signed, the Royal Navy had regained the initiative. During the peace and for most of the subsequent war with France, Anson remained at the Admiralty, reforming and leading. By this time he was serving with the great William Pitt, whose strategic grasp of naval power was unparalleled as he led Britain to the spectacular victories of 1759–62. Little more needed to be said – heroic leadership had made the critical difference.

**Fig. 4:** Leadership network: 1741.

Whereas the role of Pitt, Anson and others is certainly important, this explanation ignores why their leadership worked better than their predecessors'. Seen as a changing social network, the reasons for the collapse of effective leadership in the early 1740s and its reconstruction in the second half of the decade become clearer.

Above is a simple leadership network as it looked in the spring of 1741. The three squadron commanders were Sir John Norris (Channel), Nicholas Haddock (Mediterranean) and Edward Vernon (West Indies). The administration was headed by Sir Charles Wager. The professional head of the navy, the Admiral of the Fleet, was Sir John Norris. While there was some professional jealousy between Norris and Wager, they had worked well together since 1739. As a whole, the professional and administrative systems of the navy were working efficiently. The connections of this naval leadership with the political and social leadership of the nation were equally strong. The ministry of Sir Robert Walpole was on good terms with King George II and although political jealousies existed between Walpole and the Secretary of State for the Southern Department, the Duke of Newcastle, these had been largely submerged after the outbreak of war. Newcastle and the King were strongly in line with public opinion in their support for the war, although Walpole had far more reservations and his enthusiasm for the war was a weakness that could be exploited politically by his opponents. In 1739 the expectations about the war at sea, and the perceived operational problems, were similar among these three networks – the war would be fought at sea, and it would be short and victorious.

However, between 1739 and 1744, the war did not progress according to those expectations. Operations in the West Indies failed to achieve the decisive results predicted. From the summer of 1740, France was acting in conjunction with Spain and by the early part of 1741, France and Spain were acting together against Austria. British naval power was being stretched to cover far more than had been anticipated in 1739. By the end of February 1744, Britain was formally at war with France as well as Spain, and the Brest squadron had penetrated up the Channel to support an invasion force assembling in the Low Countries. Although the war did not cause Walpole's fall from power in February 1742, his well-known lack of enthusiasm for it became part of the rhetoric that accompanied his resignation and the reconstruction of the new ministry. By this time, Sir Charles Wager had resigned from the Admiralty, his own confidence in the war having been shattered. Walpole left office despite the wishes of the King, who was not reconciled to his new ministry, headed by the Duke of Newcastle. The new First Lord of the Admiralty, the Earl of Winchelsea, gained neither the support of the professional part of the service, nor the surviving part of Walpole's old ministry. Sir John Norris resigned from active service. Vernon was recalled from the Caribbean after the failure of a major expedition to that region. Haddock in the Mediterranean suffered a nervous breakdown and was eventually replaced by Thomas Mathews in a process that in itself caused some rancour within the squadron. The new ministry was itself soon riven by political differences, in which the conduct of war became a central feature by 1743. The King and his new Secretary of State for the Northern Department, the Earl of Carteret, had become more convinced that the war could be won in Europe than by overseas expeditions.

Thus, by the early part of 1744, there was plenty of evidence of failure, but precisely what role leadership failure played in this is very difficult to establish. For the most part, it has been enough to condemn the politicians and the political part of the administration as being uniquely incompetent. The senior professional leadership of the Royal Navy is seen in a similar manner – doing their best, but hampered by inept politicians, they lacked the nerve or weight to force a more effective strategy upon the decision-makers. Seen from the perspectives of leadership networks, the comprehensive nature of the problem becomes readily apparent.

There are now almost no solid lines, indicating confidence and communication, between the networks. The professional leadership of the navy, represented by Vernon and Norris, is detached from the administrative leadership at the Admiralty. They have their views on the perceived operational problem, which are not shared by Winchelsea and the Admiralty Board. This Board has not retained the confidence of either Mathews or Lestock in the Mediterranean, who, were, themselves, not working well together. The political leadership was

**Fig. 5:** Fractured leadership network: 1744.

divided. The King had confidence in Carteret, who had some confidence in Winchelsea, but Newcastle had confidence in neither and the King distrusted Newcastle and his colleagues. Public opinion was increasingly suspicious of the ministry, the Royal Navy and its administration. Newcastle remained acutely aware of this, but this did not mean that he either had the confidence of the public at large or that he could influence their views on the perceived operational problem. In sum, the leadership networks were fragmented within themselves and from each other.

The traditional account from this point is that a new leader in the heroic mould, George Anson, emerged and put right what was wrong. Anson had not been tarnished by the events of 1740–4. In June 1744 he returned from a circumnavigation, loaded with the wealth of a captured Spanish galleon. The public response after so much disappointment was jubilant. He was promoted to flag rank almost immediately, but he just as quickly resigned when an appointment he had made while on his voyage was not confirmed by the Admiralty. Anson joined the Admiralty Board in December 1744 when a new board was formed under the Duke of Bedford and finally took his flag in April 1745.

Anson was active at the Admiralty and at sea. His contribution to stimulating reform was second to none at the time. His cruises in the Western Approaches in 1745 and 1746 were not as successful as was hoped, but in May 1747 he intercepted two outward-bound French convoys with their small covering escort north-west of Cape Finisterre. By 7 pm he had captured six French warships and four East Indiamen. Later in the year, other French convoys fell victim to British cruising squadrons and on 14 October, another French escort force suffered heavily when six of their number were captured after a vigorous chase action conducted by a force under Edward Hawke. Largely as a result of these actions during 1747 the Royal Navy ended the war with far greater public and political confidence that it had enjoyed since 1740.

Although Anson deserves all the credit he is given for his actions at sea, within his profession and at the Admiralty, the explanation for how and why one man was able to achieve all this has been rather neglected. By placing Anson into the changing leadership networks of his time, it is possible to see how his talents were appreciated and supported.

The diagram below illustrates the leadership network as it existed early in 1747. Anson is clearly visible in very significant roles, but other changes have also taken place. First and foremost, the political fragmentation that had followed Walpole's fall in 1742 had been resolved during 1746. The struggle for dominance between Newcastle and Carteret had concluded in the former's favour. Since December 1744 the head of the Admiralty had been the Duke of Bedford, the leader of one of the 'New Allies' whose parliamentary influence was critical in the eventual defeat of Carteret. Bedford had come to the Admiralty convinced that Britain could win a war against the united Bourbon monarchies of France and Spain by the judicious application of seapower. Newcastle held this view, although strongly modified by his concern for Britain's Dutch allies. By 1747 the King was becoming convinced of this, and more at ease with Newcastle as his leading minister. There was, therefore, a shared perception of the operational problem. Public opinion was less homogenous and more distrustful, but generally sympathetic to the claims for maritime war. One of the most influential figures outside of the formal leadership systems was Edward Vernon, who had been dismissed in April 1746 after a series of clashes with the Admiralty. However, his opposition did not extend to the concept of the maritime war, of which he had been one of the most vocal exponents since the early 1730s.

Anson was therefore operating in a context in which leadership was far less contested and the networks were mutually reinforcing. Anson was, in practice, the professional head of the navy by this point. His potential competitors for this role had fallen away as they had been swept up in the crises of 1740-6. Most were in retirement or engaged in distant operations in the West Indies or the Mediterranean. Those officers that surrounded Anson were largely his protégés or junior to him. Only Vernon could have contested his leadership, but Vernon was broken by his quarrels with the Admiralty by this time. Anson's professional leadership was reinforced by his sea commands, which bore fruit in 1747. In turn this reinforced his standing in the eyes of the public. Anson was also linked to the political network. As a staunch Staffordshire Whig family in a predominantly Tory county, the Ansons were an important bridge between the parties at a time when Tory support was needed by the Broad

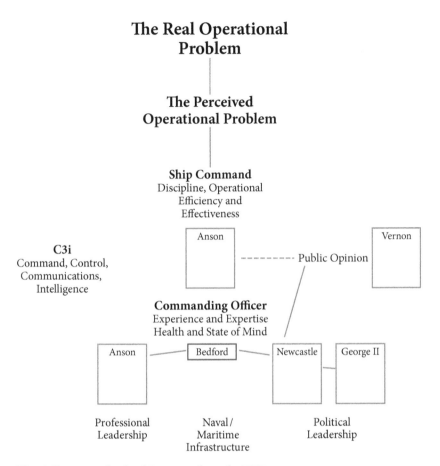

**Fig. 6:** Emerging leadership network: early 1747.

Bottom Administration. In sum, the resistance to Anson's leadership within the profession, the administration and the political networks was, by the standards of his immediate predecessors, remarkably small. The consistency with which all these networks perceived the operational problem of the Royal Navy was strong. The internal unity of the networks was strong and there was diminished inter-network friction.

The leadership context within which Anson reached the top of his profession was far more benign for him than it had been for many years for his predecessors. The frictions that might have destroyed his attempts to reform or command were greatly reduced. This does not diminish Anson. His skill as a navigator, a squadron commander, an administrator and a politician all played a part in the way he was able to work within those networks to achieve his objectives. At every level he experienced some set-backs as well as successes. He was also fortunate that he was leading at a time when the strength of the Franco-Spanish naval force was beginning to wane, worn down by the attrition of years of war conducted against it by Anson's predecessors. At the same time, British naval resources in home waters had been gradually growing, giving Anson a far greater margin of superiority than the Royal Navy had experienced since 1740.

All of these contextual factors could be described simply as 'luck', but to do so does not do justice to any of the leaders. The context is the arena within which leadership is carried out. Naval leaders and followers and those whom they fight are all parts of dynamic networks of individuals that are interacting. British admirals were part of these networks with the capacity to influence and be influenced by them. Anson brought great skills, capabilities and contacts to a situation that was, independently of him, becoming more amenable to his objectives. Anson continued to use all those advantages very effectively and is now rightly regarded as one of the most important leaders that the Royal Navy ever had. Other officers, notably Edward Vernon, also had outstanding talents as well as failings, at a time that was marginally before Anson's, but starkly different in the way the leadership networks were configured and working. Vernon, Norris and most of their contemporaries could not influence the context in the way that was to open itself up to Anson.

For most people, the facts of naval success or failure are clear in the historical record. Nelson, Anson and Edward Hawke stand out as benchmarks against which other eighteenth-century British admirals are judged. This paper has tried to argue that such judgements about eighteenth-century naval leadership are deficient. They are based on the idea that the demands of naval leadership and the definitions of success were generally unchanging during the century. This is simply untrue – they were changing all the time. This does not reduce the leader to being a passive recipient of luck, but it does change his tasks, his options, his prospects, and his resources. Each brought talents to the perceived and actual operational problems. Some leaders were able to meet the challenges spectacularly well, others were not, but they were not necessarily all facing the same challenges, nor can success or failure be attributed unconditionally to the individual leader. Far more work needs to be carried out on these officers, particularly those of the first half of the century, before we understand how they saw their tasks, how they related to the networks within which they operated, how the external contexts impinged on their options, how dynamic that context was and how they perceived leadership at flag rank. Only then will we be able to engage with the broader questions of whether there is a discernible trajectory of leadership approaches and behaviours.

# CHAPTER THREE

# The Reputation of Louis XV's Vice-Admirals of France

## Simon Surreaux
### Centre Roland Mousnier

The kingdom of France had only two admirals during the eighteenth century: the Comte de Toulouse (1678–1737) and his son, the Duke of Penthièvre (1725–93). The former was the illegitimate son of Louis XIV and the Marchioness of Montespan.[39] The Earl of Toulouse took part in only one military campaign, in 1704. During this campaign he was present at the Battle of Vélez-Málaga (24 August 1704), with the Vice-Admiral d'Estrées (1660–1737), fought against the British fleet, commanded by Admiral Sir George Rooke (1650–1709). After that battle, he never went to sea again. However, he 'had a real influence on the advancements and selections of officers'.[40] From 1669, the date of the establishment of the Secretary of State for the Navy, to 1777, when two other posts were set up, the Admiral was assisted by two Vice-Admirals of France.[41] These two general officers were entrusted with the fleet of the Ponant, for the Atlantic Ocean, and the fleet of the Levant, for the Mediterranean Sea. From 1715 to 1774, France had 18 vice-admirals and it is these men who are the subject of this paper.

Some naval officers of the reign of Louis XIV, such as Duquesne, Jean Bart, Duguay-Trouin and Tourville, are famous for their battles or for their

**How to cite this book chapter:**
Surreaux, S. 2017. The Reputation of Louis XV's Vice-Admirals of France. In: Harding, R and Guimerá, A (eds.). *Naval Leadership in the Atlantic World.* Pp. 35–47. London: University of Westminster Press. DOI: https://doi.org/10.16997/book2.d. License: CC-BY-NC-ND 4.0

leadership. The same is true of some officers of the reign of Louis XVI: for example, Suffren, d'Orvilliers, de Grasse, La Pérouse and Kerguelen -Trémarec. However, the historiography of the nineteenth and early twentieth centuries is overwhelmingly negative with regard to most of Louis XV's vice-admirals, or has even forgotten them completely. Their rehabilitation happened only with Michel Vergé-Franceschi's thesis, in 1987, and Étienne Taillemite's *Dictionnaire des marins français* in 2002.[42] Professor Vergé-Franceschi demonstrated the importance of family ties in the rise of general officers in *La Royale*, the French Royal Navy. He researched their careers, chiefly in the 'titles office' of the *Bibliothèque Nationale de France*. By reading the prosopographical and biographical data in each of these works, two facts became clear. First, with a few exceptions, the reputation of these men is almost unknown. Second, their ability to command and to lead maritime campaigns, and thus their leadership, has not been systematically analysed.

But why should we take an interest in 'reputation', which is a sketchy and rather subjective notion, as a means of examining their leadership? This chapter tries to go beyond the usual studies in leadership, in which the focus is on tactics, strategies or the numbers of opposing forces. Leadership is assessed by such facts, but equally important are the memories of the battles and campaigns evoked: that is, the reputation of the commanders involved. Furetière, in 1690, defined the word 'reputation' as: 'the good opinion the people have of persons, or things', and he went on: 'a captain just needs a victory to have a reputation of courage, and a rout to have ill repute'.[43] The first edition of the *Dictionnaire de l'Académie française*, in 1694, described 'reputation' as fame, esteem, in the public opinion.[44] 'Réputer' derives from Latin 'reputare', which means 'to appraise', and, until the sixteenth century, 'reputatio' meant appraising. Breaking with the verb, the noun acquired the meaning pointed out by Furetière and the French Academy. In 1982, Littré perfected the definition, specifying that reputation is 'the opinion that people have about someone'.[45] During the eighteenth century, the word had a favourable connotation, which differs from Littré's definition, in which people's opinion can be either favourable or critical. To assess a reputation implies an evaluation of the opinions of many protagonists such as the State (the dispenser of favours and promotion), naval officers and seamen (who contributed to their chief's reputation), other contemporaries, and succeeding generations (who absorbed recollections of the vice-admiral, and built these in a body of historical scholarship).

This chapter uses two sources in this search for reputation: the *letters patent of provision*, or *provisions*, of the Vice-Admiral of France, and evidence left by contemporaries regarding the ability of these officers to command. The letters *patent of provision*, which confirmed the appointment of an officer, listed the career of the officer concerned. They give the viewpoint of the State and of the royal institutions about the quality of these men who have been raised to the office of vice-admiral. Other contemporary witnesses provide different lights on the subject.

After several months' research in the records from the *Archives Nationales'* deposits and from the *Bibliothèque Nationale,* the resultant data is slim. After having scrupulously analysed all the probate inventories of 18 vice-admirals, attempting to find some traces of their deeds in the papers recorded after their deaths, only seven copies of the letters confirming their appointments were located. The historian cannot know exactly where else such documents may have been preserved. There are many likely places. There is some evidence suggesting that these letters were stored in the Great Chancellery.[46] However, not one has been found in that archive. Either they have been preserved elsewhere or they have vanished. Only one letter patent was found in the series *Courts of Accounts of the Parliament of Paris,* where it had been reconstituted in the *Memorials* (series P).[47] The archives of the French Admiralty were examined,[48] as well as the personal records of each vice-admiral in the series *Marine* of the *Archives Nationales of France.*[49] Only seven letters of appointment were located, permitting us to see the State's view of the reputation of these vice-admirals. Four of them had been promoted to the rank and dignity of field-marshal, which increased the available sources as it is possible to trace their maritime careers from these letters of appointment as well.

How do these letters of appointment and the remarks of contemporaries help us understand the reputations of the vice-admirals at a time when *La Royale* was no longer the force it had been under Louis XIV? The letters *patent of provision* provide a view of the careers of the new vice-admirals and an important insight into the key factors that made up the reputations of these men.

## I – The letters of provision to the Vice-Admiralty of France

To become a Vice-Admiral of France at a time when there were only two of these posts implies that these men were highly regarded by the monarchy. The appointment was a reward for meritorious service. Thus their leadership or their capacity to command was already recognised in their past success.

Letters of provision give us a clear view of the promotion criteria to the vice-admiralty and to the marshalship. Before they were issued by the War Office or by the Secretary of State of the Navy, the new Vice-Admiral or Marshal of France sent a memorandum regarding his services so that the secretaries could accurately re-transcribe his career into the letters. Most of these surviving letters have been kept as reconstituted copies on parchment or vellum in the registries of the Memorial of the Accounts Chamber, series P, at the *Archives*

| Themes/Expressions | | NB | Names of vice-admirals | Promotions |
|---|---|---|---|---|
| **A distinction** | Merit, deserve, 'to adjust rewards according to merit', 'a so well-deserved reward', 'distinguished merit', 'distinguished himself', 'distinguished himself through several glorious feats', 'distinguished services', 'lot of distinction', 'served with so much distinction' | 8 | d'Estrées, Château-Renault; Coëtlogon; Salaberry de Benneville; Court de La Bruyère; Cresnay; Macnémara; Conflans | 1703; 1730; 1750; 1755; 1756; 1758 |
| | 'Best choice', 'in better hands than his the command of our naval armies/our maritime strength' | 5 | Salaberry de Benneville; Court de La Bruyère; Cresnay; Macnémara; Conflans | 1750; 1755; 1756; 1758 |
| | 'Reward' | 5 | d'Estrées, Château-Renault; Coëtlogon; Cresnay, Conflans | 1703; 1730; 1755; 1758 |
| **Qualities of a war leader** | 'Experienced in warcraft and navigation', 'proven experience in navigation', 'acquired experience and capacity' | 5 | d'Estrées; Salaberry de Benneville; Court de La Bruyère; Cresnay; Macnémara | 1684; 1750; 1755; 1756 |
| | Victories: 'happy successes' | 5 | Salaberry de Benneville; Court de La Bruyère; Cresnay; Macnémara; Conflans | 1750; 1755; 1756; 1758 |
| | 'Fortunate dispositions' | 1 | d'Antin | 1731 |
| | 'Courage' | 2 | Coëtlogon; Court de La Bruyère | 1730; 1750 |
| | 'Good conduct' | 5 | Salaberry de Benneville; Court de La Bruyère; Cresnay; Macnémara; Conflans | 1750; 1755; 1756; 1758 |

| Themes/Expressions | | NB | Names of vice-admirals | Promotions |
|---|---|---|---|---|
| | 'Prudence', 'vigilance' | 5 | Salaberry de Benneville; Court de La Bruyère; Cresnay; Macnémara; Conflans | 1750; 1755; 1756; 1758 |
| | 'Reputation he legitimately gained', 'so much cleverness' | 1 | Court de La Bruyère | 1750 |
| | 'Valour' | 7 | d'Estrées; Château-Renault; Salaberry de Benneville; Court de La Bruyère; Cresnay; Macnémara; Conflans | 1684; 1703; 1750; 1756; 1758 |
| | Zeal | 5 | Château-Renault; Coëtlogon; Salaberry de Benneville; Cresnay; Conflans | 1703; 1730; 1750; 1755; 1758 |
| Service to the King and King's grate-fulness | Mentioned wounds | 2 | Cresnay; Conflans | 1755; 1758 |
| | 'Affection to our service' | 5 | Château-Renault; Salaberry de Benneville; Court de La Bruyère; Cresnay; Conflans | 1703; 1750; 1755; 1758 |
| | Faithfulness to the King and to the Crown | 1 | d'Estrées | 1684 |
| | 'Confidence we rightly placed in him", 'extreme confidence that we always placed in him' | 2 | Salaberry de Benneville; Cresnay | 1750; 1755 |
| Social origins, tradition and family memories | 'Birth', 'advantages of birth' | 5 | d'Estrées; Château-Renault; Coëtlogon; d'Antin; Conflans | 1703; 1730; 1731; 1758 |
| | 'Ancestors', 'ancestor' | 1 | Château-Renault | 1703 |
| | Reminder of the character of father or of a marshal or vice-admiral's relatives | 2 | d'Estrées; d'Antin | 1684; 1731 |

**Fig. 1:** Analysis of the reputation of vice-admirals through promotion criteria to vice-admiralty or marshalship in their letters of provision.

*Nationales* and in paper form in the individual files of the vice-admirals in the *Archives Nationales*.

As official acts, they are all written in the same form.[50] Eight copies of letters of provision to the vice-admiralty and four copies of the letters of provision to vice-admirals appointed as marshals were found.[51] The standardised nature of the letters might suggest a document that was a matter of form rather than an accurate assessment of an individual officer's career. Nevertheless, searching for terms and expressions, or even connotations and facts not mentioned in other examples, may help distinguish between the more or less consistent promotion criteria. These criteria express the reputation and the leadership abilities of vice-admirals. Figure 1 aims to establish the promotion criteria as they appeared in the letters. These terms or expressions enable us to assess the profile of a 'good' Vice-Admiral of France. Letters of provision include four types of useful information for an historical analysis of the sources of distinction: data related to reward, data related to qualities and skills as war leader, data related to service and commitment to the King, and expressions qualifying the social origins, tradition and family memories of the newly promoted, as though, in the last case, the blood flowing in his veins confirmed the accuracy of the monarch's decision.

### Vice-admiralty: A distinction

Out of a total of 12 letters of provision (vice-admirals and marshals together), eight feature specific terms related to the 'merit' of the character. From the Latin *meritum*, 'merit' derives from *merere* and means 'earn', 'get as a prize or a reward'. In common Latin, the word has been associated with the meaning of 'value'. In ancient French, the word had more meanings than are in modern use. Though in the first texts it means 'salary, punishment or reward', modern use was established in the seventeenth century when merit was associated with 'skills, wholly respectable moral and intellectual qualities'. More specifically, it refers to talent, seamanship (1668 'gens de mérite').[52] According to Furetière, merit falls within 'the putting together of several virtues or good qualities, in any person, which attracts consideration and admiration on him'.[53] But merit can also be associated with 'the price, the value of actions and things compared with their good or bad content'.[54] Therefore, vice-admiralty is considered in most cases as the prize for the military actions of those promoted. This criterion of distinction seems essential during the reign of Louis XIV.

Reward is found next to merit. Five patent letters claim that the granting of vice-admiralty was not an honour but a reward. 'To reward' means 'recognize the merit of someone through a favour' (Montaigne, 1580) and refers to a fortunate consequence which constitutes a gratification (1671).[55] Furetière defines the reward as 'the price, the salary, the gift to someone or the advantage he is granted in return of services done or for a good action'.[56] Merit and reward therefore seemed intertwined, which imposes the conclusion that only merit should have secured promotions to vice-admiralty.

### Qualities of the naval war leader

The qualities that made up a naval leader, such as being an accomplished sea-man and distinguished among other general officers, also came into considera-tion. Valour (in seven cases) was often accompanied by experience and leader-ship qualities (five cases). In equal numbers, prudence, good conduct and zeal (five cases) were often added, while courage (two cases) was also considered. The term of zeal, however vague ('ardour, affection, passion in something'), may have referred to the aptitude to command troops and to serve the King faithfully by complying with orders.

Behind the word 'courage' lies a reference to the heart. As a matter of fact, 'courage' features in a very general sense in ancient and middle French. Until the seventeenth century, it particularly defined the strength of soul, moral vir-tue in any field and, more specifically, the qualities of an elite nature, which were synonymous with 'heart', in a figurative sense.[57] A courageous vice-admiral was therefore a man different from his fellows because of the nature and strength of his soul. The corollary of these moral virtues is prudence, which is, according to Furetière, 'the first of the cardinal virtues which teaches one to manage one's life and customs and to guide one's actions according to right reasoning. Prudence's main function is to assess what has been done, what has to be done and what must be avoided'.[58] Courage is intertwined with prudence and also with valour, defined by Furetière as 'a firmness of soul which makes one look on the perils of war with cold blood, that is with fervour for real glory'.[59] Then comes zeal, defined as 'ardour, affection, passion in something'.[60]

The case of Dubois de La Motte (1683–1764) epitomises these criteria. He entered the *Garde de la Marine* in 1698 and was a lieutenant from 1709 to 1727. Sieur Duguay-Trouin (1673–1736) recommended him to the Secretary of State of the Navy, the Comte de Maurepas. Duguay-Trouin wanted to see him promoted to captain, stating: 'this officer is not only able skilfully to command any ship, but also several of them at the same time'. This opened the possibility that he might, in future, become a good squadron leader. Duguay-Trouin praised 'his valour', 'his prudence' his '*sang froid* in action'.[61] In 1746–7, Dubois de La Motte com-manded the ship *Le Magnanime* (74) on a voyage to the West Indies and back. He emerged from this campaign with great credit. He then protected a convoy of 40 merchant ships with the frigate *L'Etoile*. He was chased by four British ships and came under fire from a couple of them. At three o'clock the next morning, the British gave up; Dubois had not lost a single ship from his convoy. On 1 August 1747, Maurepas noted for the King's attention that 'M. Dubois de la Motte gave the utmost care for the security of the fleets he led to and from Santo-Domingo, and he distinguished himself in the two fights he waged on this occasion'.[62] The

Chambers of Commerce were satisfied with Dubois de la Motte's actions. Michel Vergé-Franceschi describes him as an 'excellent, energetic and daring tactician'; 'he reminds us of the privateer under Louis XIV [Duguay-Trouin], his fellow countryman, for whom he was often the appreciated subordinate'.[63]

So the four main qualities of the naval leader are courage, prudence, valour and zeal. On the other hand, outstanding courage and seamanship do not seem to have been essential to reach vice-admiralty. Only Claude-Élisée de Court de La Bruyère (1666–1752) was identified as a courageous clever man of good reputation. Aged 78, he led the French squadron in the fight at Cap Sicié (Battle of Toulon) on 22 February 1744. In *Le Terrible* (74), he commanded a squadron of 13 ships whose objective was to assist a Spanish squadron of 14 ships under Admiral Juan José Navarro (1687–1772) to get out of Toulon Harbour, in the face of a British squadron of 30 ships under Vice-Admiral Thomas Mathews. In the action that followed, the Franco-Spanish squadron succeeded in breaking through the British force and away towards Spain.[64] Thus it seems from the official notifications that, excluding courage and reputation, the main leadership skills could be summed up by these four words: experience, prudence, valour and zeal.

### From King's service to the recognition of family merits

Battle wounds were the proof of the gift of one's body to the king and to the nation. If a vice-admiral had fought and shed his blood, it was a distinctive criterion in the letters of provision. However, it was not crucial since only two vice-admirals' letters mention their wounds. Nevertheless, mentioning these wounds was significant, especially for Félix de Poilvilain de Cresnay (1693–1756), vice-admiral for six months before his death, who almost lost a hand at the Battle of Dettingen on 27 June 1743, while he commanded the guards company of the Admiral's boat.[65]

Then come affection (five cases), trust (two cases) and faithfulness (one case) to the King and to the crown. These terms reveal the close link between those promoted and the monarch. Such qualities referred to the personal, almost privileged, relationship between the King and men judged suitable to be granted the power of Vice-Admiral of France, as they were to command warships and troops in the name of the monarch. Finally, there was social origin, tradition and the family history of the vice-admirals. Five individuals promoted to be Vice-Admiral of France are noted for their birth, their ancestors and their families.

To sum up, being promoted to the dignity of Vice-Admiral of France in the course of the eighteenth century was, therefore, considered as a reward for military merit. Each new vice-admiral possessed at least one of the qualities derived from the four main themes considered here. He was distinguished through his own eminent qualities, his dignity, as a deserved reward, and as recognition of his family's and his own proven services to the crown. We now turn to how the leadership reputation of these men was assessed, through one case where it was stained by defeat: that of marshal and vice-admiral Hubert de Brienne, Comte de Conflans (1690–1777), whose reputation was to be severely damaged by a single, but devastating, defeat.

## II – A tarnished reputation and questioned leadership? Hubert de Conflans and the Battle of Quiberon Bay

Defeat in naval operations is undoubtedly the worst possible fate for a naval officer and disgrace logically followed from it. However, several vice-admirals were not disgraced despite their failures. During the Seven Years' War (1756–63), Vice-Admiral the Comte d'Aché de Serquigny (1701–80) was sent to India to support the French East India Company forces against the British along the Coromandel Coast. He was criticised for his failure to support an attack upon Madras or to support the defence of Pondicherry, both of which ended in defeat for the French. Nevertheless, with the support of the Secretary of State for the Navy, Nicolas Berryer, Comte de La Ferrière, he escaped prosecution, leaving his reputation and leadership untarnished – unlike the army commander at Pondicherry, Lally-Tollendal, who was executed for the disgrace in 1766.[66]

By comparison with Marshals of France, few naval officers were recalled after a failure. Although not a marshal at the time, the Prince de Soubise (1715–87) kept his position after the disastrous Battle of Rossbach on 5 November 1757, as did the Marquis de Contades (1704–95) after his defeat at the Battle of Minden on 1 August 1759.[67] However, François Duc de Villeroy (1644–1730) and Louis La Feuillade (1673–1724) both lost their military careers during the War of the Spanish Succession, although Villeroy went on to occupy a high position of state under the Regency. La Feuillade never served again after his defeat at Turin in 1706. Similarly, the Comte de Broglie (1671–1745) suffered military and political disgrace after his defeat in Bavaria in 1741. Both La Feuillade and de Broglie were exiled despite the fact that they had done nothing particularly blameworthy in leading their armies in very difficult circumstances. In the navy, only Conflans was recalled and never employed again at sea after his defeat at the Battle of Quiberon Bay (21 November 1759).

### i. Conflans: A skilful general officer in a forsaken navy

Hubert de Conflans was described in the corps as a 'good officer, skilful at doing his job, brave but slightly quick-tempered and excessively proud of his birth; pretends to descend from the Kings of Jerusalem'.[68] He joined the *Gardes*

*Marine* in 1706, was sub-lieutenant in 1712, ship lieutenant in 1727 and commander of the company of the *Gardes Marine* in Brest from 1741 to 1746. He was kept busy with the concerns of the Chambers of Commerce of Nantes and La Rochelle, and with the poor coastguards in Brest. 'Humane, ready to teach and clever, Conflans tried, to the extent of his resources, to improve the quality of the navy'.[69] As a war leader, commanding the ship *Le Content* (62) from 1740 onwards, he seized the *Northumberland* (70) in 1744. In 1746 he commanded *Le Terrible* (74) and safely escorted a convoy of 90 ships between Santo Domingo and Europe. On 29 October 1746 he met a British force and seized the *Severn* (50). On Christmas Day 1746, Maurepas, then Secretary of State for the Navy, presented to the King an account of the conduct of Conflans in his different assignments:

> 'He carried out his task with as much conduct as valour. He led and brought back to safe harbour numerous fleets which provided great wealth within the State. He successfully waged several campaigns'.[70]

In 1752, he was the eldest lieutenant general in the navy. At the top of his military career, as Vice-Admiral of Ponant in March 1756, Conflans proved a skilful general officer and he was deemed the best to fight the Royal Navy. He was therefore granted his marshal's baton in March 1758, much to Vice-Admiral Barrailh's displeasure.[71] For the first time in 55 years, a vice-admiral was promoted to the position of marshal. (The previous cases had been d'Estrées and Château-Renault in 1703.) The title was aimed at providing Conflans with additional authority. He was to 'command the Brest fleet, made up of 28 line ships, the smallest of which still features 64 cannons, and are considered as magnificent ships'. [72] Luynes noted:

> 'He is an officer of great reputation in the navy [...]. It was fair that the King gave the navy a Marshal of France, as there had not been any since the late Marshal d'Estrées. Such a well-composed corps, which has distinguished itself for a long time, is more than ever necessary in the present circumstances'.[73]

He was assigned the difficult task of preparing the ships in order to invade England at a time when the French navy was not functioning well.

### ii. The Battle of Quiberon Bay: A failure of leadership?

Conflans understood the importance of the navy. On 27 September 1757, he wrote to the Duke of Aiguillon, commander-in-chief in Brittany: 'the interest of the navy shall not be overlooked for a single moment, otherwise the fate and the advantages of the Kingdom might be at stake'.[74] This statement alone should, according to Vergé-Franceschi, 'rehabilitate this general officer accused of incapacity after the Cardinals disaster'.[75]

In 1759 Conflans flew his flag in the *Soleil-Royal* (80). His squadron was 'in poor conditions, hastily armed with dilapidated artillery. The crew was made up of landsmen who were at sea for the first time, lacking elementary training, which may account for many wrong moves'.[76] A total of 21 ships left Brest on 14 November 1759 to embark troops in the area of Vannes in southern Brittany. Conflans tried to avoid a battle but was caught by Admiral Sir Edward Hawke with his 32 ships on 21 November, near the Bay of Quiberon, in the area of Belle-Île-en-Mer. He performed 'skilful manoeuvres but, badly seconded by some of his subordinates, he was unable to prevent his squadron scattering during a violent storm'.[77] Hawke took advantage of the disorganised flight and Conflans lost five ships. Two were seized, three were wrecked and seven took refuge in the Vilaine until early January 1760.

The loss of Quebec in September 1759, and – in practice – of Canada, the defeat at Minden in August and this failure contributed to make the year 1759 an 'annus horribilis'. The way Conflans's fleet was defeated worsened the impact of this defeat. Conflans ran his flagship, the *Soleil-Royal,* aground and it was burnt near Croisic. Some 2,500 French seamen perished while 300 to 400 English seamen were killed.[78] Hawke lost two line ships and one was seized, but the French navy could no longer face the Royal Navy in battle.[79]

Conflans was not long in coming to Court to justify himself. Barbier wrote that in December 1759, 'the Marquess[80] of Conflans came recently to Versailles to clear himself of the defeat and to accuse the Marquess of Beauffremont'.[81] He reproached Versailles for having assigned him an impossible task. He accused his ship commanders. He quarrelled with Beauffremont, one of his subordinates in the Bay of Quiberon, thus continuing to bring discredit upon the navy after the rout. While he received no official blame, Conflans was no longer welcome at Versailles. Lord Anson's brother-in-law wrote about him that 'for his behaviour, Mr de Conflans would deserve his marshal's baton to be broken on his shoulders'.[82]

In 1760, no squadron was equipped. Small divisions of ships were sent out to perform specific missions designed to divert attention, to counterbalance the defeat on the sea and to inspire troops with a renewed confidence. A few days after Conflans's journey to Versailles, on 20 December 1759, the King appointed Victor François, Comte de Broglie (1718–1804) as a Marshal of France.[83] Conflans never served on the sea again. Even if, at the end of the day, this defeat contributed to the restoration of the navy by Choiseul and Castries, no naval officer was ever again appointed to the position of Marshal of France. Conflans retired to his estates and was forgotten until he died in Paris in January 1777, in accommodation he rented on Rue Saint Dominique. The Bay of Quiberon

| Levantine Vice-Admiralty, created 1669 | | | Ponantine Vice-Admiralty, created 1669 | | |
|---|---|---|---|---|---|
| Name (birth–death) | Time in charge | Dura-tion | Name (birth–death) | Time in charge | Dura-tion |
| François Louis Rousselet de Château-Renault (1637–1716) | 1 June 1701–15 November 1716 | 15 years and 5 months | Victor-Marie d'Estrées (1660–1737) | | 30 years and 7 months |
| Alain Emmanuel de Coëtlogon (1646–1730) | 18 November 1716–7 June 1730 | 13 years and 7 months | | | |
| Charles, Earl of Sainte Maure (1655–1744) | 8 June 1730–23 September 1744 | 14 years and 3 months | Antoine François de Pardaillan de Gondrin, mar-quess of Antin (1709–1741) | 28 December 1737–24 April 1741 | 3 years and 4 months |
| Gaspard de Goussé de La Roche-Allart (1664–1745) | 1–7 January 1745 | 6 days | François de Briqueville, marquess of La Luzerne (1665–1746) | 1 May 1741–29 September 1746 | 5 years and 4 months |
| *Vacancy between 1746 and 1750* | | | | | |
| Vincent de Salaberry de Benneville (1663–1750) | 7 February 1750–30 December 1750 | 10 months | Claude Élisée de La Bruyère de Court (1666–1752) | 7 February 1750–19 August 1752 | 2 years and 6 months |
| Pierre de Blouet, Knight of Camilly (1666–1753) | 17 May 1751–22 July 1753 | 2 years and 2 months | François Cornil Bart (1677–1755) | 1 September 1752–24 April 1755 | 2 years and 7 months |
| Jean André de Bar-railh (1671–1762) | 25 August 1753–25 August 1762 | 9 years | Félix de Poilvilain de Cresnay (1693–1756) | 25 September 1755–20 May 1756 | 8 months |
| Emmanuel Auguste de Cahideuc, Earl Dubois de la Motte (1683–1764) | 13 October 1762–23 October 1764 | 2 years | Jean-Baptiste Macnémarra (1690–1756) | 17–18 October 1756 | 1 day |
| Claude Louis, Mar-quess of Massiac (1686–1770) | 4 November 1764–15 August 1770 | 5 years and 9 months | Hubert de Brienne, Earl of Conflans (1690–1777) | 14 November 1756–27 January 1777 | 20 years and 2 months |
| Anne Antoine, Earl of Aché de Serquigny (1702–1780) | 24 August 1770–11 February 1780 | 9 years and 5 months | | | |

**Fig. 2:** Louis XV's vice-admirals (1715–74).

defeat, his behaviour and the overall circumstances of the kingdom in 1759–60 put an end to his career. This man, after having reached the highest military position in a couple of years (1756–8), saw his social status and his reputation destroyed by a single defeat.

Conflans was the only Marshal of France to have experienced such an end.[84] Military incompetence was a necessary but insufficient criterion to explain his disgrace, since no rule seems to have existed in this matter. Thus, according to Vergé-Franceschi, Conflans might be considered to have been 'a very severely judged officer.'[85]

## Conclusion

If the French navy during the reign of Louis XV was weaker than under Louis XIV and Seignelay or Louis XVI and Castries, the general officers who commanded this navy were nevertheless skilful men. They deserved their titles of vice-admirals even if they did owe it in part to a seniority rule and they were often appointed late in their lives. The recognition of their leadership by the King in their letters of provision was based on recurring qualities: experience, valour, zeal and prudence. During this period, a good naval officer was a prudent seaman who was anxious to preserve his ship and his men at a time when only a small budget was allocated to the navy.[86] The Seven Years' War and the defeat at the Battle of Quiberon Bay resulted in important changes in attitudes which, from then on, saw the quality of training for seamen and officers rising significantly.

# CHAPTER FOUR

# Types of Naval Leadership in the Eighteenth Century

## Michael Duffy
### University of Exeter

Ever since his death during his greatest victory in 1805, Horatio Nelson has been the international benchmark for naval leadership. Even Napoleon on St Helena lamented that if Suffren had lived on 'I would have made him our Nelson and our affairs would have taken a different turn. Instead I spent all my time looking for such a sailor and never found one.'[87]

Could a Nelson have flourished in a Napoleonic system that subordinated maritime affairs to the will of a soldier with little understanding of such matters, and whose admirals lacked the support of a powerful Admiralty containing expert professional naval advisers, provided with sufficient funds to secure the best materials for building and maintaining a navy, and with experienced officers and trained seamen inspired by a tradition of naval success? The fleets of the great European naval powers were operating to different systems and with different requirements, best displayed in the composition of their fleets. The British designed sturdy, bluff-bowed warships capable of both keeping to the seas for long periods and fighting. For the latter they included in their fleets far more three-decked warships whose size and guns could dominate a battle. The French on the other hand built a mission-orientated navy to carry or

---

**How to cite this book chapter:**
Duffy, M. 2017. Types of Naval Leadership in the Eighteenth Century. In: Harding, R and Guimerá, A (eds.). *Naval Leadership in the Atlantic World*. Pp. 49–57. London: University of Westminster Press. DOI: https://doi.org/10.16997/book2.e. License: CC-BY-NC-ND 4.0

escort troops and supplies to French possessions overseas, and hence put more emphasis on sharp-lined, lighter-framed, speedy ships to reach their destination rapidly, but at the expense of their durability in storms and battles; in the mid-eighteenth century they excluded three-deckers since their emphasis was on the mission rather than winning battles. The Spanish meanwhile had large, solidly built ships, including three-deckers, to defend their imperial trade, which financed Spanish power. The two Bourbon powers built for defence rather than attack. The first orders to the main French fleet to seek out and destroy the main British fleet were given to d'Orvilliers in 1779, when he was to be joined by the Spanish fleet as the preliminary to the invasion of Britain. Neither the French nor Spanish fleets were powerful enough in themselves to defeat the British, and the usual French invasion plan was for a surprise attack before the British were prepared, or to create a diversion which would lure the British fleet out of area and leave the way clear for the intended invasion force – as was Napoleon's plan in 1804–5.[88]

The Nelsonian model was not universally applicable. Naval leadership has to be judged in relation to circumstances – on the ability of an admiral to make the best possible use of the resources he had available so as to accomplish the stated ends of national policy – and both the means and the ends differed from country to country.

There were also differing views on how to prepare officers for naval leadership. The British and the Dutch had gone the way of the apprenticeship system. Aspirants joined ships as captain's servant (volunteer first class from the 1790s) at the ages of 12–16 to learn their trade from a captain at sea. The French from 1682, followed by Spain and the Baltic powers, sent their aspirants to naval academies between the ages of 16 and 20 where as *gardes de marine* they receive a heavily theoretical education in mathematics, hydrography, naval architecture, and English and Spanish, and time was also allotted to fencing and dancing: they were educated as gentlemen as the main attribute of an officer's authority, and their sea time was short.[89] The British also created a naval academy at Portsmouth in 1733, but its 40 places were seldom full, as most preferred the practical opportunities to learn from the example and under the eye of a serving officer who might patronise their advancement, and their path to lieutenant specified six years' sea time including two as a midshipman.[90] The main need of all navies was for lieutenants – 67% of commissioned sea officers in the British navy in 1790, 61% of the French (1789) – for which practical sea experience equipped them better than scientific theory. The British apprenticeship system brought them to command more quickly and enabled those who rose through the ranks to do so at a considerably lower age than their continental counterparts, with all the consequent advantages of experience and the boldness and robustness of younger men (see Figs 1 and 2).

Successful British admirals such as Jervis and Collingwood advised would-be officers to read history, and there was an abundance of books on naval history and biography to provide inspiration and give them a common doctrine. We

| | Hawke | Boscawen | de la Clue | Conflans |
|---|---|---|---|---|
| Born | 1705 | 1726 | 1696 | 1690 |
| Joined | 15 | 12 | 18 | 16 |
| Lieutenant | 24 | 20 | 34 | 37 |
| Captain | 28 | 30 | 45 | 43 |
| Rear Adm | 42 | 35 | 59 | 59 |
| Vice-Adm | 45 | 43 | 67 | 62 |
| Admiral | 52 | 46 | | 68 (Marshal) |
| Died | 1781 | 1761 | 1764 | 1777 |

**Fig. 1:** Age at advancement of leading admirals of the Seven Years' War.

| | Rodney | Howe | De Guichen | De Grasse |
|---|---|---|---|---|
| Born | 1717 | 1726 | 1712 | 1722 |
| Joined | 15 | 14 | 18 | 19 |
| Lieutenant | 22 | 19 | 34 | 32 |
| Captain | 25 | 20 | 44 | 40 |
| Rear Adm | 42 | 44 | 64 | 56 |
| Vice-Adm | 45 | 50 | 67 | 59 |
| Admiral | 61 | 66 | n/a | n/a |
| Died | 1792 | 1799 | 1790 | 1788 |

**Fig. 2:** Age at advancement of leading admirals of the American War.

know that mid-century admirals Sir Peter Warren and Sir Edward Hawke read works such as Josiah Burchett's *A Complete History of the Most Remarkable Transactions at Sea* (1720) and Thomas Lediard's *The Naval History of England* (1735), and, as John Hill explained in the preface of his *Naval History of Britain from the Earliest Periods* (1756), 'The use of history is, by recording actions of the dead, to set examples before the living… Our former successful enterprises will afford sufficient instances of what future commanders should pursue; and the fate of our enemies will teach them what they should avoid.'[91] James Ralfe's *Naval Biography of Great Britain* (1828) avowed the same didactic purpose, following on from a series of naval biographies – above all John Campbell's *Lives of the Admirals and Other Eminent British Seamen*, whose four volumes of 1740–2 were expanded by continuators to eight volumes by 1817. Ralfe also repeated the national view of the importance of the navy, constantly expressed in all of these books and in the Navy Acts of Parliament of 1660 and 1749, that 'upon the navy has depended the prosperity and independence of the Country; and upon the navy this kingdom must always chiefly rely for the preservation of its safety and glory.'[92] No other officer corps had such a clearly expressed view of its purpose nor so much literature showing how it had been achieved by its predecessors.

While these works substituted for leadership manuals for officers, the nearest job description of the qualities demanded of an admiral is in William Falconer's 1769 *Universal Dictionary of the Marine*. After pointing out that a fleet is unavoidably exposed to a variety of perplexing situations in a precarious element, and that a train of dangerous incidents necessarily arises from a sudden change of climate, infection or unwholesome provisions which threaten as much to destroy the health, order and discipline of his crews as tempestuous weather or dangerous navigation threaten the condition of his ships, he advised that an admiral:

> '…ought to have sufficient experience to anticipate all the probable events that may happen to his fleet during an expedition or cruise, and by consequence provide against them. His skill should be able to counter-act the various disasters which a fleet may suffer from different causes. His vigilance and presence of mind are necessary to seize every available opportunity that his situation may offer to prosecute his principal design; to extricate himself from any difficulty or distress, to check unfortunate events at the beginning, and retard the progress of any great calamity. He should be endued with resolution and fortitude to animate his officers by force of his example, and promote a sense of emulation in those who are under his command, as well as to improve any advantage, as to frustrate or defeat the efforts of ill-fortune.'[93]

Nelson would have agreed. When once asked what he thought was the key to his success, he replied: 'being fifteen minutes beforehand', and Martin van Creveld puts it succinctly in *Command in War* (1985) that '90% (at least) of good command consists of things that never happen'.[94]

Where could ill-fortune come from? Where could things go wrong beyond an admiral's control? Some things are clear: the number and quality of the ships and men provided; the quantity and quality of his naval stores and provisions and the facility of resupply; the availability of adequate repair facilities; the amount and accuracy of available intelligence; the unity and coherence of the naval administration; the unity of the officer corps within the fleet – there were notable feuds within the British navy (Mathews/Lestock in 1743–7, Keppel/Palliser 1779–80, Jervis/Alexander Hood 1779–1800), but these were as nothing compared with the divisions in the French fleet, whose personnel were parochially divided between the three major naval arsenals, three naval academies, the reds (the uniform of the academy-trained officers) and blues (the uniform of officers recruited from the merchant navy), or between officers whose noble origins lay in the military or the state bureaucracy. Their Minister of Marine Berryer summed up his experience in 1758–9 – 'in the navy they all hate each other'.[95]

Many of these factors were to a large extent known before operations and might be taken into account, but another remained lurking to happen at any time – the inherent tendency of fleet cohesion to degenerate from 'top downwards' to 'bottom upwards' controlling forces, that Sam Willis has explained so well in *Fighting at Sea in the Eighteenth Century* (2008), and which resulted from the inability or unwillingness of captains to keep station and act to a common plan. Cohesion depended on catering for the speed of the slowest ship; the variability of speed between and within different classes of ship; their different speed requirements and crew capacities for tacking or wearing ship; ship seamanship in the face of unpredictable wind, weather and sea conditions; fleet seamanship in keeping to a common speed and direction and avoiding collisions; differing weather conditions along a line of battle which might extend as far as ten miles; the different extent of battle damages and the capacity to repair them (which brought the Battle of Ushant to a halt in 1778); and the ability of captains to see and interpret signals, as well as their ability or willingness to obey them. In all this there was the danger that the worst captain or ship could end up controlling the actions of the best admiral or fleet.[96]

Over time, the adoption of copper bottoms and the reduction in the number of ship types within the line of battle helped reduce some of these problems, and the performance of ships and captains could be tested and ameliorated through training cruises (e.g. those by the French in 1772–3), and by the conscientiousness of good commanders who exercised their fleets in manoeuvres while voyaging to operational zones. (Anson and Hood had reputations for this, while Villeneuve was blamed for not doing so in the voyage of the combined fleets to Martinique and back in the Trafalgar campaign.) Fleet seamanship was built up over time and with constant sea experience – something that enabled the British, who kept their ships at sea far longer, to improve fleet performance while the fleet performance of the French, who didn't, went down in each war, as they were unable to keep up the supply of skilled and trained officers and seamen to replace earlier losses.[97] The prize for bad seamanship must go to the Chevalier de Gras Préville, captain of the 74-gun *Zélé*, who managed 14 collisions in 13 months in 1781–2, four of them between leaving Martinique and the defeat at the Saintes four days later, the last with the flagship of his commander-in-chief, the Comte de Grasse (whose own collisions in the training squadron in 1772 had led his admiral to comment that 'there is something lacking in his judgement by eye')![98]

The revealing leadership diaries of Captain Graham Moore comment in 1799 that 'There is something in the nature of the seaman's profession which many men of superior endowments never acquire and which many comparatively dull men frequently excel in. This is what the French call *gros manoeuvre* and what very few of the French navy officers of the old regime knew anything at all about. They affected indeed to despise it, which men often do when they find those whom they deem their inferiors more perfect in an art than themselves.

The superior skill, however, in practical seamanship is one of the causes of the unrivalled eminence which the British navy has attained.'[99]

Those admirals who anticipated and tried to deal with the 'bottom-upwards' erosion of their command tended to do so in one of two ways, summed up by Captain Mahan when he wrote that 'Each man has a special gift, and to succeed must needs act in accordance with it. There are those who lead and those who drive. Hawke belonged to the one class. Rodney to the other.'[100] Rodney tried to fight it. He ordered rather than explained, and enforced his orders by intimidation: 'My eyes on them had more dread than the enemy's fire, and they knew it would be more fatal,' he boasted after one battle.[101] He achieved noteworthy victories, but on at least two occasions (the Moonlight Battle and the first battle of Martinique) his failure to explain the situation to his captains thwarted him of the victories he hoped to achieve. Failure to communicate effectively facilitated 'bottom-upwards' situations.

The admirals most admired and loved were those who accepted the likely 'bottom-upward' trend in action and sought to work with it, having explained their thinking and expectations in advance. We know of Hawke's address to his captains in taking over the Mediterranean fleet from Byng in 1756, and of his willingness to give his captains their head in chase actions when opportunity offered. Likewise Howe calling his admirals and captains together before sailing to relieve Gibraltar in 1782, explaining 'his intention and manner of attacking the enemy if we should find it necessary to engage them', and of his addition to his signal book in 1794 for passing through the enemy line that 'The different captains and commanders not being able to effect the specified intention … are at liberty to act as circumstances require.'[102] On his arrival before Cádiz in 1805, Nelson had two dinners, one with his admirals and senior captains and the other with junior captains, at which he explained his intended battle plan, and he followed it up by sending them all his plan in a memorandum in which he set out this management method clearly:

> 'Thinking it almost impossible to bring a fleet of forty sail of the line into line of battle in variable winds, thick weather, and other circumstances which must occur, without such a loss of time that the opportunity would probably be lost of bringing the enemy to battle in such a manner as to make the business decisive…
>
> 'Something must be left to chance, nothing is sure in a sea fight beyond all others. Shot will carry away the masts and yards of friends as well as foes…
>
> '…in case signals can neither be seen or perfectly understood, no captain can do very wrong if he places his ship alongside that of an enemy.'[103]

Commanders who could manage to contain the drift to 'bottom-upwards' leadership were then in a position to use their fleets positively, and in the book which the present writer co-authored with Ruddock Mackay, *Hawke, Nelson and British Naval Leadership 1747–1805*, we set out twelve criteria for leadership excellence.[104] However, it is worth focusing here on the one which was the essential prerequisite to all the others. Effective naval leadership required moral courage: to be prepared to risk failure to achieve positive results. Among many notable command decisions, at least six stand out in the eighteenth century as having been made in difficult circumstances, which might have ended in total disaster, but which were in their own ways the game-changers their national policies required.

Three of these come from the Seven Years' War and signify the moment at which the British navy made the decisive step-change in its capacity for power-projection that out-matched all of its rivals – establishing an expertise in operating on enemy coasts and waterways that made it a formidable 'brown water' as well as a 'blue water' navy. Two instances triumphantly demonstrated British long-distance amphibious warfare capacity and ensure it became the nightmare of all powers with colonial empires. In 1759 Sir Charles Saunders took 20 ships of the line, 20 other warships and 180 transports carrying 8,500 troops 420 miles up the St Lawrence River to capture Quebec. Such an enterprise had been tried before, in 1711 when Admiral Hovenden Walker's fleet of 11 warships and 60 transports had been shattered and wrecked amidst the difficulties of the passage. The St Lawrence was tidal, with strong currents, strewn with hidden rocks and shoals, and frequently fog-bound between its rocky shores. It was a navigational nightmare, quite apart from French opposition with the guns of the fortress of Quebec, fireships and their removal of navigation buoys. Lacking charts, Saunders sent small boats ahead to sound and mark channels to reach Quebec, and when the attack faltered took his ships upstream, past the batteries of the fortress, to cut off its communications with upper Canada and support Wolfe in his final dangerous but successful landing.

Saunders's moral courage, careful leadership and maintenance of good relations with the army (a leadership quality particularly necessary in British naval warfare) were replicated three years later by Sir George Pocock in the capture of Havana. In order to achieve surprise, instead of taking the long windward way round the island of Cuba, he took his 31 warships and 200 transports with 11,000 men through the leeward passage and along the Old Bahama Passage on the north coast – a route unknown to British navigators and thought by the Spanish to be impossible for Pocock's 20 ships of the line. The project was Anson's, but it was left to Pocock to take the decision to risk his expedition by implementing it, again by sending boats ahead to take soundings and mark the passage by fires on boats and islands. The result was complete surprise and an unopposed landing.[105]

The third of this Seven Years' War trio was Sir Edward Hawke who, in the same year as the capture of Quebec, undertook a continual close blockade of the main French fleet at Brest in order to prevent a planned invasion. As late as

1756 an Admiralty memorandum discounted this as a possibility. Charts of the French coast were lacking to the navy whereas the French knew their own coasts perfectly and could keep near the shore and in shoal water 'where we dare not follow them'. The supply and maintenance problems of a fleet constantly at sea on the rocky French coast and the storms sweeping in from the Bay of Biscay also loomed large.[106] Yet Hawke decided to attempt it, and his leadership powers on the coast and Anson's organisation of the logistical backup from home enabled the blockade to continue for six months, until the French finally came out and Hawke caught up with them off Belle-Isle, from whence they sought safety in Quiberon Bay, not believing Hawke would follow them. But in the fading daylight of a late November afternoon and amidst a raging gale on a lee shore, and without pilots and mostly without charts of the coast, Hawke took the main British battlefleet into the cul-de-sac of Quiberon Bay, itself strewn with hidden rocks and shoal water, and achieved a crushing victory. 'No British admiral ever ran such navigational risks or gained so dramatic a victory', is the verdict of Nicholas Rodger.[107]

France was nevertheless capable of showing that positive results could still be achieved in the face of such an aggressive foe. The Comte de Grasse may have been a collision-prone seaman and was disliked by his subordinates, but he had been picked out by the squadron commander d'Orvilliers during the 1772 training manoeuvres as 'An officer of first distinction, made to be a general officer and capably direct the squadrons and fleets of the King'.[108] In 1781 he took a decision that decided the fate of a nation. When the imminent onset of the hurricane season led both the British and the French to withdraw their fleets from the Caribbean, Rodney sent just over half of his fleet to support the war in North America and took much of the rest home, escorting the rich West Indian convoys whose wealth helped sustain the war effort. He expected de Grasse to do likewise, but the latter decided to respond to an American call for aid against Lord Cornwallis's army, which had invaded Virginia, by taking his entire fleet thither, leaving only one 64-gun ship to escort France's equally valuable trade home. It was a decision that could have led to double disaster – if Rodney had taken all his fleet to America, and if the weakly escorted merchantmen had been captured and French credit ruined. Fortunately, neither happened and de Grasse's fleet closed the ring around Cornwallis's army on the Yorktown peninsula, and his repulse of the outnumbered British fleet coming to its relief decided the fate of the land campaign and of American independence. '[A]n indifferent tactician but a commander whose strategic vision made possible the most important naval victory of the 18th century', is Jonathan Dull's verdict.[109]

In May 1794 Louis Villaret-Joyeuse, newly appointed commander of the main French battlefleet – itself recently restored to discipline after mutinies, freshly mobilised in preparation for an attempted invasion, and lacking training in fleet manoeuvres – sailed from Brest in the knowledge that the British

Channel fleet was at sea, and with his orders to prevent it from intercepting a massive French convoy bringing North American grain and West Indian sugar to hard-pressed France. Failure might destabilise further the already unstable revolutionary republic; it might involve losses that would prevent its ulterior mission, and it might lead to the loss of his head! When he encountered Lord Howe's fleet, he took the decision to fight and to use his fleet as bait to lure Howe away from the path of the incoming convoy. In three actions, on 28 and 29 May and 1 June, he succeeded, in the last two leading with his flagship to the rescue of damaged ships threatened with capture. He lost seven of his 26 ships of the line, but saved the rest while so damaging Howe's ships as to render them unable to get back in front of Brest to prevent the escape of either his damaged ships or the convoy.[110]

Lastly, and despite the cautions at the start of this essay, we do come back to Nelson and his performance in the Nile campaign in 1798. In his first major command, when the French fleet sailed from Toulon in June escorting Napoleon's army and vanished into the Mediterranean, he took the decision to take his fleet a thousand miles off station to look for it off Egypt – so fast as to get there ahead of them and return disappointed to Sicily, only to find his instinct had been right and to sail back again, this time to find the French fleet anchored in a strong defensive position in Aboukir Bay. To attack a fleet at anchor, when it had had time to prepare its defences and when he lacked charts of the anchorage, was a hazardous task, and in the American war had led to bloody repulses – of d'Estaing at St Lucia (1778), Byron at Grenada (1779) and de Grasse at St Kitts (1782), yet Nelson attacked at once and was rewarded with the most decisive battle of annihilation of the eighteenth century, one that seared the minds of the French naval leadership throughout the Napoleonic Wars.[111] Leadership showing great moral courage could produce massive results for whichever national policies were being pursued.

# CHAPTER FIVE

# Naval Leadership in a 'Fleet in Being': The Spanish Navy and 'Armed Neutrality' in the Mid-Eighteenth Century

Catherine Scheybeler

Multiple ideas for the strategic function of the Spanish navy were tried and tested in the course of the eighteenth century. 'Armed neutrality' was but one of them and in place for only a brief period, during the reign of Ferdinand VI (1746–59), but it marked a significant phase in the development of eighteenth-century Spanish naval doctrine. Also, like many of the Spanish navy's strategies at this time, it was defensive, devised at the heart of government by the King's ministers and then communicated down to Spain's naval bases and officers. The command structure developed for this transmission as well as the defensive nature of the strategy itself affected naval leadership and how it was exercised by Spain's squadron commanders and ship captains. It is this relationship – between the command structure, a defensive policy and naval leadership – which will be studied here in the context of Spain's European squadrons at a time when a new idea for the function of the fleet was being introduced.

Ferdinand VI implemented 'armed neutrality' beginning from 1748 at the suggestion of his chief minister, Zenón de Somodevilla y Bengoechea, Marqués de la Ensenada (1702–81), who, in turn, had devised the policy partly to

**How to cite this book chapter:**
Scheybeler, C. 2017. Naval Leadership in a 'Fleet in Being': The Spanish Navy and 'Armed Neutrality' in the Mid-Eighteenth Century. In: Harding, R and Guimerá, A (eds.). *Naval Leadership in the Atlantic World.* Pp. 59–71. London: University of Westminster Press. DOI: https://doi.org/10.16997/book2.f. License: CC-BY-NC-ND 4.0

convince a pacific Ferdinand to allow him free rein in expanding and modern-
ising the fleet.[112] The arguments behind it were outlined in a series of memo-
randa where Ensenada reasoned, essentially, that the navy could be used as lev-
erage between Spain's two greatest European rivals, Britain and France, without
going to war.[113] A sufficiently powerful Spanish fleet could threaten British
superiority at sea when allied with the French and, therefore, the existence of
such a force would oblige both France and Britain to seek a Spanish alliance.
Its very existence, therefore, had a naval diplomatic value and it could act as
a 'fleet in being'.[114] While remaining neutral, Spain could wield the power the
navy would generate to protect its interests, to roll back the trading concessions
both powers had accumulated and, Ensenada even suggested, to have Gibraltar
and Minorca returned by Britain and Bellaguardia by France.[115] This was an
idea that was not original to Ensenada – others had promoted similar ideas in
the past and would continue to do so after – but this specific policy was actively
pursued from the 1748 Treaty of Aix-la-Chapelle to the signing of the Family
Pact in 1761 during the reign of Charles III (1759–88).

   While during these years Ensenada carried out his naval reform programme,
the manner in which the fleet was structured remained largely unchanged from
when his predecessor, José Patiño (1666–1736), had created the three Naval
Departments of Ferrol, Cádiz and Cartagena in 1726.[116] Each Naval Department deployed its own small squadron of two or three ships of the line for
routine cruising, adding extra ships in times of crisis and arming additional
squadrons for particular missions when necessary. In principle, tasks were
also divided by Department. Cartagena was responsible for the protection of
the Mediterranean and at the forefront of the fight against Barbary privateers.
Cádiz supervised convoying trade and the monarchy's resources to and from
Spain's trans-Atlantic empire, and Ferrol protected the Atlantic coast as far as
the Azores and the Canary Islands. In practice, this organisation was much
more elastic.

   The operations of the Mediterranean squadron commanded by Jefe de
Escuadra Pedro Mesía de la Cerda (1700–83) from May 1750 to January 1752
exemplify this. They also show the significance of the navy in the monarchy's
lines of communication. In addition to routine cruising and organisational
requirements such as turning over crews, collecting pay and repairing ships,
Mesía de la Cerda's squadron of two ships of the line also completed the following tasks:

1. Convoying a group of register ships into the Atlantic.[117]
2. Convoying 15 troop transports to Ceuta.[118]
3. Carrying troops from Cartagena to Barcelona and Mallorca.[119]
4. Collecting four newly-purchased xebecs at Mallorca and testing their sailing qualities on the return to Cartagena.[120]
5. Convoying Spanish shipping from Cartagena to Cádiz.[121]

6. Ferrying the Bishop of Mallorca from Barcelona to Palma.[122]
7. Transporting and exchanging 60,000 *vellon reals* for *vellon provincial* in Mallorca.[123]
8. Transporting the Royal Regiment of Artillery from Barcelona to Cádiz.[124]

Squadron deployment was arranged centrally at Court by the naval minister – the Marqués de la Ensenada until July 1754 and Julián de Arriaga y Ribera (1700–76) thereafter: the former was a bureaucrat who had risen through the ranks of naval administration and the latter a former naval officer.[125] Orders were then transmitted from Court to a Department's Comandante General, who would draw up formal instructions for a squadron commander or ship captain. If the planned operation was particularly important or secret, sealed orders were transmitted direct from the naval minister to the squadron commander as happened, for example, when the 60-gun *América* and the frigate *Esmeralda* were sent to convoy a group of wheat transports from Naples in 1753.[126]

At the Naval Departments, Comandantes Generales were in charge of seagoing officers and men as well as naval operations.[127] These positions were awarded to senior serving officers. At Cádiz, from 1750 to 1772, we find Juan José Navarro, Marqués de la Victoria (1687–1772) and, since his was the most senior Department, the post was combined with that of Director General de la Armada. At Ferrol, the Teniente General Francisco de Orozco (1699–1761) was Comandante General from 1755 to 1760 and, at Cartagena, the Teniente General Benito Antonio Spínola, Marqués Spínola (1687–1774) was in charge from 1753 to 1761. These officers were expected to have a thorough understanding of naval affairs in their Departments and to be well acquainted with their subordinate officers. They were the principle bridge of communication between a Department's naval officers and the Court.

This command structure was practical in light of the peninsula's geopolitical requirements. Its proximity to the Barbary states, whose privateers intruded constantly into Spanish waters harassing its commerce and coasts, required the navy to respond rapidly. Financial and manpower constraints made it difficult to have a large coastal protection force and consequently the three arsenals had to coordinate to provide this when such a threat loomed. This could not be arranged at the arsenals themselves since the distance between them made communication difficult, so it proved best to do this centrally. Its effectiveness is demonstrated by Ensenada's rearrangement of the fleet in the Spring of 1752 following news from Lisbon that Barbary vessels had been sighted in the Atlantic at precisely the time when the *Fuerte*, an *azogue* ship loaded with bullion from Cartagena de Indias, was expected in Cádiz.[128]

At that time, the *Dragón* (60) and *América* (60) were en route from Cádiz to Ferrol where they were to be laid up in ordinary so that their crews could be transferred to the newly launched *Asia* (70) and *Fernando* (70). In Ferrol, the frigate *Galga* and the packet boat *Marte* were ready to sail for Cartagena in the Mediterranean while the *Asia* and *Fernando* were still fitting out for a voyage across the Atlantic. In Cartagena, the *Tigre* (70) and *Septentrión* (70) and four xebecs (*Galgo, Cazador, Liebre* and *Volante*) were ready for sea. The *Septentrión* and the xebecs were going to be sent to America, leaving the *Tigre*, the *Reyna* (70) (once her repairs were concluded) and another four xebecs (*Ibicenco, Mallorquin, Valenciano* and *Catalan*) to cruise in the Mediterranean.

With Algerian privateers in the Atlantic, however, this arrangement provided insufficient protection for the *Fuerte*. Instead, Ensenada ordered the *Tigre* and *Septentrión* to cruise in the Atlantic until the end of May then return to Cartagena; the packet boat *Marte* and the frigate *Galga* were to remain in Ferrol until the *Fernando* and *Asia* could escort them to the Straits of Gibraltar, and the xebecs to remain in the Mediterranean and be joined by the *Reyna* once her repairs were complete. In this manner, the *Fuerte*, the packet boat *Marte* and the frigate *Galga* would be safe, cruising would continue in the Mediterranean and there would be sufficient time for fitting out the ships at Ferrol. The only inconvenience was that the *Septentrión, Galga, Marte* and four xebecs set to cruise in the West Indies that summer would be delayed from taking up their station until the end of June.

In order to maintain this system, however, the naval minister carefully monitored the seagoing fleet and its officers. Instructions were detailed and allowed for little deviation. The following, for example, were given to the Capitán de Fragata Juan Francisco Garganta in command of the packet boat *Marte* and the frigate *Galga* for a routine voyage from Ferrol to Cartagena in the Mediterranean:[129]

1. Once the vessels are ready for sea and the weather permits, the *Marte* and *Galga* will sail with the local pilots on board as far as the open sea.
2. Both vessels will follow a direct course to the Port of Cartagena without delay, the captains making the most precise observations on the good and bad qualities of both vessels. Once they anchor at Cartagena, they will make the most punctual and detailed report for the Court of what they have experienced and await the instructions that in consequence they will be issued.
3. They will inform the Comandante General in Cartagena Department of any news that is pertinent to him.
4. The packet boat and frigate will keep together during sailing, avoiding all separation, for which reason the commander will ensure that he issues clear and distinct signals so that no allegation of wrongdoing can be brought.
5. Should they encounter any foreign squadrons or ships belonging to allied princes in the course of the voyage, they will treat them with all possible

courtesy, maintaining the best correspondence and adhere to the *Reales Ordenanzas* in relation to greetings.

6. They will without fail board and search all ships from Hamburg and if they find any warlike goods or munitions they will confiscate these leaving the rest of the ships' cargoes and the ships themselves at liberty.[130]

7. Should they by chance come across any Algerian frigates or xebecs, they will attack them until they are taken or sunk depending on what is feasible. For this reason, both vessels will sail in a state ready to clear for action, ensuring that during the voyage the sailors and troops on board are trained in the use of the guns.

8. Should any blasphemers be found among the men and troops on board, these will be punished as instructed by the *Reales Ordenanzas*.

9. Should any vagrants be put on board either vessel, the captains will ensure that these men are not given any opportunity to desert and that they are trained in the profession of seamen.

All of which was left to 'the good conduct, prudence, zeal and courage of the commanders'. As can also be inferred from these instructions, the Spanish navy was governed by an additional code in the form of the *Ordenanzas de Su Magestad para el Govierno Militar, Político y Económico de Su Armada Naval* published in 1748.

These *Ordenanzas*, which condensed previous rulings into this two-volume work, dictated the formation of the fleet, its squadrons and ships, delineating each person's duties on land and at sea, the judicial code and its processes, and the government of its Pilot, Marine, Artillery and Guardias Marinas Corps. And, as Ferdinand VI stated in the foreword, it was to be followed 'infallibly' and 'without any deviation'.[131] All senior officers were obliged to have copies and were required to educate their subordinates in them so that none was ignorant of the law. Sections four and five in Volume One covered the duties of squadron commanders and ship captains in 60- and 76-paragraph entries respectively.[132] These outlined how commanders were to behave in a wide range of scenarios, and any infraction could be tried by a Consejo de Guerra, the Spanish equivalent of a court martial.

On occasions when anything out of the ordinary occurred, this was investigated by the Comandantes Generales and reported to the naval minister. When the *África* (70) lost sight of the frigate *Aguila* at sea during a storm in 1754, for example, and the two ships returned to Cádiz days apart despite being instructed to sail together, the Marqués de la Victoria, as the Department's Comandante, informed Ensenada that he had examined the journals of the officers on board both vessels and concluded that no one was to blame for the separation.[133] Similarly, when the *San Felipe* (70) was damaged in a storm in February 1753, the Intendente at Ferrol wrote to Ensenada noting:

'I had all the other officers' and pilots' journals given to me, they are all in agreement with each other and they do not differ in even the most minor detail from the account given by the ship's commanding officer which I forward to Your Excellency without finding the least action worthy of reproach in the conduct of the captain or the officers'.[134]

Joseph de Rojas y Beltran (1700–54), the captain of the unfortunate vessel, also felt the need to explain the accident in a letter written directly to Ensenada. He pleaded that it was 'the first such accident he had experienced in a long and active career and it has broken my health'.[135]

The naval minister could also intervene directly with regard to the behaviour of naval officers. One such occasion was when Ensenada issued a warning to the commander of the Cádiz squadron, Capitán de Navío Alonso de la Rosa Labassor, Conde de Vegaflorida (1700–71), for putting into port too frequently 'with the somewhat feeble excuse of needing to carry out repairs'.[136] In this situation, however, Vegaflorida could reply, rebutting Ensenada's accusations and insisting that the repairs had been necessary.[137]

The control exercised over naval commanders from the Court also extended to fighting at sea. During the era of 'armed neutrality', Spain might have been at peace with its European rivals but it remained in a state of conflict with the Barbary states of Tunis, Tripoli, Algiers and Morocco throughout. In the course of the eighteenth century, several offensive attempts were made against these, such as the capture of Oran in 1732, the attack on Algiers in 1775 and its bombardment in 1783. Even during Ferdinand's reign, an amphibious attack was planned against Algiers in 1749 but was cancelled at the eleventh hour.[138] Yet, on the whole, the Spanish navy adhered to a defensive strategy in this conflict, based on fending off intrusions. Commanders were thus regularly involved in small actions and skirmishes with Barbary privateers but their main priorities in these were to safeguard their own ships and resources as far as possible. This did not prevent there being many successes. In 1751, for example, the Capitán de Navío Pedro Stuart y Portugal (1720–89), in command of the *Dragón* (60), and Capitán de Navío Luis de Córdoba y Córdoba (1706–96), in command of the *América* (60), fought and destroyed the Algerian *Danzig* (60) and chased away the *Castillo Nuevo* (54) in a fierce action that lasted from 28 November to 2 December.[139] In June 1758, the squadron of Isidoro Garcia de Postigo y del Prado (1703–67), consisting of the ships *Soberano* (68), *Vencedor* (68) and *Héctor* (68), defeated and sank two Algerian ships of 60 and 40 guns.[140] Both were notable successes in which the naval commanders acted with daring and courage, but on both occasions the Spanish were challenging an enemy whom they outnumbered or outgunned. This was a stricture put upon them by the Court which insisted that commanders not challenge superior forces.

The forcefulness with which this was imposed can be understood from an exchange between Arriaga, as naval minister, and Teniente de Navío Joseph

Flon y Sesma, commander of the xebec squadron for 1755.[141] Flon, as captain of the *Aventurero* (30) and in overall command of the xebecs *Catalan, Garzota, Ibicenco* and *Gávilan*, defeated three Algerian vessels on 16 April 1755 – a notable victory. While being ordered back to sea following this action, Flon was instructed to be very careful and to keep close to coasts and anchorages where he could take refuge since he could not equal the five Algerian xebecs that were known to be near the Balearics. If he did encounter these, he could try to reinforce his squadron with vessels and men from Mallorca and, if he succeeded, then challenge them but otherwise he was to avoid an encounter. He could not deviate from his orders 'even if he had reliable information that promised greater success'.[142] Emboldened by his recent victory, Flon asked if his squadron could be reinforced with men and an additional vessel straight away so that he could attack the Algerian xebecs directly without having to seek reinforcements. When this was rejected, Flon repeated his request, explaining that Arriaga must know how 'all manoeuvres to flee the enemy will further stimulate their daring and tarnish the person in command'.[143] Arriaga only reiterated his original orders and added that Flon, being reassured that the King had 'as much faith in your courage as in your conduct', was to avoid exposing his forces unnecessarily and to keep in mind that 'squadrons do not refuse to sail with four to six ships even when they are aware that there are squadrons of eight, ten or twelve ships at sea'.[144] With this, Flon had no choice but to do as instructed.

This, then, was the command structure of the Spanish navy in European waters and the doctrine that the Court imposed on its naval officers through it. These officers were subject to a chain of command which, even in the case of their most mundane operations, began with the naval minister at Court, and through him the King, and provided specific instruction leaving little room for manoeuvre. Their activities were further controlled by a detailed code of conduct in the form of the *Ordenanzas*. The doctrine was mission-orientated, with great emphasis placed upon the navy's role in the crown's communications with its territories. At the same time, a defensive grand strategy existed in which the size of the fleet had diplomatic value and for which reason it was expected to act defensively like a 'fleet in being', so protective attitudes prevailed in relation to fighting at sea, and these stressed the safeguarding of resources. Naval leadership capabilities in squadron commanders and ship captains within this framework, however, remain significant.

With France and Britain at war from 1756, Spain pursued 'armed neutrality', as it had been conceived by the Marqués de la Ensenada to function within a state of European conflict, but intrinsic flaws began to emerge. Spanish neutrality and its navy were not such compelling diplomatic tools that Britain and France indulged Spanish interests against their own. Moreover, if France lost the war, which by 1759 seemed likely, there was nothing to prevent Britain attacking Spain without the prospect of French intervention.[145] As pertains to naval leadership, however, the navy was expected to enforce Spanish sovereignty and neutrality in its own waters. For this reason, the peninsula's squadrons were reinforced with additional ships, and commanders instructed to intervene to protect neutrality and trade from French or British interference. At the same time, though, they were to continue routine relations with warships from these countries, avoiding situations which could inadvertently bring Spain into the conflict.[146]

The difficulties with this soon became evident. In sailing the frigate *Palas* from Cartagena in the Mediterranean to Ferrol in November 1756, for example, Capitán de Navío Agustin de Idiázquez was stopped three times by British ships checking that his was not a French frigate. Doing so, and the manner in which it was done, was considered a violation of Spanish formalities and a challenge to Spain's sovereignty in its own waters. As a result, Idiázquez asked Arriaga, the naval minister, for a 'fixed instruction so that with its literal observation commanders can avoid acting wrongly and preserve the honour of the national flag.'[147]

Once at Ferrol, command of the *Palas* was transferred for patrolling between Cape Ortegal and Vigo to Vicente González-Valor de Bassecourt, Marqués González (1721–62), who would later become known for his heroic death at the siege of Havana. Francisco de Orozco, Comandante General at Ferrol, forwarded the instructions he intended to give González to Arriaga, asking if they conformed to the current strategy. These Arriaga, in turn, passed to Ricardo Wall (1694–1777), Ferdinand's minister for Foreign Affairs and then chief minister in the Spanish government, asking if what they instructed 'is in agreement with the current system' because there was no 'fixed rule.'[148] Four days later, Arriaga wrote that the instructions were to be modified so that there was less chance of them causing a break with France and Britain. Rather than escort into its ports ships and goods that had potentially been illegally seized by privateers or naval vessels of either nation, only Spanish ships flying Spanish colours at the time they were taken could be escorted to its ports and then, only if they had been taken by privateers. If the ships that seized the vessel were naval ships, then only a protest could be launched, and if the *Palas* was outnumbered by either naval ships or privateers then it was to do nothing.[149]

And yet, future instructions continued to press upon naval officers that they should make 'the King's flag and coasts be respected as they should be' by Britain and France.[150] This is what Andrés Reggio y Brachiforte (1692–1780) was ordered to do while in command of a grand squadron that was deployed in the Atlantic in 1758 partly to meet the incoming *flota* and partly as a show of force against the warring powers. When the Conde de Vegaflorida, his deputy, and in command of the division guarding the entrance to Cádiz Bay, complained that British warships were deliberately harassing shipping just beyond gunshot of him, thus making it against his instructions to react, he asked if something could be done. The answer from Court, however, was merely to follow his existing instructions.[151]

Thus while Ferdinand VI's government was asking its naval commanders to enforce neutrality in Spanish waters, it was also leaving them hamstrung as to how to do so. They, meanwhile, were conscious of this contradiction and repeatedly sought clarification. They did so working within the existing system that made specific instructions from Court necessary, especially when proposing a more aggressive stance that could cause the loss of naval resources. Ultimately it was the Court that had the decision-making capacity and it failed to respond to the strategic flaw that its naval officers had signalled, but the situation shows that these officers, nevertheless, needed to command Spain's ships with an understanding of the strategy.

At a tactical level too, courage, the determination to fight (within the right context), seamanship and tactical creativity, as well as coordination and communication between commanders, were vital naval leadership qualities, as demonstrated in the frequent skirmishes with North African privateers. One such instance is provided by the Cartagena xebec squadron, in an action that lasted from 29 September to 2 October 1753.[152] Having gathered intelligence that enemy xebecs were harassing shipping near the Straits of Gibraltar, the *Garzota* (commanded by Martin de Ortega), *Gávilan* (Francisco de Vera) and *Aventurero* (Martin de Lastarria) sailed to the area and there discovered an Algerian vessel. In attempting to catch it, it became evident that it would outsail them, so Ortega, who was in overall command, signalled to continue the chase but simultaneously raised the Algerian standard and veered his vessel to act as a lure. This was understood by Vera and Lastarria who immediately followed suit. The plan succeeded as the vessel turned and realised its mistake only once it reached them before attempting to escape once more. The distance closed, the chase continued with fighting into the night but both the *Aventurero* and *Gávilan* fell behind to repair broken masts and lost sight of the *Garzota*, which in the end only rejoined the group on 3 October.

The following day the *Gávilan* and *Aventurero* resumed the pursuit but calm seas made it unlikely they would reach the xebec before it reached the North African coast so at about midday they turned for the rendezvous at Torremolinos. Then, on the afternoon of 1 October, two Algerian xebecs were seen sailing towards them. Thinking that they could entice these to attempt a boarding that night and then catch them off guard, Vera and Lastarria agreed on a ruse to send off their launches noticeably full of men making it appear that, intimidated by the Algerians, they were abandoning ship. The launches were, in fact, to return quietly after dark. Meanwhile those who remained on board the *Gávilan* and *Aventurero* were armed, at their stations and divided into four -hour watches to ensure the men got as much rest as possible. Unfortunately for these commanders, those on the Algerian xebecs were evidently not fooled and did not approach until the following morning.

During the fighting on 2 October, the Algerians attempted to board first the *Gávilan* followed by the *Aventurero* but they were fought off with each Spanish xebec coming to the other's aid. Following a long gunnery and musketry battle, the severely damaged Algerian xebecs decided to abandon the fight in the early afternoon but were followed by the *Gávilan* and *Aventurero*, the gun battle continuing throughout. During this phase of the action, Vera sent his launch to help tow the *Aventurero* and moderated his own sail knowing that the *Aventurero* was a slower sailor and their instructions required that they remain grouped. The skirmish continued for several hours after this but the chase was called off once the *Gávilan* had completely exhausted its ammunition. The Algerian xebecs escaped but were severely damaged.

Both commanders praised the courage of their officers and men, and made recommendations for the future in their official reports. Lastarria in the *Aventurero* advised that eight-pounder bow chasers would be more suitable than three-pounders and that he had had insufficient men, which had forced him to choose between firing the guns and handling the ship. Vera in the *Gávilan* commented that despite his men being very raw he felt confident that he could train them up soon but that he had been issued with the insufficient amount of only 20 rounds per gun. Actions such as these, though seemingly small-scale and insignificant, are representative of when fighting at sea was permissible and the manner in which it could be carried out.

Seamanship, in both its theoretical and practical application, was accorded great significance as a feature of naval leadership in the Spanish navy. Education at the Academia de Guardias Marinas attempted to combine the British and French models in order to provide cadets with the academic knowledge to understand the workings of a sailing ship as well as give practical experience.[153] Greater emphasis was placed on the production of gentlemen officers illustrative of Spain's standing relative to the Enlightenment and the scientific revolution, but small detachments of students from the Academy were regularly sent as midshipmen on board Spain's warships, and applicants to it were encouraged first to serve in the Order of St John's galleys in Malta in order to prepare them for a life at sea.[154] The skills they learnt were tested throughout their careers as they were required to report and explain to the Court the sailing properties of the ships on which they served. This was especially the case during times such as the 1750s when the fleet was being substantially expanded – 48 new ships of the line were added to it in the 13 years of Ferdinand VI's reign – and a new system of naval construction was being introduced.[155] In addition, the Spanish navy, like many other fleets, had chronic manning difficulties and these were further exacerbated by a recruitment system that meant men served only short periods at sea and crews were constantly changing.[156] Complaints that the men were 'useless, most of them being very youthful, raised in the rivers in the practice of fishing, ignorant of how to handle themselves on the deck of a ship, manoeuvre one or climb a spar' were not uncommon and so, much pressure was put upon naval officers to instil seamanship skills in their crews.[157]

There are at present few known accounts of life at sea for ordinary seamen in the eighteenth-century Spanish navy, making it difficult to judge naval leadership from their perspective. Further research on the numerous petitions for pensions or employment preserved at the National Archives in Simancas, along with their accompanying references from commanding officers, could go some way towards filling this gap.[158] These petitions and references, however, served an official function and generally followed a specific format. Another source useful in understanding the leadership provided by officers to ordinary seamen is the previously mentioned *Ordenanzas de Su Magestad para el Govierno Militar, Político y Económico de Su Armada Naval* issued in 1748. Since these regulations provided a code of conduct for those serving in the Spanish navy, they show if not necessarily the reality then at least the ideal of naval leadership with which officers were required to provide their subordinates. From this it is possible to see that naval officers were expected to exercise many of the characteristics that are today considered vital for good leadership. It was the naval commander's duty to know the state of his ships and men, and to ensure that his subordinates knew what was expected of them. Officers had to ensure that the men were properly instructed and trained in their duties. And the men had a right to be governed justly and well, as dictated by the *Ordenanzas* in terms of daily routine, diet, discipline, etc. Any perceived violations of this code experienced by the men could be reported by them to the Comandante General of a Department who would then investigate the officers involved.

Another feature of naval leadership which was pertinent to the Spanish navy was the significant role played by the concept of the naval hero. Spain was not involved in any large-scale fleet engagements during the 1750s and therefore there were few opportunities for heroics, though commanders in small actions, such as Stuart y Portugal, who was promoted to Jefe de Escuadra for his victory over the *Danzig*, were much extolled. On the other hand, the conflicts to either side of this period, the War of Jenkins' Ear and the Seven Years' War, provide notable examples. Perhaps the most famous is Blas de Lezo y Olavarrieta (1689–1741) for his heroic leadership in the defence of Cartagena de Indias in 1741, which cost him his life while succeeding in repulsing the British attack. Also lauded for successfully withstanding the British was Juan José Navarro at the Battle of Toulon (Cape Sicié) in 1744, for which he was rewarded with the title Marqués de la Victoria, which, when translated into English as 'Marquis of Victory', becomes more revealing. In the Seven Years' War, Luis Vicente de Velasco (1711–62) and the previously mentioned Marqués González fought unsuccessfully but died courageously defending Morro Castle at Havana in 1762. Their valour was celebrated in various ways: medals were struck; their portraits were displayed at the *Real Academia de San Fernando*, and a state-run literary competition to commemorate this was won by Nicolás Fernández de Moratín (1737–80). In his *Egloga*, Velasco and González fight courageously while desperately outnumbered, both knowingly giving up their lives in the process, so that the British would not be handed 'victory cheap'.[159]

No mention is made in Moratín's pastoral poem, however, of the inept Gutierre de Hevia y Valdés, Marqués de Real Transporte (1720–72), under whose command Velasco and González lost their lives. On this occasion Real Transporte mishandled his command through his own personal failings: by making rudimentary tactical errors, consistently disregarding the opinions of his subordinate officers, and displaying a lack of personal courage. These failures saw him face a Consejo de Guerra on his return to Spain on seven counts of failing to follow the *Ordenanzas de Marina*, which resulted in the relatively light sentence of suspension from the navy and banishment from Court for ten years.[160] This was reversed within the year and he was reinstated in the navy. The difficulty with attributing Real Transporte's failings as solely personal, however, is that many of his mistakes were not only tolerated by the organisation in which he served but were even the product of it. Throughout his command at Havana, Real Transporte was convinced that with fewer forces than his opponents he could do nothing at sea; his decisions were motivated by the need to protect his forces and, despite the distance between Cuba and Spain, he still sought specific instructions from Madrid.[161] All three of these factors would have been familiar to Spanish naval commanders operating in European waters, which Real Transporte had of course been from 1756 to 1761.

At the same time, however, this same organisation produced talented naval leaders such as Juan Francisco de Lángara y Huarte (1736–1806), Luis de Córdoba y Córdoba (1706–96) and José de Mazarredo y Salazar de Muñatones Cortázar (1745–1812). These officers could operate within the Spanish system to advantage, especially once the aim of expanding the navy to threaten British naval supremacy when combined with the French finally materialised during the American War of Independence (1775–83).

During Ferdinand's reign and the years during which the policy of 'armed neutrality' was being pursued from 1748 to 1761, the navy was run in European waters through a highly-centralised command structure. Using this, the state imposed a defensive strategy which, by focusing on the protection of naval resources, further limited the independence of action that naval officers were allowed. The behaviour of squadron commanders and ship captains during these years reveals that these factors did have a conditioning effect on them. Conscious that acting without instruction or being responsible for loss or damage was viewed as suspect by the Crown and likely to make naval leaders liable, especially when perceived as the result of unnecessary risks, commanders tended to err on the side of caution on occasions when they did have the strength to achieve greater results. Despite this, though it seems self-evident, characteristics more frequently associated with good naval leadership in fleets employing more aggressive strategies and flexible command structures, such as strategic understanding, tactical skill, seamanship, personal leadership and courage, were required all the same in a fleet with a non-flexible command structure and defensive strategy.[162] Perhaps this helps explain why the Spanish navy failed to punish and remove incompetent commanders like Real Transporte but still fostered those with greater naval leadership capability such as Lángara,

Córdoba and Mazarredo. Despite a number of recent significant biographies of Spanish naval officers, there is still much that is uncertain. Who were the naval officers beyond the mere facts of where they were born, served and died? What were their personal opinions about leadership, the navy and the strategies they followed? What leadership and patronage networks did they belong to? And how were they judged as leaders by those who served under them? If this information were available to place alongside our present understanding of the command structure and the strategies practised, it would be possible to obtain a more nuanced picture of naval leadership in the eighteenth-century Spanish navy.

# CHAPTER SIX

# Admiral Louis Guillouet, Comte d'Orvilliers (1710–92): A Style of Command in the Age of the American War

Olivier Chaline

Université de Sorbonne, Paris

In 2003 Professor Nicholas Rodger noted that: 'British flag officers' styles of command might be located on a scale ranging from the most autocratic and centralized to the most confiding and delegating. Roughly corresponding to this was another scale, of training: those who put most effort into practising fleet manoeuvres seem very often to have been those who were most willing to allow captains to use their judgement in action.'[163] The same could be said about French admirals of that time. On one side were the cases of the Comte de Grasse (1723–88) or the Bailli de Suffren (1729–88), who were hated by many of their officers, and on the other side there was Louis Guillouet, Comte d'Orvilliers (1710–92), whose departure from Brest in September 1779 offered the Grand Corps a unique opportunity to display their love and admiration for him.

Like Jellicoe after him, d'Orvilliers can be described as a man who could have lost a war in one afternoon had he not stood fast against Admiral Keppel at

---

**How to cite this book chapter:**
Chaline, O. 2017. Admiral Louis Guillouet, Comte d'Orvilliers (1710–92): A Style of Command in the Age of the American War. In: Harding, R and Guimerá, A (eds.). *Naval Leadership in the Atlantic World.* Pp. 73–84. London: University of Westminster Press. DOI: https://doi.org/10.16997/book2.g. License: CC-BY-NC-ND 4.0

the Battle of Ushant on 27 July 1778. However, this is often neglected – even in France. Rather, it is his failure, in the following year, at the head of the French-Spanish fleet in the Western Approaches, that attracts attention.[164] The historiography, especially in France, has focused on the question of whether the plan for a landing on the south coast of Britain could really have succeeded. D'Orvilliers himself, who resigned soon after his return to Brest, has hardly been considered as an officer in the existing historiography.[165] This is a pity because he displayed a genuinely personal leadership style, a very different one indeed from that of his fellow French flag officers. His personal and familial archives have been lost, so to understand his leadership style one needs to turn to his correspondence with the Secrétaire d'État de la Marine, at the Archives Nationales in Paris. Three main issues can be probed on the basis of his letters: his teaching skills, his concern about his fleet's cohesion and efficiency and, last but not least, his dignity in command, even when he felt powerless against ministers, the unpredictable natural elements and an epidemic which led him to mourning and failure.

## I – Teaching skills

D'Orvilliers stands out as an admiral blessed with exceptional teaching skills. He spent a long time in charge of the instruction of the *Gardes de la Marine*, whose three companies at Brest, Rochefort and Toulon were at the beginning of their naval careers in the *Grand Corps*, the French officer corps. He had to command successively a brigade, a detachment and the whole company, while he himself was promoted from junior officer to *capitaine de vaisseau*. The bulk of his career took place at Rochefort. The Western maritime province of Saintonge happened to be the birthplace of his wife, Marie de Chesnel d'Escoyeux, daughter of a *chef d'escadre*. Although d'Orvilliers was born in Moulins, miles away from the coast, he was the son of a governor of French Guyana who had fought at Vélez-Málaga.[166] He was a typical *enfant du Corps*, entering the *Gardes de la Marine* in 1728, where he received the type of instruction he was later to provide to the younger *Gardes* members, who like himself, were of the provincial nobility, with a corporate spirit based on family ties rather than wealth.

These were dull times to enter the navy – no wars; no fast-track promotions. D'Orvilliers devoted his entire life to the *Grand Corps*. True, he took part in the Battle of Toulon, in 1744, but his main activity was the training of generations of young officers for the wars to come. It should be noted that Hubert de Conflans (1690–1777) did the same at Brest just before the beginning of the War of the Austrian Succession. Like Admiral La Galissonnière (1693–1756), commandant de la marine at Rochefort, d'Orvilliers came to the early conclusion that the best way of making good naval officers was to train them on sea rather than on land.

An important chance encounter was his meeting with the future vice-admiral, Jean-Baptiste Macnémara (1690–1756), like La Galissonnière, one of the most promising French flag officers at that time. From 1739, d'Orvilliers sailed many times under Macnémara's command and was selected, in 1750 and 1754, for two of the first *escadres d'évolutions*. These were organised for naval training, not for young officers but for selected captains. In 1754, as he was 44 years old, he was promoted to the rank of *capitaine de vaisseau* and was highly rated as an 'excellent officer despite his little fortune'. His career now seems to have assumed a rather speedy course. On the eve and at the beginning of the Seven Years' War (1756–63), d'Orvilliers was trained by good tacticians like Macnémara, Hilarion-Josselin Duguay (1692–1760) and Dubois de La Motte (1683–1764), especially in squadrons intended to reinforce and resupply French Canada. On these voyages, manoeuvres were more important than fighting. French Admirals sailing for Quebec or Louisbourg were instructed to achieve something other than the defeat of the enemy. The main objective for a navy in an inferior position was to keep sea routes open without being destroyed. However, after 1757, wear and tear, disease (d'Orvilliers was lucky enough to escape typhus in Dubois de La Motte's squadron returning from Louisbourg) and the British blockade made that objective unattainable.

D'Orvilliers didn't take part in the crushing defeats of 1759. His reputation remained thus unstained. When the time came to rebuild the navy he was one of the up-and-coming men on which a minister could rely. On 1 October 1764 he was promoted to *chef d'escadre*, the first rank of flag officer. In 1772, he was chosen to command the first *escadre d'évolutions*, or training squadron, organized since the Peace of Paris in 1763.[167] What he had achieved with junior officers of the *Gardes de la Marine*, he now had to achieve with more senior and experienced captains, and even with two other flag officers. The *chef d'escadre*, the Comte du Chaffault (1708–94), was two years older than him and offended that he had to obey a younger officer. The purpose of this training squadron of three warships, six frigates and three corvettes was to get officers and crews to practise a lot of manoeuvres together, obeying the orders and signals given to them. At this point, we should note that the Chevalier du Pavillon was present on board the new *Alexandre* (64), d'Orvilliers' flagship. For little more than three months, the squadron was trained by d'Orvilliers cruising from Brest to the Cape Saint-Vincent. He supervised a considerable number of naval exercises involving his flag officers and captains: for example, how to stand in a bow and quarter line, to chase, to tack in succession, and so on. They were required to practise again and again until they got things right. D'Orvilliers, as a clear-headed and patient training officer, only worked with a small number of rather straightforward manoeuvres, but the more practised his captains were, the better trained officers they became.

For d'Orvilliers there was another purpose to the training squadron: to single out deserving men for the next war against Britain. The admiral wrote a series of *apostils*; that is, teacher's assessments of the captains and junior officers who sailed under his command.[168] Some did not deserve promotion. Others seemed to be beginning a promising career, like his own nephew Hugon de Givry, who 'combines willpower and talents and promises to turn into a great officer'. Moreover, there were some officers who enjoyed a fast-track promotion, like the Chevalier du Pavillon:

> 'an officer who stands out as much for his wide-ranging command of the theory as his zeal and enthusiasm. With his remarkable eye for details, he belongs to the few who deserve, on the basis of a trial-and-error method, to be entrusted with a commanding position, rather than be relegated to some ancillary task'.

Given their strong personalities, three of d'Orvilliers's assistants clearly deserved praise and recognition. First was Du Chaffault. D'Orvilliers sought to treat him courteously in order to placate Du Chaffault's resentment against him. These were his simple words: 'Well above my approval; I hope to have deserved his.' About the Comte de Grasse, he wrote:

> 'He is the captain who manoeuvred the best and although his frigate was of very low quality, he nevertheless made the best out of his manoeuvres, the most precise and brilliant possible. His frequent collisions during that campaign show room for improvement (...) but in fact the comte de Grasse is a highly distinguished captain who is fit to command the King's squadrons and naval armies.'

The third officer was the Comte de la Motte-Picquet (1720–91), 'the only one who can fight with M. De Grasse for the best way to keep his station and to manoeuvre precisely. He took all the advantage possible from a very bad ship. Flag officers would be perfectly guilty not to undertake the greatest enterprises with captains of such merit.'

That training squadron was for d'Orvilliers an exceptional moment, when he had under his command Du Chaffault, Latouche-Tréville, de Grasse, la Motte-Picquet and La Clochetterie. Six years later, the last in this list was the commander of the frigate *La Belle Poule* (26), which successfully fought off the British *Arethusa* (32) on 17 June 1778 and precipitated the outbreak of war between France and Britain.

In 1773, the King and his minister were satisfied with the training cruise. The same cannot be said of d'Orvilliers. Committed as he was to his Corps, he knew how badly reforms were needed to fend off criticism (especially regarding the training of officers). Nevertheless, at the beginning of Louis XVI's reign, on 1 March 1775, he was chosen by the King and the minister of the navy, Antoine-Raymond-Gualbert-Gabriel de Sartine (1729–1801), to command the navy at Brest. Thus, he assumed the leadership of France's main arsenal and of the fleet mounting guard in front of Britain.

## II – D'Orvilliers's concern for his fleet's cohesion and efficiency

When he was promoted to the rank of *lieutenant général des armées nav-ales* in 1777, and the following year when he was given command of the great fleet concentrated at Brest, D'Orvilliers had reached the climax of his naval career. From that time on, he was addressed as Comte (Earl) in his official correspondence. He took on board his flagship his own son, the *lieutenant de vaisseau* Louis Claude d'Orvilliers de Château-Chesnel, and two nephews, the *enseignes de vaisseau* Louis Gilbert d'Orvilliers and Claude Hugon de Givry. What he hoped for was to reap glory for his family and strengthen the reputation of the Corps. At the same time, another French fleet that had been sent before the war from Toulon to North America was under the command of the Comte d'Estaing (1729–94), a general who had been appointed *lieutenant général des armées navales* by the Court immedi-ately after the end of the Seven Years' War. D'Estaing's fast-track promotion was resented by the *Grand Corps* as an interference directly attributable to favouritism. A haughty and vain demagogue, D'Estaing often behaved hor-ribly. By contrast, d'Orvilliers was highly praised for being a competent and affable officer, who was born into and grew up in the *Grand Corps*. He clearly met his fellow officers' expectations. He showed himself in the most favour-able light. He behaved courteously but he was firmly aware of issues of prec-edence and hierarchy. Maintaining his rank now was a top priority. As a *lieutenant général d'armée navale*, he kept his table on board his flagship *La Bretagne* with splendour and refinement, taking on board a thousand bottles of Margaux and Sauternes.

Unlike Suffren a few years later, d'Orvilliers went out of his way to set up a council of war with his flag officers and captains. He read them the royal instructions stemming from the *Secrétaire d'Etat de la Marine* and explained to each of them what his expectations were. In the early stages of the war, these instructions were rather vague but, for the first time since the age of Louis XIV, there was an offensive twist to them. The King and the nation expected d'Orvilliers to restore French maritime prestige. There was a general desire to avenge 1759.

D'Orvilliers clearly thought that, under his firm command, the *Grand Corps* would be in a good position to efficiently fight against the Royal Navy. But, as the former head of the training squadron, he was perfectly aware of the short-comings of his fleet and, shortly after their departure from Brest, he tried to carry out some manoeuvres. He flew his flag on the *Bretagne*, a vessel given to the King by the Brittany estates at the end of the previous war.[169] His flag captain was Parscau du Plessix and the captain of the fleet the Chevalier du Pavillon.[170] Both had fought at Quiberon Bay. D'Orvilliers himself was at the head of the White squadron, Du Chaffault at the head of the White and Blue. The command of the Blue squadron, however, was entrusted to the Duke of Chartres, which posed a problem.

Philippe (1747–93), Duke of Chartres and later of Orléans, was the King's cousin.[171] He is also known as Philippe Égalité, the prince who voted for Louis XVI's death sentence. At that time, however, the two branches of the Bourbon family were not yet at odds. The young prince of the blood was hoping to inherit his father-in-law's post of *grand amiral de France* and make his reputation out of a career in the navy. His career had soared in recent years. He had been promoted to the rank of *lieutenant général*, a status that clearly reached beyond his true naval experience.[172] In this capacity, he was flanked by the experienced La Motte-Picquet. The presence of a member of the royal family aspiring to glory could be worthwhile for the navy but it could also be a source of embarrassment for the Secrétaire d'Etat de la Marine as well as for d'Orvilliers. The duke didn't challenge the admiral's authority nor did he lack courage. Yet, at the battle at Ushant, on 27 July 1778, when the whole fleet had tacked, his blue squadron ended in the vanguard in the former place of Du Chaffault and therefore was in position to lead the movements.[173] D'Orvilliers ordered him to wear and envelop the British rearguard in an attempt to destroy it, like Tourville had done at Beachy Head and as was recommended too by Bigot de Morogues in his treaty about *Naval Tactics* (1763). But the duke didn't immediately carry out d'Orvilliers's order and lost time before trying to do so. By then it was too late. The exact reason for such a delay still remains unclear. The duke's entourage may have feared for his safety. Had Du Chaffault been in the duke's shoes, the orders would have been executed without demur. Far from inflicting the decisive blow, the aristocrat among the flag officers had blunted the efficiency and cohesion of the fleet.[174] There was nothing d'Orvilliers could do to prevent it.

While wanting a clear-cut victory, d'Orvilliers nevertheless scored a strategic and moral point. He did not lose the war in one afternoon and even inflicted heavy casualties on the enemy, who was quite surprised, especially when d'Orvilliers placed his flagship, *La Bretagne*, alongside the *Victory*. How extensive the modernisation of the French navy had been was now clear to everyone. While in Britain the acrimonious repercussions of the battle led to the infamous Keppel-Palliser affair, d'Orvilliers managed to keep his squadron in the Channel, forcing the Royal Navy to keep many ships at home, unable to strengthen British forces in North American waters. If nothing more was achieved in the Western Approaches, the Battle of Ushant was celebrated in France because of its impact in terms of restored national pride.

The Spanish alliance was badly needed in the following campaign.[175] A joint naval operation needed to be mounted. D'Orvilliers had by now become a leading naval officer in the eyes of the Court. He was held to be the best French flag officer for the job.[176] He met all the necessary requirements: the fame he had acquired through his victory, the esteem he enjoyed among the *Grand Corps* officers and his touch for diplomacy.[177] Under these conditions, his task was to sail to Spain, to link up with the Spanish navy under Admiral

Cordoba. The Franco-Spanish squadrons were then to make their way north to meet the Royal Navy. The difficulties d'Orvilliers had to cope with were considerably greater than before. The French ambassador in Madrid had warned him: 'I must warn you that Monsieur de Cordoba is a very old man, now in his mid-seventies. He is highly regarded in the Spanish navy but, as you may imagine, he suffers from the sort of deficiencies a man of his venerable age has to endure.'[178] It seems to have escaped the French ambassador's attention that his addressee was no less than 69 years old. D'Orvilliers responded with the sort of sense of humour he was expected to have 'towards that venerable old man all the attentions and care needed by his age and virtue'.[179] With true diplomatic skills and unlimited patience, d'Orvilliers gained his allies' confidence, especially that of Don Miguel de Gastón, whose help was invaluable in resupplying the French ships that were short of water and food.[180] However, d'Orvilliers was quickly aware that his allies' manoeuvring at sea was quite defective for want of training. A considerable amount of time was lost. There may be a case to be made that in 1779 the Bourbon cause needed a more daring admiral than d'Orvilliers but, to be fair, there was precious little chance of finding a French admiral with finer skills than him to command the combined fleet. In spite of divergent interests and a lack of preparation on both sides, d'Orvilliers went out of his way to explain to his allies what needed to be done, to take joint decisions and treat them well. There was little time left to enforce a true operational cohesion but he managed to lead the combined fleet up to the Western Approaches. Despite many hurdles, d'Orvilliers's leadership style allowed him to score some major points at sea, but having to deal with Versailles Court politics was quite a different story.

## III – Powerless dignity

By nature, or because of his background and education, d'Orvilliers was not the sort of man to stick his neck out politically. While admired and praised by his subordinates, he was short of friends at Court to promote and defend his reputation. Even after Ushant, he remained a discrete and competent servant of the King and never became a general with the sort of skills you need to wage war on two fronts: one against the King's enemies, another against the many intrigues of life at Court.

Problems at Court cropped up shortly after Ushant. First, the duke of Chartres returned to Brest and then to Versailles and Paris where he was celebrated like a hero. After the whole fleet had returned to port, some dissenting accounts of the events circulated, instilling a doubt as to the reality of the duke's alleged bravery. Whilst many Parisian lampoonists lambasted the duke's misconduct, d'Orvilliers sought to smooth a few feathers, and cautiously avoided commenting on the duke's conduct. However, if Chartres had done nothing wrong, it could be said that d'Orvilliers was not immune to criticism for not having followed up his tactical advantage. There was also some suspicion among d'Orvilliers's subordinates. For example, La Motte-Picquet wrote the admiral a letter in justification of the duke's conduct. More serious was the covert yet growing enmity of the Orléans family and faction. Chartres never went to sea again. The following year, after the failure of the Channel campaign when d'Orvilliers had to hand in his resignation, the prevailing opinion among the *Grand Corps* was that he had suffered the consequences of Chartres's wrath. In November 1778, when d'Orvilliers came to Versailles, he was hurt when the King himself bluntly asked him why he had failed to pursue his campaign after Ushant. A loyal servant of the Crown, he responded that he alone was to blame.

But more trouble and disillusion was to crop up the year after; swimming against the tide of political, diplomatic and naval constraints proved impossible. D'Orvilliers had to prepare the Brest fleet for a joint operation with the Spanish navy. In the first round of the secret talks, however, he was kept in the dark. Only the two Bourbon kings, their foreign ministers Vergennes and Floridablanca, and the ambassadors, Montmorin in Madrid, Aranda in Versailles, took part in the discussions. The main details of the projected naval operations were worked out without prior consultation of the naval officers.

Only after the Treaty of Aranjuez (12 April 1779) were d'Orvilliers and du Pavillon summoned to Versailles to hold talks with Vergennes and Sartine.[181] The two officers requested that the combined fleet be homogenously arranged, with separate French or Spanish squadrons, and an exclusively French vanguard able to launch a swift attack on the enemy.

Diplomatic reasons made this option impracticable. The same applied to their request to find a better meeting place than Sisargas island, off the coast of Galicia. Contenting the Spanish ally was the requirement that came top of the agenda. The two officers succeeded only in postponing the departure from Brest from 1 May to 1 June, the fleet being in no condition to sail before then. Lack of money and poor preparation led to the first of a string of fateful delays. It is a noticeable fact that, despite his naval experience, d'Orvilliers carried little weight. Nor was there anyone in the Secrétaire d'Etat de la Marine's department at Versailles, not even the Chevalier de Fleurieu (albeit himself a naval officer), to oversee naval preparations in tandem with d'Orvilliers. The difference with the British Board of Admiralty is indeed striking. The available navy was clearly insufficient too. The success of the joint naval operation depended on d'Orvilliers but it took a long time before he became privy to the project. What's more, he was shackled to royal instructions, which remained rather vague on key issues and exaggeratedly detailed in other areas. Worse, when he left Brest, his ships had received only two months' worth of water and food supplies. Now, the slightest delay was likely to foil the project of a joint assault on the Isle of Wight.

Waiting for the Spanish for a whole month near Sisargas (23 June–23 July) brought about a second fateful delay. Water and food supplies were running low. The French fleet was beset by an epidemic which greatly blunted its sailing and fighting abilities. Once the fleet was ready, unfavourable winds barred access to the Channel. Disease spread into the fleet. D'Orvilliers's only son fell sick and died on 2 August. D'Orvilliers was deeply upset and never quite recovered from this loss, but he staunchly persisted in carrying out the orders he had received. As he wrote to Sartine: 'The Lord has taken away everything I own in this world but I have enough strength left to bring the campaign to a close.'[182] Six days later he made his last will, bequeathing to his nephew maths books and instruments, maritime maps, now useless noble titles, his croix de Saint Louis and family portraits.[183] The death of his son seems to have taken its toll on him.

In the following month (from early August to early September), he persisted in wanting to lead the combined fleet into the Channel. But he had to cope with overwhelming difficulties: the constant deterioration of his crew's health, the lack of cohesion of the combined fleet and, worst of all, unfavourable winds. Nevertheless, in mid-August he anchored near Plymouth, arousing fear in Cornwall. He then received new instructions giving the fleet a new and different target: not the Isle of Wight any more but an attempted landing on the Cornish coast. He voiced his surprise to Sartine: 'Full of respect and deference for my master's and his council's wisdom, I shall carry out the orders I received with the utmost possible zeal, but I feel I ought to provide you and the Crown with the following observations...'. These few words offer a nice summary of d'Orvilliers's leadership style when, driven away from the Channel by the winds, he increasingly disagreed with the King and his ministers. All hopes of immediate victory had vanished; so had the hope of a good understanding with ministers who remained far remote from the reality of naval business. Nevertheless, abiding by his duty came as a consolation for d'Orvilliers.

In early September, however, after having failed to catch Admiral Sir Charles Hardy's Channel Squadron, d'Orvilliers decided not to resume the pursuit and returned to Brest to avoid exhausting his crews, greater difficulties and perhaps defeat.[184] Perfectly aware that he had reached the limits of his power of keeping the sea, he then wrote to Sartine: 'Let me confess that this was mission impossible for my crew. I don't see how anyone on earth could disagree with me.'

D'Orvilliers was compelled to serve as the scapegoat for a poorly prepared campaign, resigning and then going on to live the life of a recluse. Praised by public opinion a year earlier, he was turned into a laughing stock. Lampoonists in Paris ascribed his failure to his deep but now unfashionable religious faith. With no backing to be expected from the Court, he was defenceless. He withdrew with dignity, issuing neither complaints nor indictments. He never saw the King and his ministers again.

His departure from Brest in September 1779 was a unique event testifying to the extraordinary esteem in which he was held by the French navy. Scipion de Castries was later to describe it as a real triumph because of the way d'Orvilliers was escorted to the City gates by French and Spanish naval officers.[185] Farewells were so moving that he felt unable to respond. More than 200 officers accompanied him to Landerneau and some even to Morlaix. These farewells can be interpreted as a protest movement of the *Grand Corps* against the Court and ministers. And it was precisely to the officers of the *corps de la marine* that d'Orvilliers later wrote exhorting them to obey and serve with dedication and faithfulness, as they had done before.

D'Orvilliers's leadership style displays a very professional attitude made up of naval competence, esprit de corps and dedication. He can be compared with his fellow French flag officers of the American war. He was a fine tactician like Guichen or de Grasse but he lacked the wide experience of naval action of Du Chaffault and Guichen. He was firm, but neither intrepid nor particularly aggressive. Unlike de Grasse he had charisma and led his subordinates by being really able to impress them. However, this accomplished officer was unable to express himself very freely or effectively with ministers, even when he lost his grip on the situation in August 1779 and the failure was largely due to circumstances and decisions beyond his control.

Nor could he contest the monarchical order, the precedence of the *Grand Corps*, and naval tactics he had learnt and taught. But his faithfulness to the Crown left no room for doubt. During the impending tragedy at sea in summer 1779, when naval and strategic failure was deepened by mourning for his son and the loss of any family future, d'Orvilliers reached his true greatness, just before he disappeared into retreat and silence.

Appendix: D'Orvilliers as seen by the Chevalier du Pavillon in a letter to the Secrétaire d'Etat de la Marine Sartine, 15 September 1779 (AN Marine B⁴ 154).

« Monseigneur, Mon général vient de me dire qu'il est désapprouvé de n'avoir pas poursuivi l'ennemi plus longtemps et de ne pas avoir ordonné la chasse sans égard à l'ordre prescrit entre les vaisseaux de la ligne de bataille; j'avoue, Monseigneur, que ma surprise est extrême; comment pouvait-il se dispenser de courir sur une flotte signalées à plusieurs reprises par des personnes graves? Si elle se fut trouvée anglaise, on l'aurait bien mieux condamné; enfin, Monseigneur, comment mon Général pouvait-il négliger un seul instant de ressortir de la Manche puisqu'il était menacé de vents de sud-ouest, que l'événement a prouvé qu'il les aurait trouvés; qu'il manquait absolument d'eau, de vivres et même de matelots; vous devez sentir aujourd'hui, Monseigneur, puisque vous connaissez l'état et les progrès de l'épidémie qui ravage tous les vaisseaux du Roi, que quelques jours de retard dans la sortie de la Manche aurait fait perdre au Roi ses vaisseaux et le reste de leurs matelots; ce fait n'est que trop prouvé; il l'est également aux yeux de toute l'armée que jamais son Général n'a été aussi grand, aussi supérieur à l'humanité et aux adversités que dans cette malheureuse campagne, laquelle n'a manqué que parce qu'on a mal choisi le point de réunion des vaisseaux des deux puissances; quant à la poursuite que l'on prétend à

Paris n'avoir pas été assez vive, parce qu'on n'a pas fait chasser sans ordre une armée ennemie de trente-neuf vaisseaux, il est aisé de répondre à cette méchanceté absurde:

1°) les vaisseaux français n'étaient pas ni à portée ni en état de combattre seuls puisqu'ils étaient de vrais hôpitaux plutôt que des vaisseaux de guerre,

2°) les ordres du Roi étaient aussi contraires à de pareilles dispositions puisque les espagnols et les français sont entremêlés dans la ligne de bataille d'après mûr examen de la cour et quoi qu'il ait été proposé dès le principe de composer l'avant-garde de l'armée combinée entièrement de vaisseaux français.

Vous m'avez demandé mon sentiment, Monseigneur, sur tous ses objets; je vous les donne sans détour, et avec la même franchise, j'ai l'honneur de vous assurer que jamais le tableau de ce qui arrive à monsieur d'Orvilliers ne s'effacera de ma mémoire; je tâcherai d'en faire mon profit pour être plus sage et moins ambitieux, car je ne pense pas qu'on puisse montrer plus de force d'âme et de zèle pour le service du Roi que ce digne général en a montré depuis la mort de son fils; j'ajouterai à tout ceci d'après vous-même, Monseigneur, que monsieur d'Orvilliers ne peut être remplacé dans ce moment ni pour la guerre ni pour le cabinet; comment donc est-il possible que de simples propos de quelques individus méprisables puissent nuire à un pareil homme. Je suis avec respect, Monseigneur, votre très humble et très obéissant serviteur. Le chevalier du Pavillon. A bord de la Bretagne le 15 septembre 1779 ».

Translation:

Monseigneur,

My general has just told me that he has been censured for not having pursued the enemy longer and not having ordered the pursuit without reforming the line of battle. I confess, Monseigneur, that I am extremely surprised. How could he excuse himself from running towards a fleet that had been reported several times by reliable people? If it was found to be English, he would have been even more censured. Finally, Monseigneur, how could my general neglect for a single moment getting out of the Channel, as it was threatened by south-west winds. Events have proven that he was right. He had an absolute lack of water, food and even seamen. You must feel today, Monseigneur, since you know the state and the progress of the epidemic that devastates all the King's ships, that a few days of delay in the Channel would have lost the King his ships and the rest of their sailors. This fact is only too obvious. It is also clear to the entire army that never was its general so great and so superior in his humanity and his adversities than in this unfortunate campaign, which only failed because of the poorly chosen rendezvous for the vessels of the two powers. As to the pursuit, which, it is alleged in Paris, was not carried out with the proper intensity, he could not chase an enemy fleet of 39 vessels in a disordered state. It is easy to respond to this wicked absurdity:

1°) The French vessels were not in a state to fight alone. They were really hospitals rather than ships of war,

2°) The King's orders were also contrary to such an action because the Spanish and French ships were so intermixed in the line of battle. After mature consideration by the Court, it had been established as a principle that the van of the fleet should consist entirely of French vessels.

You asked me my feelings, Monsignor, on all these things. I have given you it without evasion and with frankness. I have the honour to tell you that the vision of what happened to Mon. d'Orvilliers will never be erased from my memory. I will make it my task to become wiser and less ambitious, because I do not think that we can show more strength of soul and zeal for the service of the King than this worthy General has shown since the death of his son. For you, I would add to all this that Mon. d'Orvilliers cannot be replaced at this time, not in the war nor in the cabinet. So how is it possible that a few despicable individuals could be an obstacle to such a man?

I am with respect, Monseigneur, your very humble and very obedient servant.

Le chevalier du Pavillon

On board *La Bretagne*
15 September 1779

# CHAPTER SEVEN

# Le Bailli Pierre-André de Suffren: A Precursor of Nelson

Rémi Monaque

Marine française

There was nothing about the young Suffren, when he joined the company of *Gardes Marine* in Toulon at the age of 14 in October 1743, that would have marked him out to become an innovator in naval tactics and strategy. He belonged to the high nobility of Provence, which provided at this time a quarter of the officers of the royal navy, and he followed the usual training for future senior officers of the navy, receiving the classic instruction in the doctrine that prevailed at the time. However, very soon, an event ocurred that was favourable to his training; after a 30-year interval, hostilities between France and Great Britain broke out again. In January 1744, Pierre-André left the classrooms of the arsenal in Toulon to embark on the *Solide* (64) and only a few weeks later participated in the Battle of Toulon (22 February 1744 n.s.), during which the French squadron commanded by Court de La Bruyère, a 78-year-old admiral, made it possible for a Spanish squadron which had been sheltering in Toulon to break out of the port and head back to Cádiz in spite of the opposition of the British Admiral Mathews' blockading squadron.

Except for six months on land with the naval guards at Brest, Suffren remained on board throughout the war, undergoing a thorough training 'à l'anglaise' (at

---

**How to cite this book chapter:**
Monaque, R. 2017. Le Bailli Pierre-André de Suffren: A Precursor of Nelson. In: Harding, R and Guimerá, A (eds.). *Naval Leadership in the Atlantic World.* Pp. 85–91. London: University of Westminster Press. DOI: https://doi. org/10.16997/book2.h. License: CC-BY-NC-ND 4.0

sea) with many enriching experiences. The last of them is his service on the *Monarque* (74), which, on 25 October 1747, took part in a heroic combat off the coast of Ouessant (the Second Battle of Cape Finisterre). In this battle, the eight vessels of the *chef d'escadre*, Des Herbiers de l'Etenduère, charged with protecting a huge convoy of ships towards the West Indies, were attacked by Rear Admiral Edward Hawke's 14 vessels. The French admiral succeeded in saving the convoy at the price of a seven-hour battle during which six French vessels were captured after they had defended themselves heroically. Suffren, taken prisoner on the *Monarque*, had his first experience of captivity and especially the terrible humiliation of witnessing the victory of Hawke who sailed triumphantly up the Thames with the spoils of war. This cruel experience left a mark on him that lasted all his life and maintained his unrelenting hatred of the English.

Suffren took advantage of the short period between 1748 and 1756 that separated the War of the Austrian Succession from the Seven Years' War to go to Malta to be trained as a Knight of Saint John of Jerusalem. During the whole of his adult life, Suffren performed, alternatively, his services in Malta and in the King's navy. Taking both careers hand in hand, he cleverly leaned on each of them to ensure progress in both. Was Suffren's style of commanding influenced by this double affiliation? Yes, certainly, but not so much in the domain of naval operations, because by this time the heroic conflicts of the Christian states with Turks and the inhabitants of the Barbary Coast were over. However, there remained in this history a glorious tradition of attacking the enemy with energy, and a spirit of sacrifice without taking into account the risks. Much more surely, the admiral developed, during his sojourns in Malta, a constant interest in the physical and moral health of his crew members. In his role of a good Knight Hospitaller monk, he showed great solicitude for the sick and the wounded, and knew how to take concrete measures to improve the daily life of his crew. Ultimately, he owed his fame largely to this attitude.

The Seven Years' War (1756–63) brought Suffren new and enriching experiences. In 1756, he participated in the French victory at Minorque (20 May 1756), won by the *chef d'escadre*, the Marquis de La Gallisonnière, over the unfortunate Rear Admiral John Byng, who, for his failure to do his utmost in this battle, was judged by court martial, condemned to death and executed on 14 March 1757.[186] Nicholas Rodger believes that this general officer, who did not deserve such a punishment, was the victim of 'the king's anger, the fury of public opinion and the disgust of his naval colleagues'. On this occasion, Pierre-André was able to note the fact that combat on parallel lines is ineffectual when the adversary (in this case the English), lying windward, is satisfied with a cannonade at long distance without forcing his adversary to close combat. The Battle of Lagos, in August 1759, was far more dramatic. Suffren, now a lieutenant, was aboard the *Ocean*, the flagship of Admiral M. de la Clue. The admiral, after an opening battle when his squadron was dispersed, had taken refuge with four of his vessels in Portuguese, and therefore neutral, waters in Lagos Bay. He was pursued by Admiral Edward Boscawen who, with contempt for international law, burned two of the vessels, which had surrendered, and captured the other two. Pierre-André was imprisoned once again. Some 20 years later, he was still able to remember this cynical lesson in realism and he did not hesitate, in his turn, to infringe Portuguese neutrality at the Battle of Porto Praya (16 April 1781).

During the long truce which separated the Seven Years' War in 1763 from the outbreak of the American War of Independence in 1775, Pierre-André's reputation began to grow both in the King's navy and that of Malta. He was given many commands: two xebecs, two frigates and a Maltese galley. During these years between the wars, Pierre-André, as a captain, participated in the campaigns of training squadrons where he was able to perfect his manoeuvring and tactical art. When war was declared on Britain in 1778, he was appointed to the command of the *Fantasque* (64).

During the American War of Independence, Suffren served at sea from the first day to the last. In command of the *Fantasque*, he was part of the first squadron sent to aid the American rebels under the orders of d'Estaing. This unusual admiral was from a family of the highest nobility. He had come from the army and had entered the navy with a high rank of flag officer. This undeserved promotion, like his maritime incompetence, engendered the hostility of almost all the naval officers. However, he did not lack other great qualities such as courage, tenacity and a remarkable capacity to discern the talents of his subordinates. It did not take d'Estaing long to understand that Suffren, who had a relatively low rank in the naval hierarchy, was his best captain. D'Estaing put him in charge of the most delicate missions, giving him the authority to command bigger and bigger forces. Pierre-André took advantage of these opportunities to improve his skills in managing the tactical formation of squadrons and did not hesitate, sometimes with scant ceremony, to criticise the way in which the squadron was being commanded. He distinguished himself on a number of occasions, notably at Newport by compelling five English frigates to scuttle (29 July 1778) and at the Battle of La Grenade (15 December 1778) where he took the first place in the French line, dauntlessly coming under the enemy fire of the whole English squadron.

During this campaign, when many opportunities were lost by the French, Suffren sharpened his strategic and tactical conceptions and, little by little, reached the conclusion that one can obtain definite success on only two conditions: engage in very close combat with the enemy and concentrate the greatest section of one's own fighting force on a section of the enemy squadron.

This conviction was a result not only of his own vast experience but also of his historical readings, and especially a study of the campaigns of the great Dutch Admiral Michiel de Ruyter (1607–76) for whom he felt profound admiration. From de Ruyter and his own experiences Pierre-André understood that close combat is fairly simple, at least if you have the advantage of a favourable wind, and so the possibility of getting as close as possible to one's adversary was the key to victory. Great courage and authority are all one needs: great courage to place one's vessel in an extremely dangerous position where it will receive at point-blank range the gunfire of the enemy; great authority to persuade the captains to do the same. It is much more difficult to arrive at a concentration of forces. For Pierre-André this implied renouncing fighting in one continuous line and spreading out one's squadron in several autonomous divisions capable of individual, particular manoeuvres, while still respecting the principle of strict coordination. The Commander must therefore have captains capable of taking initiatives, well-informed of the manoeuvres that are envisaged and of the intentions of the admiral. These conditions would later be realised admirably in the hearts of the famous Band of Brothers that served under Nelson. Alas, Suffren was never able to obtain a similar cohesion of minds and hearts among his officers.

After his command of the *Fantasque*, Pierre-André was put in charge of a more powerful vessel, the *Zélé* (74). He distinguished himself in this warship by taking part in the capture of a huge British convoy off the Portuguese coasts (9 August 1780). It was only in March 1781 that he at last received a command worthy of his talents. A little squadron of five vessels, armed at Brest, was put in his charge with the mission of protecting the Dutch colony at the Cape, then under threat of an English attack; then to sail on to Mauritius and join the Indian Ocean squadron commanded by M. d'Orves. This rather mediocre admiral had the good idea of dying in February 1782, leaving the command to Suffren for his famous campaign of the Indies where the *bailli* finished up having 15 vessels and holding on for two years against the English squadron under Admiral Hughes. Of this famous campaign, I will mention only two examples which illustrate marvellously the type of leadership practised by Suffren.

It was at Porto La Praya, in the Portuguese isles of Cape Verde, on 16 April 1781, in the extraordinary battle against Commodore Johnstone, that the possession of the Cape of Good Hope was settled. The British officer who had been ordered to capture this colony had left Europe a few days before Suffren. The latter, who had no information about the position of his adversary, decided to make a stop at this neutral country in order to complete his provisions and to refresh the crew members. On approaching La Praya, the leading French ship noticed spars in the harbour, turned around and informed his commander. In a flash, Pierre-André made a decision. He placed the *Héros* (74) at the head of the line, ordered the other ships to get closer to one another and clear the ships for action while making a rush at the enemy. The English, lacking vigilance, were confined without order at the bottom of the bay; warships and transport vessels all mixed together. They were completely surprised. The *Héros*, followed by the *Annibal* (74), penetrated into the harbour, firing from both sides, and placed itself in a broadside position at a short distance from an enemy vessel.

The *Annibal* did the same and placed itself in front of its leader. But her guns remained practically silent.

Captain Trémigon, who commanded the *Annibal,* thought there would be no fighting in neutral waters, and neglected to make his preparations for action. Seriously wounded from the beginning of the action, this unforgivable omission cost him his life. The third vessel of the line, the *Artésien* (64), succeeded in penetrating the heart of the enemy formation, but its commanding officer, the Chevalier de Cardaillac, was killed at the moment he ordered the anchoring of his ship. The order was not executed and the vessel, pushed on by wind and currents, sailed out of the harbour. The last two vessels were also forced out without being able to participate effectively in the combat. Thus Suffren found himself in the middle of a furnace with just two ships, only one of which was fit for battle. Overwhelmed by attacks from all sides, the only solution he had was to cut all the cables in order to get out of a deadly trap. The *Annibal*, soon totally dismasted, imitated the manoeuvre of its commander and the two vessels, helped by favourable wind and current, managed to extricate themselves and leave the harbour. With remarkable energy and sangfroid, Suffren gathered his forces together and formed a tight line with his five ships, ordering the *Sphinx* to tow the dismasted *Annibal*. Now it was a matter of confronting on the high seas the English squadron that had got over its surprise and sailed out. But Johnstone hesitated to attack an adversary who seemed extremely capable and the pursuit of whom would take him far under the winds of Praya, where he had left some of his men and a convoy in great disorder. After a chase of six days, the British commander gave up all hope of combat and sailed back to the port. He had lost the race to the Cape and was not able to accomplish his mission. Suffren had led an extraordinary action, had not been understood by his captains and had suffered heavy losses without inflicting similar losses on his enemy. Even so, his audacity and ability to make decisions had paid off. Johnstone was definitely distanced and the Cape, where the Frenchman was able to land a strong garrison force, was saved.

The Battle of Sadras (17 February 1782) will be my second example. Suffren, now at the head of 12 vessels – his squadron had been strengthened by six vessels lying at the Île-de-France and the capture of an English vessel – had arrived at the Coast of Coromandel. He knew that his adversary, Vice-Admiral Sir Edward Hughes, still had only nine ships of the line. He decided to get rid of Hughes as soon as possible. The meeting took place on 17 February 1782 off the coast of Sadras. Suffren had prepared for the battle with particular care, with the idea of a completely new technique. Instead of being content, as was the usual practice at the time, with sailing along the whole line of enemy vessels and doubling his rear guard with the three extra vessels, the 'bailli' (Dignitary of the Order of Malta) intended not to attack the three leading British vessels and, instead, overcome the following six by placing them between two lines of six French vessels. He himself, on board the *Héros*, the leading vessel, took good care to prevent the three English vessels that were not being attacked, from tacking to come to the aid of their fellows. He had taken the trouble of explaining this manoeuvre in writing to Tromelin, the senior captain, asking him to take the initiative, when the time came, to assure the surrounding of the enemy line from behind. Alas, this brilliant idea, which would have permitted the concentration of the French forces on six enemy vessels, was not understood by the majority of the captains and was even sabotaged by Tromelin, who just repeated the signals of the commander without executing them. Only two French vessels doubled the English line – the manoeuvre however permitted the crippling of the British ships *Superb* and *Exeter* which were almost captured. Hughes was able to escape without losing ships but had to sail to Trincomalee to repair the badly damaged vessels. The area was left free for Suffren to land the French troops in Portonovo, not far from Pondicherry, in a zone controlled by their ally, the Nawab Heider Ali.

The two examples mentioned obviously show the lack of communication between Suffren and his captains. Having an inflexible, ironic and abrupt character, he did not make any real effort to be understood by his subordinates. He even took a malicious pleasure in shocking them by wearing slovenly-looking clothes and using a language littered with Provençal swear-words, more frequently heard on the lower deck than on the quarter-deck. Pierre-André's orders, as soon as they diverged from routine, were badly understood and therefore badly executed. It is true that there were, under his orders, many captains whose professional level was mediocre and, even worse, who were very badly disposed towards him. So difficult was his character that he managed to discourage even those who had the best intentions. What is more, even when his tactical inspiration was brilliant, Suffren did not conduct the action with all the necessary rigour and precision. His ardour and impatience made him multiply orders and counter-orders, and flag signals, which were not always very clear. So there often followed a lot of confusion in the execution of the manoeuvres he had set in motion.

In short, Suffren as a tactician is disappointing. His accomplishments fell short of his original ideas. He totally lacked a pedagogical sense and disliked gathering together his captains to explain his ideas of manoeuvring, to obtain comprehension and their commitment. He had no notion of the training that is indispensable if one wants to get out of routine and achieve the unusual. On the other hand, his ardour, his tenacity and his aggressive behaviour had wonderful results and he ended up winning the respect of his captains and the sincere admiration of his adversaries. On 20 June 1783, in the course of his last battle, at Cuddalore, fighting with 15 vessels against 18, he manifested his superiority over Hughes, who was forced to give up his attempts to give aid to the attacking British army and retired to Calcutta. One circumstance, perhaps unique in naval history, crowns Pierre-André's glorious career. On 22 December 1783, the *Héros*, Suffren's flagship, arrived at Table Bay in the Dutch Cape Colony, where Commodore Sir Richard King's English squadron lay at anchor. The

British historian and Admiral, Ballard, related that a host of British officers went aboard the *Héros* 'to greet personally a master of their profession'. Suffren deserves to be ranked among the very great seamen, between Ruyter and Nelson, whose destructive injunction to 'annihilate the enemy' he could well have made his own. But his intuitions, his courage and his obstinacy brought him only limited success, as his action was so cramped by negative characteristics which prevented him from assembling all the forces around himself.

# PART THREE

# Naval Leadership and the French Revolution, 1789–1850

# Naval Leadership and the French Revolution

Richard Harding* and Agustin Guimerá†

*University of Westminster

†Instituto de Historia, Consejo Superior de Investigaciones Científicas, Madrid

On 14 July 1789, after months of economic distress and political tension, there was a popular rising in Paris to release prisoners in the Bastille, the fortress that overawed the eastern part of the city. There were few prisoners to be released, but it sparked a series of events that were to lead to seismic shifts in world history. The political, economic, cultural and military consequences of that rising are still very much with us today. By August 1792 the political shifts in France had brought about a republican government and later, in January 1793, the execution of the King, Louis XVI. The monarchical institutions of the army and navy which had been crumbling since 1790 were eventually shattered as revolutionary suspicion of the predominantly aristocratic officer corps led to the dismissal and mass migration of experienced officers. By the late summer of 1792 the simmering hostility of the other great monarchies of Europe turned into open war and by early 1793 France was faced by a coalition of Austria, Prussia, Spain, Great Britain and the United Provinces. Despite a victory at Valmy (September 1792), the position of France remained desperate.

**How to cite this book chapter:**
Harding, R and Guimerá, A. 2017. Introduction: Naval Leadership and the French Revolution. In: Harding, R and Guimerá, A (eds.). *Naval Leadership in the Atlantic World*. Pp. 95–98. London: University of Westminster Press. DOI: https://doi.org/10.16997/book2.i. License: CC-BY-NC-ND 4.0

The great achievement of the revolutionary government was to fashion a new army and a new art of war out of the crisis. It achieved remarkable success, reorganising its armies and, critically, its officer corps, so that by the end of 1794, France appeared the most powerful military state in Europe.[187] The mobilisation of the nation, driven on by an ideology of a free citizenship in arms and the energy of revolutionary government against the old feudal monarchies, provided manpower and resources that expanded the army to four times its 1792 size. By mid-1796 internal revolt had been crushed and the First Coalition had effectively broken up.

Within France's armies, Napoleon Bonaparte was excelling at his trade and rising through the officer corps. His seizure of power by *coup d'état* to become First Consul in October 1799 and then the establishment of his empire at the end of 1804 fundamentally changed the political nature of the revolution and entrenched France as a dynamic military force. Although ultimately suffering complete defeat in 1814–5, the wars of the Napoleonic Empire caused massive change in thinking about warfare. From tactics, through operations, to the understanding of strategy, the conduct of warfare across Europe went through major changes. Military analysts at the time and later historians, seeking to systematise or codify these changes, have sometimes overstated the revolutionary nature of Napoleonic warfare, underestimating the developments that were occurring before 1789 and ignoring the continuities with those reforms, but there can be little doubt that the theory and practice of land warfare was dramatically altered by 1815.[188] Looking back, with experience and hindsight it appeared to some that there was a distinct difference between the strategies employed by states before and after the Revolution. The two basic strategies that have been employed throughout history, depending on the circumstances, were most simply summed up by the German historian Hans Delbrück (1848–1929). The first was a strategy of exhaustion, in which battle was only one of many means of wearing down the enemy's capability to fight. The second was a strategy of annihilation in which the destruction of the enemy's army, and thus battle, was the central objective. The lessons of the Napoleonic decisive battle that made it impossible for the enemy to resist long after defeat in the field were clear.[189] The former suited the conditions of the eighteenth century, while the latter suited the conditions of Revolution and after.

Some of these changes, particularly those associated with the mobilisation of populations in a national cause, did not survive the end of the Napoleonic threat to the traditional dynastic states. However, most of the organisational and technological shifts were more permanent and incorporated into the armies of Europe. One of the most interesting shifts was the change of focus from the reformers of the eighteenth century, who sought the underlying principles of war at a tactical level, to those who experienced the wars of 1792–1815 and saw the need to focus on the policy and strategic principles. The evolution was evident in the work of Antoine-Henri Jomini (1779–1869) and fully developed in that of Carl von Clausewitz (1780–1831). Jomini, who experienced the great Napoleonic campaigns first hand, located the operation of military genius in the destruction of the enemy's armed force by seizing the initiative, maintaining mobility and concentration. Clausewitz's works, which gained prominence in the second half of the nineteenth century, insisted that this war of annihilation had to fit within the policy framework of the state. With the decisive victories of Prussia over Austria and France in 1866 and 1870–1, and the evident contribution of a sophisticated General Staff, the higher direction of armies became the key element in military organisation in the last quarter of the century.[190]

How did this change in military thinking and operations apply to naval warfare and officership? Of the great naval powers, France suffered the greatest organisational dislocation during the Revolution. While Napoleon made moves to rebuild his navy, employing the resources across his European empire, they could never be concentrated or sustained for a long period. After Trafalgar in 1805 the French imperial navy never recovered to offer more than spasmodic squadron operations.[191] Other navies, the British Royal Navy excepted, suffered crushing defeats, economic starvation and domestic upheavals that seriously damaged their effectiveness. The most obvious difference between the experience of European armies and the navies was that while the forces of revolutionary ideology and drive successfully rebuilt the French army and created a weapon of immense force under Napoleon, nothing like this occurred in the naval sphere. The mass mobilisation of the population and ideology could never compensate for the loss of experienced officers and administrators. The ruthless drive for administrative improvement was effective under the Committee of Public Safety (1792–94) in the short run, but not enough to recreate effective, sustainable naval forces, especially against the Royal Navy, which was operating at a level of unparalleled effectiveness.[192] Naval expertise could not be created out of revolutionary or imperial enthusiasm.

In many respects, the changes in the art of war on land identified during the revolutionary period had been taking place at sea for a while. The conditions of war that had favoured a strategy of exhaustion on land were largely to do with the relative parity of force in offence and defence that had emerged in Europe with the effective fortification of key areas towards the end of the seventeenth century. Fortifications made decisive field encounters difficult to exploit with the size of armies available. Throughout the eighteenth century the development of professional armies, with engineering and artillery expertise, was broadly balanced by the expansion of fortresses at key strategic points. The Revolution, which produced large popular armies, made the fortress less significant in both offence and defence and the strategy of annihilation became more important.[193]

On the high seas there were no *points d'appui* like the fortress. However, from the mid-seventeenth century, the disciplined line of battle in combat acted like an impenetrable artillery line. Getting around it or breaking through it to annihilate the enemy was an ambition or fear of naval officers from the late seventeenth century onwards. The problem was how to surround or break through in the face of a determined enemy. Really significant results were only achieved in chase actions, such as the two battles off Finisterre in May and October 1747 or at Quiberon Bay in 1759, or when the enemy was at anchor (Battle of Chesme, July 1770 and the Nile, August 1798). Of course, there were differences between officers in the enthusiasm with which they pursued the annihilation of the enemy and differences in the expectations of their political masters as well. In Britain, the expectation of destroying the enemy was so strong that even a moderately creditable performance was sometimes inadequate to protect the officer from censure, as William, Lord Hotham and Sir Robert Calder found out in 1795 and 1805 respectively.[194] On the other hand, for French and Spanish officers, who almost always faced a numerical and qualitatively superior enemy, the option of breaking the line seldom presented itself. Furthermore, for the most part they sailed under orders to achieve a particular operational objective, not to seek out and destroy their enemies. Thus, French and Spanish navies had to be more committed to a strategy of exhaustion. It did not prevent brave, resourceful and sophisticated operations on the part of their officers, but it did present them with a more challenging context and thus, different approaches to their duty and conduct.

# CHAPTER EIGHT

# Leadership in the French Navy during the Revolution and Empire. The Optimist and the Pessimist: Louis-René de Latouche-Tréville (1745–1804) and Pierre Charles de Villeneuve (1763–1806)

Rémi Monaque

Marine française

The Revolution of 1789 brought about a profound and lasting disorganisation of the French navy. Its officer corps, mostly consisting of nobles, was forced to take part in a massive emigration. Some of them, due to family traditions, considered their fidelity to the King more important than their fidelity to the Nation, but many, although open to new ideas, left the country just to save their lives. The awful atmosphere that existed on board ships made it impossible for them to exercise authority over their crews who had lost all confidence in the 'aristocrats' whom they suspected of betrayal. Some rare noble officers managed to stay in service for a while. However, by November 1793 they were all dismissed. After the Reign of Terror, which ended in 1794, successive governments started the reintegration of the old noble officer corps but this procedure

**How to cite this book chapter:**
Monaque, R. 2017. Leadership in the French Navy during the Revolution and Empire. The Optimist and the Pessimist: Louis-René de Latouche-Tréville (1745–1804) and Pierre Charles de Villeneuve (1763–1806). In: Harding, R and Guimerá, A (eds.). *Naval Leadership in the Atlantic World.* Pp. 99–106. London: University of Westminster Press. DOI: https://doi.org/10.16997/book2.j. License: CC-BY-NC-ND 4.0

concerned only a limited number of individuals. To solve the problem of the huge lack of officers, all kinds of improvisations were necessary. Many officers of the merchant marine were enrolled and the best qualified petty officers in the navy promoted. But these measures had their limits, all the more so as the elementary training of young officers was no longer assured since the suppression of companies of *Gardes Marine* by the Revolution. One had to wait till 1810 to see the rebirth of schools for officers. Besides, the French squadrons, weakened by the defection of their best-trained officers and the complete disorganisation of naval dockyards, now found themselves hampered by the superiority of the Royal Navy against which it had battled on equal terms during the American War of Independence. Moreover, the handover by the Royalists of the port of Toulon to the Anglo-Spanish forces in 1793 had cost the French navy 13 vessels, that is to say, a loss exactly equal to that suffered at Trafalgar. All this explains why the Revolutionary and then the imperial navy was completely dominated by its ancient adversary and spent most of its time in harbours blocked by the British navy.

Serious training and the opportunity of forming new, competent commanders was not possible. Very often, it is among the old sailors of Louis XVI's navy, survivors of the Revolution, that one has to look for admirals capable of conducting effective operations. Two examples concern us in this paper – one happy and successful, that of Louis-René de Latouche-Tréville, who has left a bright and unforgettable reputation in the French navy. The other, that of Pierre Charles de Villeneuve, a profoundly sad character, who is linked to the most tragic event known to the French navy.

Latouche-Tréville (1745–1804) was from a family ennobled in the reign of Louis XIV for work accomplished in the West Indies at the beginning of French colonisation. From this colonial past, the future admiral, himself the son of one of the King's naval officers, inherited a spirit of adventure, a great capacity for speaking without constraint and a total absence of prejudice. All his life, Latouche had a network of friendly relationships with people of all conditions, from the princes of royal blood to his village carpenter. He had a great love for his profession and his country, but no political convictions whatsoever. He served all the regimes with the same enthusiasm and, from being a good royalist, became a convinced Jacobin and then a devoted subject of the Emperor without the slightest remorse. He is one of the rare officers of the nobility who succeeded in retaining the confidence of his crews during the campaign, in the Mediterranean Sea, of the first squadron which sailed under the Republican flag (October 1792–March 1793). He had just been promoted to the rank of *chef d'escadre* (Rear Admiral) and, far from being offended by observing the growth of committees of seamen, he took advantage of them to influence the morale of the crews. By giving loyal Republican instructions, he used the committees to spread confidence in him, his ideas and his orders. On his flagship, *Languedoc*, Latouche overcame without difficulty the crew's attempt at rebellion by appealing to the patriotic feelings of the mutineers.

Louis-René was one of those rare naval officers who knew how to exercise their uncontested authority while, at the same time, being adored by their crews and their officers. He showed in a brilliant fashion that a chief need not be harsh and unpleasant in order to be obeyed. His good humour, optimism and benevolence brought him results far superior to many of his peers who were satisfied with cold severity. Jurien de La Gravière, one of Latouche's subordinate officers, relates in his memoirs how he became forever attached to this admiral. [195] In 1802, at Rochefort, Jurien commanded a frigate in the squadron sailing out to Saint-Domingue and, on the first day of his service, he made a grave error in manoeuvring under the eyes of the admiral, which he managed to correct brilliantly. He writes:

'Latouche was an accomplished seaman and the least movement of his squadron did not escape his observation. Far from blaming me, he had the kindness to congratulate me for the manoeuvre with which I had got back from a difficult situation. From that day onwards, my heart was his. I felt I had just met a man worthy of commanding French officers and sailors.'

Latouche's benevolence extended even to his enemies. Louis-René was one of those eighteenth-century men who engaged in warfare without hatred, considered their adversaries as colleagues doing the same job, maintained courteous relationships with them during the conflict and, once peace was re-established, could become their friends. Twice in his career, Latouche was able to congratulate himself for having adopted such an attitude. Taken prisoner, in the last months of the American War of Independence, by the Commodore Keith Elphinstone, after having scuttled his frigate on the American coast, Louis-René became a friend of his gaoler, was received by him in England and ended up by asking him to get him a two-seat coach (pretty without being splendid) for which he did not want to spend more than 40 Guineas! Later, in the course of the terrible Campaign of Saint-Domingue (1802–3), Latouche owed his survival to the quality of the relationship he had established with Admiral Duckworth, the commander of the naval forces of neighbouring Jamaica. The two men, without ever having met each other, had exchanged letters and presents and had soon come to feel mutual appreciation and friendship. The war having begun again in March 1803, Duckworth, learning that Latouche was dying, gave him permission to go back to France on a treaty vessel. This very kind action reminds us of the favour of which Admiral Rodney was the beneficiary, imprisoned for debt in Paris at the beginning of the War of Independence and freed thanks to the generosity of his French friends who must therefore take the responsibility for our defeat at the Saintes!

Latouche-Tréville, who distinguished himself during the War of Independence as commander of several frigates, is the only French admiral who could boast that he kept Nelson at bay. In August 1803, while he was at the head of the Boulogne flotilla, he drove back on two occasions the attempts of the British hero to destroy or capture little landing ships moored off Boulogne. The second attempt, at night between 15 and 16 August, ended in a bloody failure. The destinies of Nelson and Latouche crossed once again, a third time, on 16 June 1804 off Toulon. On that day, Nelson, who had five ships and two frigates, decided to capture two French vessels moored at the north of Porquerolles. Latouche, who observed the manoeuvre from the Cape Cepet observatory, immediately ordered his squadron to get under way and left the port with his eight vessels at record speed. Nelson retired, followed by Latouche, till nightfall. This non-event led to a report that pleased the First Consul Napoleon Bonaparte and was published in the official journal. It didn't take long for Nelson to become aware of it and he flew into a towering rage. He wrote to the whole world to defend himself against the charge of fleeing before the enemy and used many insulting expressions against Latouche, to whom he swore he would make him eat his report after having imprisoned him. Did the great man sometimes lack humour and a sense of fair play? As for Latouche, he did not feel any hatred for his adversary and spoke in his letters of his great desire to 'have another confrontation with his colleague, Nelson' – a striking difference of character but also of mentality between the two men. Nelson had in his heart, from the time of his youth, a hatred of the French. This feeling was exacerbated by the ideological passions that inspired the admiral. Since the beginning of the revolutionary wars, Nelson made war not only against his country's enemies but also against regicidal and irreligious Republicans.

The death of Latouche in August 1804 brought an end to the Homeric duel between the two champions. Louis-René, exhausted by his campaigns and the fervour to which he had had recourse in order to train his squadron in Toulon for combat, died of sickness in the harbour of Toulon on board his admiral flagship, *Bucentaure*, after having refused to be transported on land: 'A sailor,' he had said, 'is only too happy to die under his flag.' His demise deprived Napoleon of his finest asset for conquering Great Britain. Latouche, to whom the Emperor had confided the principal role in his great strategy of invasion, believed in his mission and had already succeeded in building up his squadron's morale and was preparing it for the decisive confrontation. The friendly and even affectionate relationship which Louis-René had developed in Brest in 1800 with the Spanish Admiral Federico Gravina would have been a valuable asset during the manoeuvres of the campaign of 1804–5, in the course of which Franco-Spanish cooperation would become essential.

Finding a substitute for Latouche at the head of the squadron of Toulon was a very difficult problem for the Emperor. The number of admirals capable of succeeding Nelson's former 'challenger' was extremely limited. Bruix had certainly acquired a great reputation but bad health made it impossible for him to do service at sea. Ganteaume, who had brought back Napoleon from Egypt and who, since then, had played the role of naval adviser to the head of state, was already appointed Commander of the squadron in Brest, that also had an important role to play in the Emperor's plans. Decrès, the minister of the navy, excluded Missiessy, a man of great worth but whom he did not like, and proposed the name of Villeneuve, who, lacking ambition, was not a threat to his ministerial career.

Villeneuve, 42 years old at that time, was from one of the oldest and most illustrious noble Provençal families. He entered the Company of the Naval Guards of Toulon in 1778 and fought throughout the American War of Independence, experiencing with Grasse the glory of the Battle of Chesapeake (5 September 1781) and the setbacks at the Battle of the Saintes (12 April 1782). At the time of the Revolution, he held the rank of lieutenant. His family, well-established in High Provence, approved of the new ideas and did not emigrate. He, like Latouche-Tréville, managed to remain in service and had the advantage of a rapid promotion. Like all officers from the nobility, he was excluded from the navy for a short period (November 1793–May 1795) during and after the Terror. After the Reign of Terror, his rise was phenomenal, all the more so as the other contenders were weak and he was endowed with exceptional advantages: a remarkable intelligence and lucidity, great professional qualities, an affable and benevolent character, and an exemplary sense of duty. Promoted to the rank of Rear Admiral from September 1796, Villeneuve commanded the rearguard of the French squadron at the Battle of the Nile (1 August 1798). He was not attacked by Nelson and witnessed the destruction of the rest of the squadron without making any attempt to come to their aid. To justify this passivity, Villeneuve attributed his action to contrary winds and the delays in making way. It was only on the following morning that he left the port and managed to take his division safe and sound to Malta. Far from being blamed, he was praised by the French government, the Directory, for having saved from disaster a section of the French fleet. As for Bonaparte, the event made him remember the fact that Villeneuve was a lucky man, which, to his mind, was a considerable advantage. The Admiral, however, was traumatised by what happened and continued to have a deep sense of inferiority when faced with Nelson's genius. He had no wish to undergo another confrontation with this 'colleague'.

When, in Autumn 1804, the squadron trained by Latouche-Tréville was put under his command, Villeneuve felt there was an unbearable burden on his shoulders. He showed himself absolutely incapable of maintaining the activity, the confidence and the high state of morale that his predecessor had succeeded in developing.[196] On the other hand, his solitary reflections permitted him to guess, with extraordinary foresight, what a confrontation with Nelson would be like. In the instructions he sent to his captains on the 21 December 1804, Villeneuve wrote with exactitude what the Battle of Trafalgar would be:

'The enemy will not stop at creating a battle line parallel to ours and at delivering an artillery battle [ ... ]. He will seek to surround our rear guard, to cross us and carry his own divisions upon those vessels of ours that he will have separated, in order to surround and reduce them.'

The tragic aspect of Villeneuve is that this rare lucidity was accompanied by a profound pessimism. He believed that the French and soon the Spanish ships he would have to deal with would be incapable of performing complicated manoeuvres and he would have to be satisfied with opposing the enemy with a line of vessels tightly closed up to one another. His first attempt to get under way from Toulon in January 1805 convinced him of the validity of this opinion. The violent gust of the Mistral that he was subjected to as he got out of the port caused such a state of disorder in his squadron that he was obliged to return shamefully three days later. In despair, he wrote to Decrès, the minister of the navy, a profoundly defeatist letter in which there is this terrible sentence: 'The enemy will beat us even with forces inferior to ours by a third.' Following the logical conclusion of this analysis, Villeneuve declared his resignation. The minister then committed an unforgivable mistake: he did not send the letter to the Emperor and asked his friend to remain at his post. Villeneuve, in the spirit of duty, but also as someone who was passive and resigned to his fate, agreed to pursue his mission. A man afflicted with two such serious faults as pessimism and passivity should never have been invested with a such a command.

Without the space to explore all the events of the campaign that preceded Trafalgar, let us simply note a few episodes that illustrate Villeneuve's style of command and his temperament. The French squadron left Toulon on 30 March 1805. It sailed through the Strait of Gibraltar without opposition and arrived on 9 April in Cádiz where it was to be joined by a Spanish squadron. Only the *Argonauta*, the flagship of Admiral Federico Gravina, and the French vessel *L'Aigle* were in the port and ready to leave. Villeneuve stayed only a few hours in the harbour and sailed away towards the West Indies without waiting any longer for the five Spanish vessels which were not ready to sail out. This haste has something indecent about it for it shows quite plainly the pathological fear he had of a confrontation with the victor of Aboukir. It could only have been perceived as a negative quality by the French crews and even more by his Spanish allies. Once he arrived in Martinique, Villeneuve, in conformity with the orders received, waited 40 days for the rallying of the squadrons of Brest and Rochefort. This useless waiting, during which he could take no major action against the enemy,[197] brought upon him the lively reproaches of the Emperor. The Admiral was hurt by this profoundly unjust criticism and his morale was affected. After recrossing the Atlantic he met the squadron of Rear Admiral Sir Robert Calder off the western coast of Spain on 22 July 1805. An indecisive action followed. The day after this battle Villeneuve lost precious time putting his squadron into order instead of pursuing the enemy vigorously and retaking the two Spanish vessels captured by Calder. This failure was another blow to his morale as indeed it was to the rather uncertain prestige he enjoyed among his Spanish allies. Finally, on 15 August, while he had succeeded in joining the Spanish squadron in Ferrol, Villeneuve, completely demoralised, abandoned his voyage towards Brest in order to take refuge in Cádiz. He believed, not without good reason, that the enemy had now been able to concentrate impor- tant forces at the entry of the English Channel and that his own mission had become quite impossible.

To sum up, the West Indian campaign was a long Calvary for Villeneuve. His morale, faltering from the beginning, sank further without the Admiral being able to find the necessary energy and optimism to train his men and prepare them for a decisive combat. The great accomplishments at Trafalgar by several French and Spanish vessels show, however, that there was, in the Franco-Spanish squadron, a potential that Villeneuve did not know either how to mobilise or to federate. Resignation, pessimism and passivity do not make great commanders! There certainly was too great a difference between the com- bined fleet and its British adversary to hope for a victory. The precision and rapidity of firing, the monopoly of carronades, terribly efficient at short dis- tances, but, above all, the formation and training of the crews gave the British an advantage that could not be equalled. But the terrible tragedy of Trafalgar, for which Napoleon was chiefly responsible, could have been avoided. Let us remember that on 19 October 1805, the united fleet sailed from Cádiz not in order to conquer England but to reach Toulon. Let us keep in mind the fact that if Villeneuve was still at the head of the fleet, it was because the Emperor had taken the demented decision of sending a substitute for Villeneuve without informing him, thinking that the Admiral, too faint-hearted, would not dare to attack the enemy. In fact, Villeneuve was a courageous man who believed he could redeem himself only by a brilliant performance or by dying worthily.

In the end, his adversaries rendered him deep respect. Rather naively, the English officers who came across him during his captivity were surprised to meet not the slovenly and vociferous individual they expected but a very distin- guished gentleman; Admiral Collingwood presents a fine portrait:[198] 'Admiral Villeneuve is well brought-up and, I believe, a very good officer; there is noth- ing displeasing or boastful, such as we attribute too often to the French, in his behaviour.' In short, in the eyes of the English, Villeneuve was someone very easy to associate with, who even possessed abundantly the quality of fair play. What better, in fact, than to be beaten while showing consistent resistance in order to assure the glory of one's conqueror?

The admirals of the Revolution and of the Empire had the unrewarding task of combating, in terribly unfavourable circumstances, an enemy who had attained great superiority. In the first years of the Revolution, they sailed out to combat with improvised captains, crews often on the verge of mutiny, and ships badly maintained and lacking armaments. Later, when order was restored on board ship and in the naval dockyards, British supremacy was such that French squadrons, blocked in ports, had huge difficulties in acquiring a minimum of training, all the more as the seamen who had been well trained were in a state of exhaustion. Napoleon's style of command did not improve the situation. Not having confidence in his admirals, the Emperor did not inform them of the objectives he had in mind but overwhelmed them with orders containing precise details and the threat of imposing sanctions in case of laxity or disobedience, which, taking into account communication delays, no longer had anything to do with the present situation and became a source of trouble and confusion.

In these circumstances, the talents that existed outside the noble corps of the Naval Guards had neither the time to blossom nor the possibility of doing so. Certain admirals, such as Villaret-Joyeuse and Allemand, former auxiliary officers, or Martin, former petty officer in the Royal Navy, showed real qualities which could at other times, have produced great commanders. Latouche-Tréville, who defied his colleague Nelson, and Villeneuve, who was tragically trapped while performing a role he knew himself incapable of assuming, still belonged to the great navy established in the time of Louis XVI.

# CHAPTER NINE

# Admiral Antonio Barceló, 1716–97: A Self-Made Naval Leader

## Agustín Ramón Rodríguez González
### Real Academia de la Historia, Madrid

The career of Antonio Barceló y Pont de la Terra has on many occasions attracted the attention of researchers and publishers of naval history. He was a modest mail-boat skipper, who, despite not being a nobleman and having very little academic training, managed to obtain the title of Admiral (Teniente General de la Armada) at a time when such an achievement was nigh on impossible. It was solely due to his merits in action during times of war and other outstanding services.[199]

Much less attention has been paid to the perhaps inevitable fact, given his character and career, that despite being an outstanding leader in the Spanish Royal Navy at that time, prejudices of all kinds, professional envy and the inertia of the 'establishment' ensured that a large part of his efforts did not receive their due reward and his ideas were not applied, or at least not to the desired extent.

Perhaps one of the subtlest attacks on his career and legacy has been to trivialise his actions, presenting them as typical of a hard, skilled 'corsair', within a very limited operational context, based on anecdotal evidence. This chapter aims to correct or, at least, considerably clarify this accepted opinion.

**How to cite this book chapter:**
Rodríguez González, A R. 2017. Admiral Antonio Barceló, 1716–97: A Self-Made Naval Leader. In: Harding, R and Guimerá, A (eds.). *Naval Leadership in the Atlantic World*. Pp. 107–115. London: University of Westminster Press. DOI: https://doi.org/10.16997/book2.k. License: CC-BY-NC-ND 4.0

## Barceló's career

A brief summary of the career of this great sailor would not be amiss, as he was a very well-known figure who, in our opinion, did not receive due credit. Born in Palma de Mallorca on 31 December 1716, in June 1735 he was appointed by Royal Order as master of the mail boat that connected Palma with Barcelona, giving him at the tender age of 18 a position he had already held whenever his father, from whom he inherited the boat and position, was absent or ill.

In November 1738, at 21 years old, he was rewarded with promotion to Lieutenant Junior Grade (Alfarez de Navio) for the bravery and skill with which he repelled an attack by two Algerian galiots during one of his crossings. Another of his services was to supply Palma with bread and flour during a severe 'supplies crisis', during which, to encourage his crew to work faster and to gain more cargo space on board, he got rid of the water tank. He rose to Sub-lieutenant (Teniente de Fragata) in May 1748. He also took command of a squadron of armed privateering xebecs, which had to act together with the navy ships against the Barbary corsairs, but the results were poor due to bureaucratic problems, indolence and a lack of coordination.

In June 1753 he was promoted to effective Lieutenant, as a result of repelling the attack of two Algerian galiots with his xebec, capturing one and damaging the other one until it fled. After 15 years, during which his bravery could have been put to much better use, our man entered the Spanish Royal Navy through well-earned references, at the unusually old age of 39 years old.

In August 1753 he was promoted to acting Lieutenant (Teniente de Navío) after providing another outstanding service which he combined with his postal duties: with his xebec and another under his command, he managed to capture an Algerian galiot and burn a Majorcan ship the Algerian privateers had just seized.

There followed some years of relative obscurity for Barceló, in which we have not been able to find any relevant services or promotions. Perhaps this was due to the difficulty for such an unusual sailor in the Royal Navy to gain acceptance, not to mention his service in the xebec, which became an efficient antidote to the similar Barbary ships and galiots, rather than the more prestigious ships of the line or frigates in royal service.

Nevertheless, Barceló's continuous successes between 1762 and 1769 confirmed that too much time had been lost in accepting the obvious: during those seven years, Barceló, at the helm of his xebec, accompanied by one or several others, captured or destroyed no fewer than 19 Barbary corsairs, of 6 to 30 guns, with a total of 1,600 prisoners, and freeing almost 1,000 Christian captives of all nationalities.

In order to better understand this, we have to remember that these Barbary sailors were not armed merchants, who defended themselves more or less weakly, but corsairs who literally fought to the death because, among other reasons, they knew there would be no exchange of prisoners for them and they could only hope for a short, difficult life of hard labour.

This series of successes was accompanied by the corresponding promotions for Barceló. He became Commander (Capitán de Fregata) in June 1762 and Post Captain (Capitán de Navío) in March 1769. The successes continued: such as on 22 October 1769, for instance, with a division of six xebecs, another 4-gun Algerian ship was conquered and captured near Melilla. That same year, on 24 November, a pension of 12,000 *reales* annually for life was granted by Royal Order for his outstanding services. In February 1775, Barceló rose to Commodore [Brigadier].[200]

His expertise in that style of naval warfare was more than proven, as was his personal courage, shown by several wounds, one of which was a very serious shot to his mouth that ripped out several teeth and became infected. He had a high temperature and could not eat or drink for almost three months, but he remained in charge of his xebec on a patrol mission. Whether due to the difficulty of his constant services or for other reasons, he was also said to be extremely deaf, yet despite this he remained in active service.

In the same year as he was promoted to Commodore, Barceló took part in the unfortunate expedition against Algiers. He was in command of a division of xebecs, with nine ships of between 20 and 32 guns, as well as the squadron and convoy, under the overall command of *Teniente General* don Pedro González Castejón for the naval part and Conde O'Reilly for the landing party. Barceló criticised the actions taken by these two commanders for landing on a beach near the corsairs' port, but they did not pay any attention to him. However, when the situation for the landing party became critical, Barceló did not wait for orders and covered the threatened flank of troops by firing from his xebecs, whilst *Jefe de Escuadra* Juan Acton did the same on the opposing flank with other units, thus avoiding greater disaster.

Spanish public opinion severely criticised the commanders for their ineptitude, and praised Barceló, who shortly after was promoted to Rear Admiral (Jefe de Escuadra). But this reward, and the fact he received so much praise and had exposed the ineptitude of senior officers, made him many enemies, with unpleasant consequences, not so much for his career – although it had some effect – but rather in terms of the influence of his leadership.

In spite of everything, he had risen to Rear Admiral by April 1779, in time to be involved in a new dispute against a very different type of enemy: the British Royal Navy.

His new mission was to take light blockade forces to Gibraltar, to oppose the British squadron there under the command of Rear Admiral Robert Duff. A blockade was always tedious, and more likely to highlight virtues such as patience and tenacity than brilliant acts of strategy and courage. On the other hand, completely closing the Strait, with its typical weather conditions, to any ship, whether an enemy or neutral, was an almost impossible task during the age of sail. The situation was made worse by the usual damage and operational withdrawals in Barceló's fleet, and above all the impatience and inexperience of the commanders and officers of the army entrenched at La Línea. Thus criticism rained down on Barceló, aggravated by the failure of his attack with a fireship, to such an extent that he was put under the inspection of another admiral, Rodríguez de Valcárce, a situation that was both embarrassing and wrong.

Such a harsh judgement was not meted out against other Spanish leaders who, for one reason or another, let three successive large convoys pass during the war and the siege. Each had been guarded by powerful squadrons and was much more important and decisive for the fortune of the besieged town than any small ship that managed to enter port, which is all that Barceló could be reproached with. However, the leaders who commanded squadrons were not reproached in any way; some were even promoted, such as Lángara, despite losing a large part of his own squadron in a battle against Admiral Rodney's squadron on 16 January 1780.

Barceló's difficult situation is corroborated in a letter sent from the Court to the new Commander-in-Chief, the Duke of Crillón, informing him that Barceló, due to his advanced age, deafness and limited academic training, was not a trustworthy leader.[201]

But while they lost ships, money and men with the controversial 'floating batteries' designed by the French engineer D'Arçon, which had such an unfortunate end, Barceló's luck began to change. He had the idea of designing gunboats to bombard the town from the sea. These were large rowing boats armed with a 24-pounder cannon and reinforced, first with cork and later with iron, although it was soon discovered that this overloaded the boat unnecessarily. These gunboats were particularly useful in the night attacks against Gibraltar, probably being the weapon that most concerned and disturbed the besieged. However, there were never enough of them, partly due to focusing on the batteries, and partly from pure indolence.

And so it was that, once the war ended, the King was satisfied with Barceló's tireless service. He had been continuously in action, and he was promoted on 16 February 1783 to Admiral Teniente General as part of a big promotion, justified because the war was deemed to be a victory, with the exception of Gibraltar. It must be said that of the four main promotions, the minister Floridablanca stated in a letter to Crillón that Barceló's was the most deserving, and reminded the Duke of Crillón that, despite reports discrediting Barceló, Crillón himself had been the most interested in Barceló's promotion.

Once the war with Great Britain had ended, interest was reignited in the continuing war with Barbary corsairs. Barceló's system was so effective that both Tripoli and Tunisia decided to sign a peace treaty with Spain. Only Algiers continued the fight, despite the Arab commanders or corsair captains insisting that their mission was now almost impossible.

It was obvious that only a masterstroke could dissuade Algiers from continuing with its policy of confrontation, and Barceló was given command of that mission. Believing that a new landing like that of 1775 was excessively expensive and dangerous, he planned a systematic bombardment of the town and port with his gunboats and newer types, such as bomb-ships armed with howitzers. They were trained in boarding to repel the counter-attack of the light enemy boats. All were guarded by ships of the line, frigates, the inevitable xebecs and many others.

The squadron of 85 vessels subjected Algiers to a series of nine heavy bombardments in July 1783. Despite serious damage and very few Spanish losses, Algiers did not cede and the expedition had to be repeated the following year, on a larger scale and with support from galleys of the Knights of St John of Malta and vessels from the kingdoms of Naples and Portugal joining for the first time. Despite his age, Barceló was personally involved to such an extent, covering the line of fire aboard a felucca, that his ship was in serious danger of being hit by an enemy projectile and sinking, despite which the bombardments continued.

The tactics that he used were as severely criticised by some as they were celebrated by others who had not forgotten the disaster of 1775. He was completely successful: Algiers could not hold up against such a series of attacks indefinitely, which besides the damage they caused (always limited due to the artillery of the time), forced Algiers to focus all its efforts on defence, and not on privateering, which was its way of life. Thus, after preliminary talks, and faced with the threat of a third expedition, peace was signed in 1786, one of the Spanish envoys being none other than José Mazarredo, who had been under Barceló's orders during the attacks.[202]

Although relations with Algerian corsairs in particular, and the Berbers in general, had some flare-ups over the following years, they were no longer the threat they had been to Spain since the sixteenth century. This enabled the repopulation of the east coast from Catalonia to Granada, and the significant economic boom of this region, which had previously been under threat of corsairs. It was definitely the most important and decisive Spanish victory of the eighteenth century.

Despite this, Barceló was barely rewarded, except for the confirmation of his promotion to Admiral and the award of the Grand Cross of the Order of Charles III, as well as other minor rewards. No doubt the reason was that he could only rise further to become Admiral of the Navy, a title that many of the Courtiers deemed excessive for his humble origins.

The last few years of his life passed uneventfully, with the exception of being passed over for command of a similar expedition, although much smaller, against Morocco, which was given to Francisco Morales de los Ríos, an inept man, who had been previously disqualified due to his cowardice as second-in-command of the frigate *Hermione* (26), which was lost in battle with a British frigate in May 1762. Nevertheless, Morales was promoted and given the title of Count of Morales for his small bombardment of Tangiers, which was a skirmish compared with those in Algiers. Morales was to demonstrate this ineptitude again in the Battle of San Vicente in February 1797, but his career shows the significant difference in treatment that officers could experience.

Barceló died from natural causes in his home in Palma on 30 January 1797, a fortnight before Morales's failure in San Vicente that led to him being dismissed from the service and demoted.

## Xebecs: a tough school for sailors

Nicholas Rodger reminded us some time ago that most eighteenth-century sailors on men-of-war had a strange profession as they only worked during wars. Once peace was achieved, all the navies stripped the ships of the rigging and sails, cannons and equipment, and anchored them in the dockyards, with very few small ones staying in active service, exclusively for scientific exploration and surveillance tasks.

But that was not the case for the xebecs, at least until the Treaty of 1786: they continually patrolled in search of their slippery and dangerous enemies, the Barbary corsairs, staying in port only for essential work such as repairs or renewing supplies and ammunition. Therefore it was a formidable school for young officers who, instead of settling on land in more or less bureaucratic postings, had the chance to learn and grow in their profession.

To cite two well-known names, none other than Federico Gravina and Antonio Escaño carried out many of their first battles and campaigns in xebecs, directly under Barceló's command or under his inspiration and protection. Gravina, a modest ensign (*alférez de fragata*), sailed in *Pilar* and *Gamo*, distinguishing himself later in command of the *San Luis*, in which he began to stand out. He took part in the two bombardments of Algiers, commanding the *Catalán* and dealing with the intelligence for the expedition. Escaño, a simple midshipman (*guardiamarina*), was under the direct orders of Barceló on the *Vigilante* in several battles; then he passed on to the *Atrevido* and even commanded a division of xebecs under the flag of the frigate *Casilda*.

Barceló's relationship with these and other great sailors of the time was close, as is shown in a personal letter from Gravina to Barceló upon hearing about his rise to Admiral:

'No one has more reasons than I to celebrate the satisfaction and advantage for Spain... I am most pleased for the promotion you have just received, for which I send you my warmest congratulations.'[203]

People of the calibre of Escaño, Grandallana and Alsedo, and many others, also wrote in similar terms.

Among these there may also have been the great Mazarredo, who was under Barceló's orders in Algiers, and signed the peace treaty that Barceló won.

Mazarredo used his gunboats brilliantly to harass the ships blocking Cádiz in 1797. But the many huge merits of this great Basque sailor did not include acknowledging debts to others who were not loyal subordinates. What was for some a promotion and apprenticeship, was for others a punishment. An officer condemned for dishonourable conduct before the enemy was often offered the chance to 'redeem' himself by voluntarily boarding as an 'adventurer' in the xebecs. Sometimes it was done with entire crews: on one occasion, three Spanish galleons were shamefully beaten by a sole Algerian xebec that captured one and made the other two flee. It was considered that the best way to 'retrain' the crews and officers was to put them under Barceló's command.[204]

It must have greatly surprised these fellow officers to be faced with such a rough and uneducated man, with little culture, who shouted a lot and took off his wig at the slightest occasion. A man who was capable of joining a boarding, or of carrying out an order himself. On one occasion, upon capturing an Algerian ship, orders forbade taking anything from it on board, for fear of an epidemic. A sailor took a liking to a beautiful wide red belt and Barceló himself snatched it out of his hands and threw it into the sea, a gesture that shook his much primmer subordinates, who would have sent a petty officer to do it.

But they soon realised they were with a real 'sea dog', a professional forged by long, hard service, resourceful and with common sense, friendly and modest, who became a legend not just for his crews, but for the whole Spanish east coast, a fact proven by many folk songs and poems. There is no doubt he was the most popular and admired Spanish sailor of the eighteenth century.

Barceló was also a man who took care of his own and did not allow other authorities to interfere with his subordinates, something that is mentioned many times. He dealt with things as a 'family affair'.

As might be expected, Barceló was strongly in favour of meritocracy in promotions and mentions in despatches, in a navy where careers were based on seniority of service and the King's favour. Thus, with his typical frankness, he wrote to Charles III in November 1784, while preparing his third expedition against Algiers:

'But before leaving the Court I find a big obstacle that, no doubt, will make this venture difficult, this being that I will not find officers willing to serve under my orders as there will be no reward no matter how much they risk their life in action. Your Majesty knows better than I that no General among those that have been heroes would have achieved such successful actions if they had not had brave corporals and subordinates who, obeying their orders, earned their deserving rewards through hard work and sweat.' …

'Having seen men promoted who were not there (in the second expedition to Algiers) or, if they were, had only been promoted earlier, am I, perhaps, to blame for many recent officers having been put under my command so that after having risked everything, they are not promoted due to a shorter length of service? And if length of service were the only deserving reason, what would be the point of fostering and stimulating young men to attempt glorious actions if they are not going to receive their due reward for a lack of it?'

He summarised:

'How am I to attempt glorious actions for the State when I can see from the start the hurdle of not duly rewarding Your Majesty's vassals, who have tried hard to serve you?'

Finally, he argued that he was the person who best knew which subordinates were the most suitable for the job and which deserved to be rewarded, not the bureaucracy or the narrow regulations.[205]

What Barceló so insistently proposed to King Charles III was little short of revolutionary for the time, and very little or nothing could be done in that sense. However, there is no doubt we are in the presence of a true leader, a man who trained his subordinates, who demanded everything from them and who requested on their behalf the rewards that were their main motivation. And in light of the history of the Spanish navy, many more like Barceló were needed at that time, when efforts were not rewarded, and defeats, including the most shameful, often had little influence in sailors' careers.

## Barceló's other activities

Barceló was not just the leading commander of a new kind of ship, the xebec, and expert in its suitable use, but he was also concerned with design changes: from the originals with around 20 cannons and lateen-rigged (*aparejo latino*), to the final ones with over 40 guns and with a pole-masted square rig (*aparejo redondo de polacra*). In this race the Algerians could not match the Spanish, although they tried. Barceló constantly experimented with changes and improvements. Some were carried out at his own expense, such as those called 'galleons', lighter and more streamlined for hunting the enemy. He examined the best among the captured Algerian boats and proposed and obtained their incorporation into the navy.

He also developed the gunboats and their derivatives, creating a weapon that would give the navy many of the modest successes it achieved in the tragic years from 1797 to 1805, and which later on would be of great importance in the decisive defence of Cádiz from 1810 to 1812. For all of them he planned tactics that were deemed unorthodox, generally passing from boarding to pounding with artillery.

However, he also had unusual sensibility and real concern for the service and for people. After the recovery of Menorca in 1783, which had been the Royal Navy's base for many years since the War of Spanish Succession, with the logical benefits for its inhabitants, he was the driving force behind the creation of new buildings in Port Mahón. In a letter to the King he wrote:

'With this, Sir, I promise not only to teach the Moors a lesson, but to favour the locals of Mahón who I see to be somewhat uprooted from that island, as they have not had their main trade and are lacking active business, thus managing to consolidate the serenity of these vassals and their families...' [206]

That was not all. Enriched by his many captures, he did not hesitate to invest part of his capital in shipping companies. However, not being interested in money, it is known that he handed out large amounts to the dockyards so they could finish building ships that had been stopped due to a lack of state funding, and he even refused to receive payment for expenses and statutory compensations. This wealth and generosity could well have been another reason for envy among many colleagues.[207]

## Conclusion

The figure of Antonio Barceló, although well-known and popular, has been excessively trivialised, being seen as nothing more than a rough sea dog who beat the Algerian corsairs in epic combats between xebecs. Some of that can be seen in the Spanish navy which regularly gives his name to light units: from torpedo boats to patrol boats.

But as we have seen, Barceló's achievements significantly surpass those achieved by his xebecs and gunboats, providing a much more complete professional image of the man. And that a man with his limitations knew how to train and lead many of the best Spanish sailors of the eighteenth century, who fought to eradicate the damaging system of rewards and punishments of the age, despite which, and on his own merit, he managed to obtain the highest ranks combat after combat, is by no means the least of his contributions.

As the popular folk song says:

'If the King of Spain had
Four like Barceló,
Gibraltar would be Spain.
And for the English, no.'

The fact that this simple verse contained so much truth is something that some would never forgive.

CHAPTER TEN

# Naval Leadership and the 'Art of War': John Jervis and José de Mazarredo Compared (1797–9)

Agustín Guimerá

Instituto de Historia, Consejo Superior de Investigaciones Científicas, Madrid

'This trinity [of war] is composed of primordial violence, hatred, and enmity ... of the play of chance and probability, within which the creative spirit is free to roam; and of its element of subordination, as an instrument of policy, which makes it subject to pure reason.' (Clausewitz, *On War*, 1780–1831)

In his final book, entitled *Nelson, the Admiral*, Colin White explored the great British naval officer's gift for leadership – his strong emotional ties to the profession, and his dedication to the service of his King and country, as well as his ability to build an outstanding team of officers with whom he shared these concerns and to whom he provided not only an example, but also affection and even friendship. Nelson's great sensitivity to the harsh conditions endured by the crews of his ships and fleets won the admiration of even the least of his subordinates.[208]

There can be no doubt that the quality of leadership in the three great maritime powers of the period – Great Britain, France and Spain – affected how international conflicts unfolded at sea between the years 1750 and 1850.

**How to cite this book chapter:**
Guimerá, A. 2017. Naval Leadership and the 'Art of War': John Jervis and José de Mazarredo Compared (1797–9). In: Harding, R and Guimerá, A (eds.). *Naval Leadership in the Atlantic World*. Pp. 117–130. London: University of Westminster Press. DOI: https://doi.org/10.16997/book2.l. License: CC-BY-NC-ND 4.0

The present paper will compare two naval officers who faced each other at the culminating moment of their careers: the British admiral John Jervis (1735–1823), commander of the Mediterranean Fleet, and the Spanish lieutenant general José de Mazarredo (1754–1812), commanding officer of the *Escuadra del Océano* and Spain's premier naval officer in the eighteenth century. The arena for their confrontation was the close blockade of Cádiz by Jervis's fleet between April 1797 and August 1799, during which Mazarredo was the architect of the port city's defence. The former was a typical example of a great fleet commander in a highly efficient naval organisation such as the Royal Navy. The latter was a naval leader *par excellence*, whose career coincided with an acute economic and political crisis in Spain, when the navy was in rapid decline.

Andrew Lambert has reflected on the true 'admiral's art', emphasising the importance of military command, management and leadership as key factors in the effective use of naval power in numerous spheres, such as diplomacy, deterrence and the projection of that power, among others.[209] Modern leadership theory also clearly distinguishes leadership from authority, administration, charisma and heroism. A military leader goes beyond these. It is not sufficient to exercise control and wield great social influence, or to be effective in an organisational sense. To be effective in war, he must have a clear sense of what will bring victory and must wisely apply the values of his time to inspire collaborators, create a sense of teamwork and determination to win in the most unforgiving of competitive environments.[210]

After situating the blockade of Cádiz in its strategic context within the Anglo-Spanish confrontation of 1796–1802, this paper will consider one aspect of the leader's role: the choice of strategic pathways. That choice was between attritional warfare and a war of annihilation; between humanitarianism and extreme violence. For Mazarredo, this was expressed in the protocols he observed in his interaction with his adversary John Jervis.

## Jervis and Mazarredo, parallel lives

Both Jervis and Mazarredo were effective fleet commanders within the military context of their time. They were both good seamen and exhibited unremitting concern for the training of their crews and the health and welfare of their subordinates. They had mastered all the areas of their profession: navigation, strategy, tactics, logistics, organisational structure, naval intelligence, armaments and such like. They had also distinguished themselves in important campaigns throughout their careers. They even both participated in the Battle of Cape Spartel on 20 October 1782, during the American War of Independence. In their confrontation during 1797–9 they turned their respective fleets into efficient machines – in Jervis's case for destruction and for Mazarredo deterrence.[211]

While Jervis was a magnificent fleet commander, he was not, in a sense, a true leader – he did not try to lead his subordinates, but to command them. His manner was harsh: he imposed a savage discipline on his crews, implacable towards mutineers and fierce in response to officers who voiced objections. According to Lambert, he was inflexible – always adopting a strategy of confrontation rather than cooperation.

This can be seen clearly in his term as First Lord of the Admiralty (1801–04), which is generally considered to have been disastrous for the Royal Navy.[212] Some of his other defects had come to light earlier during his campaign in the Caribbean in 1794. Here, he revealed a rapaciousness for the booty of prize ships and a readiness to mistreat neutral ships in pursuit of this end.

During his tenure as commander of the Mediterranean Fleet (1795–9), his inflexibility made it impossible to create a true team. He was highly critical of the divisional commanders who were under his orders and merciless towards those whom he considered to be ineffective captains. He was only able to connect with a small group of young and ambitious officers, such as Nelson, Troubridge, Collingwood, Fremantle, Miller and Hood. It is true that he was genuinely concerned about the health and welfare of his crews and that he was sometimes generous with the common sailor. However, these gestures were in stark contrast to the public mistreatment of his men, which exacerbated the social antagonism between his officers and sailors.

Mazarredo was entirely different – displaying what might now be considered a true naval leadership. In the words of a contemporary, he was phenomenal, 'the Hercules from Biscay', displaying boundless energy and capacity for work. A well-educated philanthropist, he was part of Spain's enlightened military elite. He perfectly combined knowledge of science and maritime warfare. He was a sponsor and organiser of the most important scientific institutions and expeditions of his time. He was also a distinguished author of seven books on naval warfare, in addition to the famous naval ordinances, published in 1793. As ambassador to Algiers, he was responsible for the signing of the preliminary peace accords with the Regency in June 1785. He was also a good diplomat for naval affairs to First Consul Bonaparte in Paris, when the *Escuadra del Océano* was stationed in Brest from 1799 to 1801.

His gifts for leadership allowed him to put together teams that made the most of the abilities of some of his subordinates. The list of illustrious officers who served with him in the *Escuadra del Océano* (1797–1801) is impressive: officers such as Gravina, Álava, Churruca, Alcalá Galiano, Valdés, Vargas, Uriarte, Cisneros, Villavicencio, Nava and Espinosa were among many who were later to become heroes at Trafalgar.

Standing out above them all was the future lieutenant general Antonio de Escaño (1752–1814), who was for decades Mazarredo's inseparable collaborator. The pair operated perfectly together on many campaigns and left a deep impression on their fellow naval commanders. Together they built an innovative team that exemplified the spirit of service to their country.

However, there was a further difference between Jervis and Mazarredo –
Mazarredo lacked Jervis's political sense. Jervis's antipathy towards the nobility did not stop him from seeking their support in order to realise his professional and political ambitions. He made good use of his family and political
connections, being a member of Parliament from 1783 until his death.[213]
Mazarredo, on the other hand, followed a very different trajectory. In contexts
that were favourable to the navy, he was able to work effectively with the political leaders of the state. This was the case in his collaboration with Secretary
of the Navy Antonio Valdés (1783–95) and Secretary of State Mariano Luis
de Urquijo (1798–1800). However, Mazarredo's character and professionalism
were incompatible with bending to the sensibilities of powerful men where he
felt the interests of the navy were at risk. He was incapable of submitting to his
superiors when he believed that he was in the right, and his candour at times
mingled with naivety. All of this created difficulties for him, including being
politically outcast during some of the most crucial years of the Spanish-British
War (1795–7 and 1804–8), the very times when the disastrous battles of Cape
St Vincent (14 February 1797) and Trafalgar (21 October 1805) took place.
This crisis for the Bourbon dynasty was a long and trying time for a leader like
him, forced to watch the decline of a navy that on so many other occasions he
had helped save from disaster.

## Context of the Anglo-Spanish War (1796–1802)

When Spain declared war on Great Britain in October 1796, the country was
pursuing political aims that were consistent with a huge shift in its diplomacy.
Throughout the eighteenth century, the Spanish Empire was caught between
two giants that were often at war with one other: France and Great Britain.
With countless territories and interests spread all over the globe, long-term
neutrality was an impossible policy for a nation as significant as Spain. In 1796,
faced with limited options for manoeuvre on the international stage, the Secretary of State, Manuel Godoy, chose the lesser of two evils, an alliance with
France, through the instrument of the Treaty of San Ildefonso, a defensive pact
signed in August of that year. It was an 'unnatural' agreement, between a Cath-
olic monarchy and a regicide, secular republic, but it arose out of the specific
political situation of the moment. Through it, the Spanish monarchy sought to
check French expansionism. For Spain it would have been suicide to remain at
odds with such a powerful neighbour, which throughout much of the century
had been restrained through the so-called 'Family Pacts'. Another of Spain's
political objectives was to thwart British 'ambition' in European and colonial
seas, which had led to over 100 years of friction, most recently evidenced in
the Nootka Sound incident in 1790. Spain continued to have many grievances
against Great Britain: the centuries-long English contraband trade with Spain's
American colonies, corsair activity in Corsica – to which Great Britain turned

a blind eye – and the restitution of Gibraltar. Moreover, the Spanish monarchy accused its erstwhile ally in the war against revolutionary France of disloyalty.[214]

In this war, Spain's military objective was consistent with the traditional idea of attritional warfare associated with the *ancien régime*.[215] When the Spanish monarchy declared war on Great Britain, it was a preventive move. Spanish policy was not to seek out and destroy British power at sea, but rather by the presence and cooperation of the allied fleets present a strong means of deterrence – a 'fleet in being' – to act as a restraint on the superiority of the Royal Navy. During the talks in Basel in 1795, the French had encouraged the Spanish to form a confederation of maritime powers of Northern Europe to further counteract British superiority at sea. It was essentially a defensive policy aimed at maintaining the status quo in Europe and the Americas.

Great Britain's military objective in 1796 was very different from that of her opponents. Once war had been declared, Great Britain worked tenaciously to get Spain to end its alliance with France. Another of its political goals – a constant theme in its foreign diplomacy – was opening Spanish colonial markets to British shipping and trade.

During the second half of the eighteenth century, Great Britain had increasingly practised the war of destruction: 'absolute war' or 'the absolute of war', which Clausewitz would define years later. The wars of the French Revolution and their consequences accelerated this process. The defence of British national interests and the Napoleonic Wars would soon crystallise in a total war between nations. The 'hostile intentions' of a government towards the enemy would become 'hostile sentiments' among its people.[216]

During the period 1797–9 the Royal Navy once again pursued the destruction of Spanish fleets in decisive battles, in addition to inflicting great damage to her maritime trade, through privateering and the blockade of her principal ports. Special emphasis was put on the traditional policy of interrupting Spanish colonial trade to the Americas, which, for two centuries, was a key source of financing for the Spanish monarchy. The ultimate goal of this strategy was to starve the Spanish economy of bullions thereby limiting the capacity of the monarch to finance the war and exerting pressure on public opinion so that the people would demand peace from their government.

## The strategies of Jervis and Mazarredo, 1797–9

With these different strategic objectives, the strategies deployed by the two antagonists were also very different.[217] With Spain's declaration of war in October 1796 and the advance of the French armies in Italy, Jervis was obliged to abandon his bases in the Mediterranean, including the important bases in Corsica and Elba. In December of that year, Jervis was in Lisbon, which would serve as the winter base of the Mediterranean Fleet for a time. This withdrawal served only to incite discontent among his crews and British public opinion, which now supported war of annihilation with Spain more than ever.

Jervis was subsequently the architect of the close blockade of Spanish ports in 1797, especially Cádiz, the key to colonial trade. With this blockade he continued the same strategy that he had employed in Toulon and Leghorn (Livorno) during the previous year. The blockade was intended to force Mazarredo to bring his squadron out of Cádiz and engage Jervis in battle. The British admiral had full confidence in his fleet of 23 ships of the line, after the victory over the Spanish fleet in Cape St Vincent in February 1797.

The blockade of Cádiz began in April 1797 and continued after the end of Jervis's command until 1808, when Britain started backing the Spanish rebellion against Napoleon. Jervis anchored a squadron very close to Cádiz, the Inshore Squadron, initially under the command of Rear Admiral Horatio Nelson, with the bulk of the fleet continuously making long tacks out to sea, like a military parade of naval power, in sight of the Bay of Cádiz. On other occasions he anchored at Rota. During the winter season, Jervis took his fleet to Lisbon, leaving the surveillance squadron off Cádiz. Sometimes, bad weather forced him to draw near to the Bay of Tangiers. It was an enormous feat of navigation, logistics and naval intelligence. The blockade was so effective that 1797 was the worst year for Spanish-American trade in all of recent history.[218]

Moreover, Jervis had to carry out other missions. He had to prevent the allied squadrons at Toulon, Cartagena, Cádiz and Ferrol from rendezvousing; protect Portuguese trade and sovereignty; neutralise possible threats to Gibraltar; and carry out cruising missions in the Mediterranean to diminish French pressure on the Kingdom of Naples and the Two Sicilies.

Jervis's strategy was to compel the Spanish into a decisive battle, in order to diminish their operational capability. He tried to force Mazarredo to come out of the bay with his fleet and engage in battle by shelling Cádiz on the nights of 3 and 5 July 1797. Action against enemy trade was another facet of this war of annihilation. The abortive assault on Santa Cruz de Tenerife by a squadron under Nelson's command at the end of July 1797 is the most significant example of this policy.

For his part, Mazarredo recognised the weakness of his fleet at Cádiz. The Spanish navy in 1797 was a shadow of its former strength. The Cádiz squadron could effectively arm only 21 ships of the line and later had to lower this number to 19. Mazarredo's response, therefore, had to be nuanced. In the first place, he accepted the inevitability of the Cádiz blockade by Jervis's fleet. However, he sought unceasingly to wear down both its physical power and the combat morale of the enemy through a strategy of active defence. To protect the city and the fleet he developed what were called 'subtle forces', which followed the model of the *flotille a la hollandaise* and which had had so much success in the Great Siege of Gibraltar (1779–82). Within two months of having taken command, Mazarredo had more than 100 smaller vessels, armed with cannons and mortars, the most important being the gunboats.[219] He was thus able to neutralise the shelling by the British in July 1797, and these units were a thorn in the side of the enemy throughout the blockade.

He also made the most of the few opportunities that arose in this war of attrition to prevent the total interruption of Spain's trade with its colonies and to weaken the enemy's naval power. With the help of Escaño and his team, he organised a fleet of 21 ships in Cádiz also within two months, although it was a 'fleet in being' only since there were severe shortages in terms of seamen and gunners. He never granted Jervis the opportunity of a decisive battle, but he did surprise his rival when he took his fleet out to sea on the night of 6 February 1798. For a week it sailed towards Cape St Vincent in pursuit of the British surveillance squadron, and then returned to its base. This sortie raised the morale of the fleet and the people of Cádiz and was applauded by the government.

## Leadership values

In the Anglo-Spanish conflicts between 1776 and 1815 there seems to have been a shift between two traditional conceptions of armed conflict; away from attritional warfare towards a war of annihilation and the concept of total war. Attritional warfare was the *ancien régime*'s customary form of armed conflict. It was dynastic and conventional in nature, waged between kings, and limited in duration. It was a 'war of cabinets', where strategic manoeuvring took precedence over battle. It had concrete objectives, such as the defence or break-up of a commercial system, redrawing of borders or the conquest of territory. Once this objective was met (or could not be met), the parties promptly negotiated peace to limit their losses. The war of annihilation goes far further. It pursues the destruction of the enemy's material and military resources through decisive battles, burning down dockyards and warehouses, dismantling fortifications, plundering settlements and harvests. The objectives or ambitions could be far wider, encompassing the collapse of the enemy as a political or economic entity. The eighteenth century saw both types of conflicts. Neither conflicted with the values of the Enlightenment, but the strategy of annihilation became more prominent as the French Revolution produced more implacable hostilities at a fundamental ideological level and mobilised societies which had the resources to prosecute wars more ferociously over time.

The French Revolution and the Napoleonic Wars thus mark the dawn of total warfare, which was to become an increasingly common form of armed conflict in centuries to come. These conflicts involved a country's entire population, by way of universal and compulsory enlistment, and the use of all the resources belonging to a community, which had become united around the ideology of the nation. War was now a conflict between peoples. This shift coincided with the emergence in European society of new sentiments of a pre-Romantic variety.

This evolution of violence was studied in detail by Clausewitz in the decades following the war. For this military theorist, 'absolute war' or 'the absolute of war' was the not the same as 'real war'. The former gave primacy to the political realm while the latter was the day-to-day practice of war which tended towards pure violence, in which the political end was subordinate to the paroxysm of fighting. The annihilation of the enemy was a product of the reality of war itself. For Clausewitz, the effective conduct of war depended on establishing a balance between the components of the trinity of war mentioned above: violence, the game of chance and instrument of policy.

Depending on the duration and importance of a particular conflict, the transition from hostile intentions to hostile sentiment occurred with greater or lesser ease. Daily life had a direct influence on the emotional world of the fighters. It was a context in which threat and uncertainty reigned. In battle – 'the first-born son of war' – this tension reached a climax. As the scene of survival, death and destruction, battle catalysed hostile sentiment among the protagonists, as well as their ambition and their eagerness for glory. The conduct demonstrated by Jervis and Mazarredo during the Cádiz blockade of 1797–9 corresponds respectively to the conception of the war of annihilation, in the case of the British admiral, and that of attritional warfare in the case of his Spanish counterpart.[220] This naval operation also allows us to examine the change in Jervis's day-to-day conduct: that is, his transition from conducting 'absolute war' to 'real war.'

## Attitudes towards the enemy

Under the circumstances of the blockade, the British admiral alternated between two extremes. On the one hand, he was frustrated by having been expelled from the Mediterranean and by not being able to destroy Mazarredo's fleet, which lay out of reach at anchor in Cádiz. On the other, he praised the virtues of the Spanish crews.

One of his protégés, Rear Admiral Nelson, epitomised the hostile sentiment. In November 1796, in spite of the allies' superior numbers, he was confident that Jervis would defeat the enemy and make Spain pay dearly for its interference in the Franco-British conflict. When Jervis's fleet pulled out of the Mediterranean in January 1797, Nelson again demonstrated his rancour towards the Spanish – referring to them pejoratively as the *Dons* – for having declared war on Great Britain.[221]

Yet Nelson and Jervis admired their opponents' courage. The former praised the valiant conduct of Jacob Stuart, the commander of a frigate captured in December 1796, and Miguel Tryason, the leader of a flotilla of gunboats, whose barge was taken by Nelson after a tough hand-to-hand struggle in the course of the famous night action that took place on 3 July 1797, in Cádiz Bay.[222] In the spring of 1797 Jervis defended the magnificent performance of Moreno, a division leader of the Spanish fleet during the Battle of Cape St Vincent, at his court martial in Cádiz.[223]

For his part, Mazarredo also alternated between criticism and admiration of his enemy. In August 1795, at the time of the Peace of Basel and the end of the Spanish alliance with the United Kingdom, he criticised Great Britain's zeal for overseas domination through the destruction of the Spanish and French navies:

'England with its sea moat, England with its industry and its navy, will be master of the world for many years hence, and the stronger its dominion becomes the longer the calamities will continue on the continent of Europe. It will pay for these calamities with money, cementing her superiority.'[224]

But in the same letter he recognised the positive qualities of his adversary, the British virtue of fostering scientific study and technical advances in the service of naval warfare – in sum, the search for perfection:

'But beware, her Navy is formidable. It is what matters to her. It's her great object of study… There is nothing that she will not put to the test. There is no new advance that she will not immediately adopt… Let us not deceive ourselves with flattering ideas about honour, pride, and goodwill. Will alone is not enough in the Navy. It is necessary to distil the means of making will fruitful, as the English do…'

## War of destruction

All was fair in the conflicts at the end of the century of the Enlightenment. For example, the British used a false flag to take a Spanish merchant vessel by surprise at the beginning of the blockade.[225] We also witness a change in Jervis's attitude towards the war. In May 1797 he worried about the shots fired by his fleet at the gunboats and batteries in Rota doing harm to the civilian population.[226] But two months later, he gives a series of justifications for his decision to shell Cádiz.[227]

Among Jervis's fleet there were crews that had participated in the general mutiny in England during April and May 1797. This was true of the ship *Theseus*, whose command was handed over to Nelson when it arrived in Cádiz that spring. It was necessary to keep these sailors occupied and disciplined, and operations such as the bombing of Cádiz served this purpose.

Jervis also attempted to sow panic in the civilian population through the destruction of property and the killing of some of the city's inhabitants. This strategy was intended to influence public opinion to pressure Mazarredo into leaving the bay and engaging in battle.

From the invention of the bombship in the 1680s, the threat of or the actual shelling of towns from the sea had been common practice in the eighteenth century, but this was the first time in living memory that the British had shelled a city in metropolitan Spain, attacking the property and the lives of civilians, and it was strongly denounced in Spain. It is symptomatic that there is an ominous silence in the documentation of the two antagonists at this juncture: there was no correspondence at all between Jervis and Mazarredo during most of the month of July. A letter written by Nelson to his commander in the midst of the operation provides an accurate reflection of the hostile sentiment that motivated the British, who were frustrated at not being able to force the enemy fleet into a sortie:

'News from Cádiz, by a Market-boat, that our Ships did much damage; the Town was on fire in three places; a shell that fell in a Convent destroyed several priests (that no harm, they will never be missed); that plunder and robbery was going on – a glorious scene of confusion ...'[228]

Although this news was false, it confirms that Nelson was a staunch advocate for war of annihilation.

Everything said up to now contrasts with the view of war taken by Mazarredo. Nelson was powerfully influenced by his Christian faith, but also by his unmovable determination to win against those whom he saw as heretics and atheist regicides. Mazarredo, on the other hand, was guided by his Christian spirit in a different way. He sought to wear down his powerful and arrogant enemy through whatever damage could be done to his commerce and his navy. It was necessary to combine bravery and mercy. The object of war was not to kill one's opponents but to defeat them in order to achieve peace. Unnecessary death was to be avoided and the defeated were to be treated with generosity.[229]

## Humanitarianism

War, whether it was of attrition or annihilation, should have its countervailing forces. The strong emotions that it aroused demanded the existence of a plan to harmonise them, according to Clausewitz. With respect to the blockade of Cádiz, this was manifest in two different aspects: the humanitarian treatment of the adversary and the observance of protocol.

The exchange of prisoners was dictated by practical considerations. The care for and surveillance of numerous enemies on board a ship already brimming with people was a difficult task. The return of prisoners also constituted an act of reciprocal generosity towards individuals who had suffered hardship and thus tempered the horrors of war.[230]

This situation is reflected in Jervis and Mazarredo's correspondence, which served to clarify misunderstandings and helped to facilitate coastal fishing, coastal trade and neutral commerce:

'Your Excellency will understand perfectly that on both points I adhere closely to the tacit convention of nations, that proper mutual consideration should not be disregarded by reason of being at war.'[231]

Once the close blockade of Cádiz was established in April 1797, Jervis moved quickly to permit neutral commerce, at Mazarredo's request.[232] The same was true of coastal fishing. Jervis also gave permission for fishermen to perform their labours in the bay and on the Cádiz coast. He reprimanded his captains when they were guilty of excesses towards the fishermen and punished a privateer from Gibraltar for his poor treatment of a fisherman. He also dictated terms for tuna fishing in Conil and sardine fishing in Ayamonte. Jarvis's tone in these letters is highly significant:

'I am engaged in hostilities, by the orders of my Sovereign, whose highest displeasure I should most certainly incur if I did not exercise every degree of humanity towards them in acrid military operations … nothing will give me greater satisfaction than to soften the scourge of war, between the people of two nations who are formed to live in the friendship and esteem of each other, by every means in my power.'[233]

In contrast, Mazarredo was very cautious in this matter and prohibited deep-sea fishing, since some fishermen made deals with the enemy. For example, he arrested the owners of fishing boats who arranged to sell produce to Jervis's fleet.[234] The same happened with coastal trading in basic necessities. For example, Jervis released two Moroccan ships that were carrying meat and grain to Cádiz and the Spanish fleet.[235]

However, war should not only be licit but also appear to be so. In accordance with the tacit laws of belligerent nations, Mazarredo conformed to the principle of not using merchant ships to relay messages between belligerent parties. From the beginning of the blockade, he refused any communications from the British relayed through fishermen or neutral vessels, even if related to matters of the utmost importance. To exchange letters, he alerted Jervis to have a ship of truce drop anchor in the entry channel, two miles beyond the shoals at the mouth to the Bay of Cádiz. There it would wait for a Spanish messenger to collect the document on board.[236]

Despite this fact, a fishing boat availed itself of this polite treatment at the hands of the British fleet to venture beyond the fishing grounds near the coast.

Nelson then accused the fisherman of spying and threatened to sink any and all ships that surpassed the agreed-upon limits.[237]

Mazarredo intervened in this matter, alleging that it was a Portuguese fisherman, who was fishing without his authorisation. As proof of good faith, he pointed out that the prohibition against using private citizens to carry out naval intelligence missions had allowed a brigantine from America to be captured by the blockading fleet.[238]

## Protocol

In this theatre of war, the two naval leaders staged a performance – concerning honour and public image – of the gallant conduct that two civilised enemies should show one another.

The blockade of Cádiz and the bombing of the city did not prevent Jervis from commending Mazarredo's good judgement and shrewdness, or the latter from extolling the humanity of the former, in highly obsequious language.[239] The two exchanged gifts throughout the campaign. On one occasion, Jervis sent Mazarredo some boxes with illustrations of plants and birds from America addressed to Charles IV that had been found on the frigate *Ninfa*, which had been captured by the British.[240] At another point, the British admiral presented him with a box of cigars, with his emblem and card.[241] Mazarredo sent Jervis a barrel of wine. Jervis in turn sent Mazarredo 36 bottles of beer and a barrel of salted meat, along with a recipe for curing it.

For the two antagonists, this show of courtesy is compatible with the war that they were waging. Mazarredo expressed it thus, when presenting Jervis with a hunting gun for his wife:

> 'Since the Countess of St Vincent takes so much pleasure in her duties in the countryside, and in accompanying her, her husband the Admiral might find it expedient to divert himself with hunting quail, Don Joseph de Mazarredo ventures to present Your Excellency with a Spanish piece for such an occasion and to beg him to deign to accept it as a reminder of his friendship, wholly reconcilable with their respective obligations in any circumstances.'[242]

The courtesies between the two foes began at the outset of the blockade. For example, Nelson sent word to Mazarredo that on 4 June, 1797, the fleet would perform a salute in honour of the birthday of the King of Great Britain, at 8 pm, and adds:

> '...and has desired me to mention it to your Excellency, that the Ladies at Cádiz may not be alarmed at the firing.'

In response to which, after praising the urbanity expressed in Nelson's letter, Mazarredo replied in the same cordial tone:

'The Ladies of Cádiz, accustomed to the noisy rounds of salutes of the vessels of war, will sit and will hear what Sir John Jervis means to regale them with, for the evening of the 4th current, in honour of his Britannic Majesty's birthday; and the general wish of the Spanish nation cannot but interest itself in so august a motive.'[243]

Today it seems strange to us that two weeks before the shelling of Cádiz by Jervis's fleet, the latter would have asked for permission for a British officer and his wife to visit Cádiz, as if it were a stop on the Grand Tour. The Spanish commander refused, with utmost diplomacy, citing reasons that tell us much about the nature of conventional war:

'… making me equally regretful that, due to the appearance of the particular situation, it is not at my discretion that Madame Manfield and this gentleman be satisfied in their curiosity to see Cádiz; since among the public, unacquainted with how the movements of individuals might be combined with the duties of arms, it would cause a sensation, characteristic of this lack of acquaintance, for a lady to appear, especially one of her distinction, and in particular since the General would not be deprived of honouring her as would befit the occasion.'[244]

In August 1797, Mazarredo's diplomacy was again on display, when he enquired after the health of Rear Admiral Nelson and Captain Fremantle, both wounded in the recent attack on Santa Cruz de Tenerife. Jervis in turn extolled the sentiments of honour and humanity in his opponent.[245]

## Epilogue

In conclusion, Jervis excelled as a fleet commander and Mazarredo as a naval leader in the period of transition to total war. Jervis perfected the strategy of the close blockade, utilised by Great Britain during that period to such disastrous effect for her adversaries. He was also one of the promoters of the professionalisation of the Royal Navy. For his part, Mazarredo helped to save the Bourbon navy from further disasters. In spite of innumerable difficulties, the Spanish navy was able to fulfil its function as deterrent in contemporary international relations. What is more, Mazarredo inspired an entire naval ethos among his subordinates, a legacy that would remain part of the institution for many years to come.

Notwithstanding this, there remains much to be explored around the values of a leader. The war of annihilation, developed by the British during the Cádiz blockade, reached its fullest expression in the shelling of the city in July 1797. Fortunately, it did not extend to its logical conclusion, the destruction of the city, but it represented a ratcheting up of hostile sentiment – a preliminary to total war during the Napoleonic period. Spain would have first-hand experience of this new state of affairs before long, during the Peninsular War.

Some historians argue that war of annihilation was an inevitable development during the decades around the turn of the nineteenth century, since the survival of nations such as Great Britain depended on this new view of warfare and its strategy. The ruthless bombardment of Copenhagen in 1807, which was, curiously, criticised by Jervis, constitutes ample proof of this.[246]

From this perspective, attritional warfare was becoming a thing of the past. Mazarredo and those who thought like him did not anticipate this new international state of affairs. The violence wrought by incipient nationalism and total war, beginning with the French Revolution, demanded a new approach to waging war in which the end justified the means. Once again, as had been the case in the vicious religious wars of the sixteenth and seventeenth centuries, inflicting terrible collateral damage on the civilian population was, once more, part of the game.

# CHAPTER ELEVEN

# Luis María de Salazar, Ángel Laborde and the Defence of Cuba, 1825–9: A Study in Combined Leadership

Carlos Alfaro Zaforteza

King's College London

On 9 December 1824 the last Royalist army in the American continent was defeated at the plateau of Ayacucho. The battle caused the fall of the Viceroyalty of Peru and is generally considered the end of the Spanish American wars of independence. It is generally less well known that hostilities went on in the Gulf-Caribbean area for a further five years. Once free from Royalist forces in the mainland, the Colombian government started preparations for a combined attack, together with Mexico, on Cuba and Puerto Rico. The objective was two-fold: to eliminate a serious threat to the independence of both states, and to end Spanish rule in America. The critical military element in this enterprise was seapower. This paper analyses the actions of two men who led the Spanish navy at that time; they succeeded in providing adequate defence for the island of Cuba in particularly difficult conditions. It is true that the United States, Britain and France opposed such an alteration of the Caribbean status quo. Yet it was not clear how far they were willing to go in this direction, nor if they would be able to act in time. The Colombian and Mexican governments, as well

---

**How to cite this book chapter:**
Zaforteza, C A. 2017, Luis María de Salazar, Ángel Laborde and the Defence of Cuba, 1825–9: A Study in Combined Leadership. In: Harding, R and Guimerá, A (eds.). *Naval Leadership in the Atlantic World.* Pp. 131–139. London: University of Westminster Press. DOI: https://doi.org/10.16997/book2.m. License: CC-BY-NC-ND 4.0

as the Spanish, harboured serious doubts as to whether these powers could or would effectively deter patriot plans. The Spanish government, therefore, rightly assumed that it must rely on its own means.

Spanish historiography has largely ignored this achievement, even though it was arguably the most creditable performance put up by the navy during the Spanish American Wars of Independence. The two key personalities concerned were the Navy Minister, Luis María de Salazar, and the commander of the *Apostadero de la Habana* (Havana Station), Ángel Laborde. This paper is made up of three sections: the nature of the threat, the situation and main actors, and the response. Success was the result of effective leadership and close cooperation, despite the obstacle of distance – 4,000 nautical miles between Madrid and Havana, and the appalling state of the navy and the country.

## The threat

When Britain recognised Buenos Aires, Colombia and Mexico, the Spanish government was concerned that they would enjoy easier access to credit. This was essential to acquire and operate a sizeable naval force. Colombian Vice-President Francisco de Paula Santander was especially sanguine about naval affairs. He planned to use the fleet to help Mexico take the fortress of San Juan de Ulúa and blockade or destroy the Spanish squadron in Havana. For this purpose, he purchased one ship of the line and one frigate from the Swedish navy and ordered two powerful frigates to be built in the United States.[247] The Mexican government, for its part, fortuitously came into possession of the Spanish ship of the line *Asia*. In June 1825 the crew mutinied and went over to the insurgents. By September, as the *Asia* started on its long journey from Monterrey to Veracruz, the only units of any consequence in the port of Veracruz were a converted merchant frigate and two brigs, which had been acquired through a London firm. Mexico also had some minor vessels being built in the United States, and was in negotiations to buy a frigate and 84-gun ship from Sweden.[248] These ships presented an imposing array, since it was assumed that they would soon be ready for combat. By comparison, the only major ships of the Havana squadron were two frigates.

Initially, difficulties in getting reliable intelligence caused confusion and alarm. In September the consul in New York reported on the ships being built locally for the patriots. The two Colombian 64-gun frigates were especially worrying; they were superior to anything the Spaniards had. A Swedish ship of the line had also arrived, to be converted into another large frigate. The Mexican government was erroneously reported to have another 64-gun frigate under construction and several minor vessels.[249] Incoming information about the Patriots' capabilities was also unsettling. A report received in August 1825 stated that one of the big Colombian frigates would be ready in a month. Salazar hoped to have three frigates ready by the end of the year. He had originally planned to send two to Cuba, as escorts of a troop convoy, and leave one in metropolitan waters. Yet he could not afford to run the risk of an attack on the convoy; a Colombian squadron including the new ship was more than a match for the two frigates and a brig of the escort, so he chose to add a third frigate. The decision was difficult, as it meant leaving metropolitan waters with nothing larger than a sloop, but reinforcing Cuba was top priority.[250] Almost simultaneously, another event raised the threat level. In September Laborde's last attempt to relieve San Juan de Ulúa failed. His force of two frigates, one sloop and two transports ran into a storm. Laborde's flagship, the *Sabina*, was dismasted and had to return to Havana. Although damaged, the rest carried on, but turned back without a fight when a Mexican squadron interposed itself between them and the fortress. The battered ships took more than a month to repair. During this time the *Apostadero's* largest serviceable units were two brigs. Cuba and its commerce were practically defenceless against naval attack. Of course, no ships were available for another relief expedition to San Juan de Ulúa, which finally surrendered in November. This caused an invasion panic in Cuba, dealt a heavy blow to Spanish morale and increased the sense of urgency about Cuba's defencelessness. In December Salazar received another piece of intelligence: the patriots expected to have a fleet of two ships of the line and seven frigates ready for action in a month's time.[251]

The difficulties which precluded the materialisation of these plans were not yet apparent in March 1826, when Mexico and Colombia concluded a formal treaty to constitute a combined fleet based at Veracruz. It was to be commanded by an American naval officer, David Porter, a hero of the War of 1812; operations were to start at the end of May. The main objective was to destroy the Havana squadron.[252] Due to lack of resources, the whole plan started falling apart almost from the outset. Yet some time elapsed before the Spanish authorities realised it. The view from Madrid was gloomy; distance magnified the problem; the country had no effective allies and few resources to draw on.

## The situation and the men

By 1825 Spain was an impoverished country, not yet recovered from the ravages of the war against Napoleon (1808–14). The staggering foreign debt, the end of the American silver supply and recurrent political strife precluded reconstruction. The navy's condition was no better. During the French invasion most ships were disarmed and the crews fought ashore; the dockyards were despoiled of every single valuable item, and the ships were allowed to decay for lack of maintenance. After the war, no ships were available to fight the American insurgents. In 1817 the government had to resort to purchasing a squadron of five ships of the line and three frigates from Russia. By mid-1825 not a single ship of the line was in commission, and the number of frigates was reduced to three. Only Cádiz Dockyard, the main naval base, was able to support this meagre force; new construction was out of the question. Only the personnel remained. A small core of naval officers had preserved their skills through continuous service afloat and action against the insurgents. However, they were demoralised by the old, worn-out materiel, bleak career prospects and erratic pay. In those years, the navy got only a fraction of its official budget. The resulting malaise added to Salazar's material difficulties.

Only the *Apostadero de la Habana* had a regular budget and punctually paid its personnel. It was financed by the Cuban treasury, but the war brought new commitments, such as the relief of the fortress of San Juan de Ulúa, on the Mexican coast. By 1825 the island's income could barely meet ordinary expenses, let alone wartime obligations. Help from the worse-off metropolitan treasury was out of the question. The dockyard, which had built so many ships in the previous century, was capable of only limited repair work; it lacked a dry dock, had a poor supply of naval stores, and labour costs in Havana were much higher than in the Peninsula. Moreover, the *Apostadero*'s naval administration was notoriously wasteful. Additionally, the island's naval budget was burdened with the salaries of many retired and half-pay officers, which left little for materiel expenses. In order to protect Cuban commerce, the island's trading community had contributed generous sums to make up for the deficit, but without noticeable results.

Even if all of the station's ships were kept fully operational, 11 ships were far from enough to defend Cuba and Puerto Rico against invasion, escort relief convoys to San Juan de Ulúa and protect Spanish trade in the Gulf-Caribbean area. The station's commander, Brigadier Miguel Gastón, considered that an adequate force should be made up of 26 ships, which meant more than doubling the cost (see table).

The man in charge of coping with this situation was the navy minister, Luis María de Salazar y Salazar (1758–1838). He started his career as a naval officer, but soon ill health forced him to abandon service afloat. Nevertheless, his work as a naval administrator was outstanding. In 1792 he was called to serve in the Navy Ministry, under his relative General Mazarredo, one of the most

|  | Existing | Required |
|---|---|---|
| Ships of the line | none | 1 |
| Frigates | 2 | 5 |
| Sloops | 3 | 3 |
| Brigs | 4 | 10 |
| Schooners | 2 | 7 |
| Total | 11 | 26 |
| Annual cost (*pesos*) | 650,000 | 1,500,000 |

**Table 1:** Spanish naval strength in Cuba, March 1825.[253]

influential naval officers at the turn of the century. In 1803 he was appointed Intendant of Ferrol Dockyard, where he continued to hone his skills. During the War of Independence, he was already so highly regarded that he was appointed finance minister of the Regency and later governor of Seville.[254] After the war, Salazar served his first term as navy minister (1814–16). In 1820 the Liberals offered him the post, which he declined, but he accepted it from the Absolutists three years later. During his second term (1823–32) he ably ran the service for almost ten years under extreme penury and complex political circumstances. He enjoyed the respect of his fellow cabinet members and most of the officer corps. Though Salazar was a conservative, but not a recalcitrant one, most of the latter were Liberals. He was thus one of the few who could liaise with practically everybody, which made his work much easier.

Ángel Laborde y Navarro (1772–1834) was the commander of the *Apostadero de la Habana*. He arrived in the Caribbean in 1820, to take command of a squadron based at Puerto Cabello, until the town was evacuated in 1823. He was then based at Havana, as deputy commander of the *Apostadero*. During these years he earned a reputation as a proactive, successful leader among friends and foes. Once he was appointed commander of the Havana Station he reversed traditional practice: he spent most of the time afloat, while his deputy took care of the dockyard and logistic support. Laborde always made sure that his men were punctually paid and well cared for, but he also expected them always to do their duty.

Two examples illustrate this attitude. He would select only the ablest men in critical posts. An officer who had served under Laborde, and was in half-pay, managed to get a commission as commander of one of his frigates through his political connections in Madrid; he hoped to get his full pay again, which would allow him to maintain adequately his nine-child family. Laborde, who knew him well, rejected the appointment for two reasons. The officer had some ailments that impaired his health; his professional skills and knowledge lagged behind those of his colleagues, because he had shown no interest in nurturing them.[255] This behaviour does not mean that he was not humane. During the two heavy storms cited below, officers lost most of their personal belongings, including expensive items such as chronometers and other navigation instruments. Presumably on Laborde's advice, the Havana Intendant provided the money to buy replacements, and Salazar approved the measure.[256] In the distance, Salazar had to rely on Laborde's professional judgement and leadership skills; it seems that he never regretted it.

## The solution

Salazar's response to the threat was to appoint the right man to lead the Havana squadron, trust him and provide him with the necessary materiel. His choice of Laborde was not exempt from controversy. The latter's capabilities were evident, but, as a captain, he was too junior for the post. Salazar allayed this difficulty by lowering the required rank, ostensibly to save expenses. In doing this he alienated several officers who believed that they were entitled to the post. Further, Gastón had not finished his full term; he was dismissed because the other island authorities, notably the Captain General, were dissatisfied with him.[257] What Salazar expected from Laborde was not only first-class operational command, but also the effective implementation of administrative reform. To optimise operational readiness, all non-essential expenses were to be cut. This included sending back redundant personnel who had taken refuge there during the Liberal period (1820–3) to secure their pay.[258] Laborde's appointment met with wide approval in Cuba and boosted the morale of the *Apostadero*'s personnel. He had a rapport not only with Salazar, but with the other Cuban authorities, which made for smooth, close collaboration.

Shortage of ships in the Peninsula posed larger difficulties. The Captain General and the Intendant, as well as Laborde, asked for naval reinforcements to be sent urgently; to start with, they needed one ship of the line and two frigates.[259] The few ships still worth repairing needed substantial work to make them serviceable again. However, before this was possible the dockyards themselves had to be refurbished, supplied with stores and provided with skilled labour. There was neither money nor time to do this; only the bare essentials could be restored. The dry docks at Cádiz and the channel that linked them with the harbour were silted. To refit the two ships of the line they had to be dredged and their doors repaired.[260] Cádiz was the main naval base of the fleet; Ferrol and Cartagena were simply abandoned. To have the ships repaired within time and cost, Salazar resorted to private contractors. They used the dockyards' existing facilities, brought their own equipment, materials and personnel, and did the job.[261] In this way Salazar obviated the need to restore the costly dockyard infrastructure; he had only to care about paying for each individual task.

An unexpected circumstance produced the necessary funds: a failed crop threatened famine in Andalusia and the Mediterranean coastal areas. To prevent this, the government temporarily lifted the ban on foreign grain. The duties levied on the import licences were allocated to the navy. Had he not benefited from this windfall, the resourceful Salazar would presumably have come up with a solution. Thanks to this fortuitous event, he was able to kick-start the construction of the frigates *Iberia* and *Lealtad*, and begin refit work on the ships of the line *Guerrero* and *Soberano*.[262] The first two had been laid down at Ferrol Dockyard in 1821, but construction had stopped for lack of money; *Guerrero* and *Soberano* were old eighteenth-century 74-gun ships which had been lying in utter neglect for years at Ferrol Dockyard.

Due to the extreme penury of the treasury, competition for money among the different government departments was intense; corruption was rife at all levels, and the state administrative machinery was in disarray. In these circumstances it was not unusual for sizeable amounts to be diverted from their original purpose, or simply disappear. Salazar knew this only too well to trust the existing bureaucracy. Navy paymasters in the port towns were supposed to collect the proceeds of the said import licences and transfer them directly to the contractors. Salazar issued strict orders for the money to be transferred directly to Madrid instead. There it was to be kept by the Navy Paymaster General in a special safe with two keys (the second was to be kept by another trusted official) in his office; Salazar was to be instantly informed of every movement in and out. To keep a permanent watch on the safe, the paymaster was instructed, as well, to stay overnight in the building, together with a naval infantry guard of hand-picked men.[263] This episode illustrates the administrative chaos and the feeling of insecurity in Spain at the time. Salazar also had to cope with the resulting malaise.

After 1808 the number of ships and the naval budget were greatly reduced, but the Navy List was still packed with officers. Although only a small proportion could actually be employed, the rest were still entitled to their salaries. Salazar found out that the pay distribution was haphazard; some inactive officers were getting paid more regularly than their colleagues in active service. The latter were not getting more than six payments a year. Occasionally, some officers were reluctant to sail unless they were paid some of their arrears; unlike seamen, they had to buy their own food. Salazar dealt with this comparative injustice through a tighter control of the paymasters and a clear set of priorities. He made sure that personnel serving afloat were paid punctually. A comparative grievance, and a major cause of low morale and lack of discipline, was thus removed.[264] These reforms in the materiel and the personnel were indispensable to supply Laborde with the necessary means for action.

In December 1825 three frigates and a convoy arrived in Havana. Shortly after, the frigates *Sabina* and *Casilda*, from the *Apostadero de La Habana*, were repaired after the damage they sustained trying to relieve San Juan de Ulúa. Hence, by the beginning of 1826, Laborde was able to deploy a squadron of five frigates, soon reinforced by a ship of the line. At last he could conduct the offensive strategy that he was used to.[265] As soon as the *Guerrero* (74) joined his squadron, in March 1826, he sailed to Cartagena (Colombia), where the enemy fleet lay. It was made up of one ship of the line, three frigates, two sloops and four minor warships, but the ship of the line and one frigate were not combat-ready, and there were not enough personnel to man the rest.[266] The Colombian squadron, therefore, was unable to leave the harbour and meet Laborde's challenge. The Spanish fleet was left free to sail along the Venezuelan coast, to encourage Royalist guerrillas and politically destabilise the country. This political mission was of the utmost importance, both to keep the enemy busy and as part of a plan to restore Spanish rule. Four months later Laborde set sail again with the same objective. General Páez, the governor of Venezuela, had rebelled against the central government at Bogotá; these political dissensions made the country more vulnerable to Royalist action. Laborde was to collect a battalion and money in Santiago de Cuba to support the Venezuelan Royalists. Yet the operation was aborted by an unexpected event. As the squadron sailed through the Bahama Channel, it ran into a hurricane. The ships were dispersed and heavily damaged; they limped back to Havana under jury rig.[267] Due to the limited facilities of Havana Dockyard, the repairs took two months. The large number of masts and spars required were not available in Cuba, and had to be ordered from the United States. In the meantime, Commodore David Porter, in the service of the Mexican navy, seized the opportunity to harass Cuban commerce. He took advantage of the benevolent neutrality of the US government to base his squadron at Key West, but Spanish forces blockaded him there and captured his best ship.[268]

The next time that Laborde received demands to support Royalist guerrillas in Venezuela, he waited until December, when the hurricane season was over. He cruised off the Venezuelan coast until February, but was unable to establish contact. This time his force was reduced to the *Guerrero*, *Iberia* and a brig. He did not expect substantial opposition now that the real capabilities of the enemy were known. By 1827 the shortage of officers, seamen and money had become so acute that the Colombian navy had had to disarm most of its ships; it was no longer a combat-worthy force. The Mexican navy experienced the same difficulties. After a long journey around Cape Horn, the ship of the line *Congreso Mexicano* (formerly the Spanish *Asia*) finally arrived in Veracruz, only to be decommissioned.[269] On the other hand, the *Apostadero de la Habana* went from strength to strength.

In 1828 Salazar sent the ship of the line *Soberano* and the frigate *Restauración*, and the Cuban treasury could now comfortably support its increasing naval strength. The naval superiority thus achieved enabled the setting up of regularly scheduled convoys between Havana and Cádiz without unduly weakening the defence of Cuba. Additionally, a fully fledged expedition against Mexico was planned for the following year. The landing at Tampico in July 1829 was supported by just one ship of the line and two frigates, just a fraction of the station's total strength. The enemy navies lay disarmed in port. With enough ships and soldiers in Cuba, and no opposition at sea, another attempt at the re-conquest of Mexico was planned for 1830. Salazar even sent a third ship of the line. However, the outbreak of revolution in France diverted the Spanish government's attention away from America. Colombia and Mexico were also absorbed by internal troubles: they had neither the capability nor the intention to continue hostilities. For all practical purposes, the war was finished.

## Conclusions

The successful leadership displayed by Salazar and Laborde was instrumental in preserving Spanish rule in Cuba and Puerto Rico for the rest of the century. The former's acumen in selecting the latter, trusting him, and providing him with the ships and men to do the job, succeeded in the face of apparently insurmountable difficulties. The legacies of Salazar and Laborde, in naval policy and operational command respectively, exerted considerable influence in nineteenth-century naval policy. The new emphasis on merit and results introduced a new ethos. The excessive forbearance of the previous-century establishment towards an officer's failings or misconduct was at an end. During the reign of Queen Isabel II (1833–68), able administrators created an effective steam navy, run by experienced, competent officers, which effectively contributed to the defence of Cuba. Admiral Castro Méndez Núñez (1824–69) was the outstanding officer of this period. A worthy successor of Laborde, he ably led his men to victory in Mindanao, Santo Domingo and Callao.

# CHAPTER TWELVE

# Napier, Palmerston and Palmella in 1833: The Unofficial Arm of British Diplomacy

## Andrew Lambert
### King's College London

Captain Charles Napier's service in the Portuguese Civil War combined a brilliant individual performance in the service of the Portuguese Constitutional Party with a vital contribution to the furtherance of British policy.

### The British Problem

In the long eighteenth century, relations between Britain and Portugal were based on the interconnected interests of trade and strategy. Britain had long maintained a leading position in Portuguese commerce: exchanging woollens for wine, and in return providing security guarantees. The relationship was essentially symbiotic, as occasional attempts to alter it invariably revealed. While Britain was the more powerful, her need for the trade of Portugal and her empire, and access to the vital strategic harbour of Lisbon, were of such importance that Portugal could expect help in times of crisis, even if her government did not require it.

This relationship became more complex in the 1820s and early 1830s, as the old consensus at the heart of Portuguese politics, a politics complicated and

**How to cite this book chapter:**
Lambert, A. 2017. Napier, Palmerston and Palmella in 1833: The Unofficial Arm of
British Diplomacy. In: Harding, R and Guimerá, A (eds.). *Naval Leadership in
the Atlantic World*. Pp. 141–156. London: University of Westminster Press. DOI:
https://doi.org/10.16997/book2.n. License: CC-BY-NC-ND 4.0

compromised by the long years of war and the loss of Brazil, began to frac-ture.[270] Following the death of King Joao VI in 1826, his elder son Dom Pedro, the Emperor of Brazil, had renounced the throne in favour of his daughter Donna Maria, and issued a constitutional charter. Donna Maria was to marry Pedro's younger brother Dom Miguel, the Regent, when she came of age. In the event Miguel, who had already attempted to assume power in his father's lifetime, encouraged by his mother, reneged on the agreement. The charter was unpopular in Portugal, and alarmed the King of Spain, who had his own prob-lems. In 1828, after Prime Minister Wellington had removed the British troops sent by Canning in 1825, Miguel returned to Portugal, and broke his oath to Dom Pedro by proclaiming himself King. Miguel had the support of the great mass of the people, the clergy and the aristocracy. Wellington was preparing to recognise Miguel, if only for the sake of Portuguese stability and British influ-ence, but the Whigs, influenced by Portuguese liberals, loathed Miguel and attacked Wellington's policy.

Before any decisions could be taken Wellington's Ministry was defeated, and replaced by Earl Grey's Whig/Liberal coalition in late 1830. The new foreign secretary, Lord Palmerston, was Canning's political heir. While he was unable to act against Miguel, British resources being stretched by the Belgian Crisis and other concerns nearer to home, Palmerston declared that he would not give Miguel's regime official recognition. Palmerston favoured the use of force, and lending support to the Constitutionalist movement led by Dom Pedro, since April 1831 the former Emperor of Brazil. However, Prime Minister Earl Grey was not prepared to go so far. Grey disliked Pedro as much as his brother.[271] Furthermore the majority in cabinet were opposed to any overt action, while the Tory opposition, led by Wellington, marshalled an impressive assault on the ministers over this issue. The impasse led to a marked reduction in British influ-ence in Portugal and Spain, reopening concerns over the increasing penetration of French trade in the hitherto largely British-controlled Portuguese market.

The domestic politics of the Reform Crisis would exert a powerful influence over policy towards Portugal, as would the concurrent crisis in Belgium, and a marked deterioration in Anglo-Russian relations after the Polish Revolt. Palm-erston favoured a change of regime in Lisbon, but could not secure it by force, not least because of the complex relationship with the emerging Orléans regime in France. Consequently, he and Grey could only offer covert aid to the Pedroite invasion of the Azores, and then the landing at Oporto, which they were pre-pared to disavow in Parliament. The key intermediary between Palmerston and the Constitutional Party was Marquis Palmella, who was often in London. He worked on Palmerston's fears of another war across the Iberian peninsula, with the concomitant rise in French influence, to secure concessions, including the release of embargoed ships and men destined for the Constitutional forces. Unfortunately Palmella, among the most advanced members of the liberal coalition, was not trusted by Pedro. Consequently, while British policy-makers favoured the liberals generally, they were almost equally anxious to promote the cause of Palmella.

In the spring of 1832 Grey agreed to increase the naval force stationed in the Tagus, ostensibly to deter Spanish intervention in support of Miguel. Still optimistic, Palmerston hoped this would secure the success of the Constitutionalist attempt at Oporto. Instead Pedro and his troops were trapped in the city, besieged by a larger Miguelite army. Portugal had not risen to be liberated; if anything the war confirmed the popularity of Miguel, who, for all his personal failings, espoused many of the core values of a proud people. Attempts to resolve the problem by bringing Spain to support the Constitutional case were doomed by the equally troubled succession crisis then looming in Madrid, where the imminent death of King Ferdinand would place his infant daughter on the throne, while her uncle tried to establish a superior claim.[272]

By mid-1833 British government policy was in tatters, condemned in the House of Lords. Fortunately the House of Commons supported the ministers, but that was only a breathing space. Palmerston was close to despair. Anticipating that the final defeat of Dom Pedro was imminent, he instructed the Admiralty to send additional ships into the Douro, to protect British lives in case Oporto fell to a Miguelite assault. The Miguelite foreign minister Santarem was advised that any interference with the British ships would be deemed *casus belli*.[273] These were desperate times, and they called for desperate measures and desperate men to execute them.

## Charles Napier

The British problem would be solved by an unusual hero. Captain Charles Napier RN even looked unusual:

'about 5 feet 8 inches in height, spare made, black hair and whiskers, straight nose, and sallow complexion, and fifty years of age. There was no regard to personal appearance, but he looked most intent on what he was about.'[274]

Napier (1786–1860) had earned a brilliant reputation in the Napoleonic wars and the War of 1812. He combined seamanship, daring and initiative in the best Royal Navy tradition with a mastery of coastal and amphibious warfare. His quickness of perception and extensive study, allied to intuitive understanding and coolness under fire, revealed a true 'genius' for war. The coming of peace left little scope for such skills, and after marrying and conducting a 'Grand Tour' Napier had sought new challenges in cutting-edge technology and commercial speculation. Between 1820 and 1827 he committed his prize fortune to creating a flotilla of iron steam vessels, providing a commercial service on the River Seine. The financial failure of this venture forced him to return to the Royal Navy, and to seek another fortune.

In mid-1832 Napier had just paid off the frigate HMS *Galatea*, and was seeking a new field of endeavour. He contested the Parliamentary seat of Portsmouth as a radical, knowing that success would give him a claim on the government for a post or some other preferment. In the event he was defeated by powerful vested interests, the local brewer and the leader of the Baring family. Defeat and consequent financial losses forced him to solicit rewards from his government.[275] It also led him to offer his services to the Constitutional Party in Portugal.

Napier had little choice but to become a mercenary; there was simply no other career open to him. Not that the choice was an easy one; under the Foreign Enlistment Act he risked losing his commission, and with that his naval career. The choice was eased by his own knowledge of, and sympathy for, the Constitutional cause. Napier had twice obtained personal experience of the political problems of Portugal while commanding HMS *Galatea*. In mid-1829 he had been sent to Lisbon to demand redress for various offences committed by the Miguelite regime. In mid-1831 he was in the Azores to protect British interests during the Constitutionalist conquest of the islands. He conducted the latter task with a marked partiality towards the invaders.

In August 1832 Napier wrote to Marquis Palmella, then in London, offering to command a converted East Indiaman in the Constitutionalist fleet. Such extemporised warships, converted from the largest merchant ships, were often used when regular fighting ships could not be obtained. Palmella was delighted with the offer, having already decided to buy such a ship. If Napier would serve under Captain George Sartorius RN, the current Constitutional commander, he would be most welcome: 'nothing could be more fortunate for the cause of Portugal than to secure your services, even for a short time.'[276] From this point Napier was involved, initially assisting Palmella to equip the 800-ton Indiaman, *Lord Wellington,* renamed *Dom Pedro.*

While Napier had no desire to supplant Sartorius, an old friend, he was soon being invited to take over the chief command afloat. The fact that Sartorius was several years junior to Napier on the Navy List would have made their working relationship difficult had he remained. Sartorius was a brave and skilful seaman, but he lacked the touch of brilliance required, being too methodical and calculating for such fluid circumstances. Furthermore, Sartorius was having a hard time dealing with the complex factional politics of the Pedroite regime at Oporto, and mounting insubordination of his unpaid, unruly British sailors. Nor were his officers any help; at least one of them had been promised the command by elements at Pedro's headquarters. Unequal to the stern task of imposing discipline on officers he did not trust and seamen with whom he sympathised, Sartorius was never going to win the war. While he had defeated the Absolutist fleet in two battles, these were mere tactical triumphs that produced no strategic consequences. He needed to capture the entire fleet to secure any strategic benefit. Finally, when he failed to support a combined attack at Oporto in January 1833, due to bad weather, Dom Pedro lost all faith, and sent officers to arrest him at the fleet anchorage at Vigo. Forewarned by Napier, Sartorius turned the tables, calling on the crews of his ships to arrest the ministerial officers, and hold them as security for the back pay owed to the fleet. This confirmed his decision to resign.

However, Napier was not going to serve for honour, or glory. He was effectively bankrupt, and his name was his last commercial asset. Consequently, he drove a hard bargain, and held out for his terms. In part his demands reflected the strictures of the Foreign Enlistment Act, but his personal financial needs overrode other concerns. The negotiations ran from late 1832 to 1 February 1833, when the Chevalier Lima was authorised to offer him the command. Palmella had introduced Napier to Lima, the 'Official' representative of the Constitutional cause in London. Their negotiations resulted in the award of six months' advance of pay, an insurance policy on his life for £10,000 and similar terms for his officers. Advised to bring his own officers, Napier took his stepson and a handful of hand-picked junior officers and warrant officers to command the ships of his new fleet.[277]

The overriding attraction of Napier to his new employers was the bold and immediate course of action he had proposed to Palmella some months before. He advocated staking the whole war on a single throw of the dice, embarking part of the Constitutional army from Oporto for a bold attempt to capture Lisbon from the sea. With the Constitutional forces pinned down in Oporto, Napier's proposal was attractive, and he was initially promised 12 steamships and 7,000 troops, typically unrealistic figures. Napier advised that if a smaller force were used it should be sent to attack coastal areas. The strategic basis of his thinking was clear: 'the command of the sea is an enormous advantage, and it ought to be used'.[278]

Throughout this period Napier was in close contact with Admiral Sir George Dundas, the second Naval Lord of the Admiralty, and an important politico-military figure. Dundas was an old friend and close confidant; he was also the trusted political lieutenant of the First Lord of the Admiralty, Sir James Graham.[279] Graham had come into contact with Napier back in 1814, while serving in a diplomatic capacity with Lord William Bentinck in Italy, and formed a very high opinion of him.[280] When Graham awarded Napier a Greenwich Out-Pension in 1832 he did so on the express understanding it 'should not deprive the country of the experience and talents of superior officers'.[281] The two men had been corresponding on a range of issues. In addition, the First Naval Lord, Admiral Sir Thomas Hardy, knew Napier well, as did almost every officer in the service. Among Whigs and Liberals he was rated a great man; Tories were less complimentary. More significantly, Graham shared Palmerston's opinion on the problems of the Iberian peninsula. Consequently it can be inferred that

Napier was neither unaware of the wishes of these two key ministers, nor acting against their privately conveyed opinion. Napier's departure for Portugal with so many officers would have been impossible without the tacit complicity of the ministers, at the very least. He even had to ask Dundas to release his stepson from his studies on board HMS *Excellent*.[282]

The bright hopes of February were soon dashed by lack of money, and it was only the use of Napier's name that enabled the Constitutional financier Mendizábal to secure the £12,000 needed to raise fresh troops, seamen and steamships. By early April, Napier's plans to take Lisbon had been reduced to a force of 1,000 men in three steamboats for an attempt on the Algarve. Even so, he would take the post only if Sartorius was satisfied, and the fleet was fit to sail.[283] Napier was too professional an officer to take excessive risks, and too careful of his own name, his last asset, to hazard it without a good chance of success.

Sartorius was only too pleased to give up his command to a man he knew had the ability and resolve to complete the task. After paying tribute to Napier's 'strict and honourable character', Sartorius informed him of the conspiracies that had ruined his command.[284] He expected some of the British sailors would leave, but hoped enough would remain to man the ships, with the Portuguese sailors, who were good and more 'tractable' than the English. The Portuguese officers he condemned as 'ignorant and spiritless', save a few of the youngest. He would remain at Oporto only long enough to hand over the squadron. In the interval he prepared his men for the arrival of their new Admiral, 'a Black looking shabby fellow'. Napier was advised to bring out signal flags, battle lanterns and quill tubes.[285]

To disguise himself from the prying eyes of his Tory opponents at home, Napier adopted the *nom de guerre* Dom Carlos de Ponza, in honour of an outstanding amphibious operation he had conducted back in 1813. His officers were more pedestrian, picking alternative 'British' names.

On 22 May, Napier boarded the steamer *City of Waterford* at Spithead, only to find the newly raised sailors mutinous, having been misled by the crimps. A further mutinous outbreak at Falmouth resulted in several men being drowned when the boat in which they were attempting to desert capsized. It was hardly the most auspicious start. Recognising that he was now an Admiral, Napier left the imposition of order and discipline to Commander Wilkinson, his Captain of the Fleet. Wilkinson applied the lash with some severity, and quickly imposed control, although he could not achieve a willing or rapid execution of duty. Napier finally departed on 2 May, with five steamers, but only 137 seamen, rather than the 400 he needed to complete the crews of the fleet. He was also suffering from an agonising neuralgia that would plague him for the next month. He was accompanied by Palmella and Mendizábal.[286]

After a brief stop at Vigo, where hopes of reinforcement were disappointed, Napier arrived off Oporto late on 2 June. After meeting Sartorius and then going ashore to meet some of his acquaintances from the Azores in 1831, Napier was given a shabby reception by Dom Pedro. Pedro disliked Palmella and had not been told of the expedition. His entourage even implied Palmella was coming to remove him! Disgusted at this treatment and prevarication among the Emperor's advisors over the expedition, Napier threatened to leave.[287] His temper, never the best aspect of his complex character when on shore, was not improved by the neuralgia, or the fact that he had burnt his mouth so badly on a supposed remedy that he could not speak.[288] The threat quickly had an effect. Pedro improved his manner, and won over Napier, an easy man to flatter and given to admiring 'great men'. The Emperor accepted that something had to be done soon, and this sparked a strategic debate at headquarters. On 11 June Pedro ordered that an army of 2,600 men be embarked on Napier's fleet, under the Duke of Terceira.[289] Palmella would accompany the expedition to govern any liberated territory. Mendizábal was also on board. No target was assigned; all would be left to the commanders on the spot. Marshal Solignac, the French general then commanding at Oporto, and the chief opponent of the expedition, finally resigned on 12 June. He had argued for a direct attack across the Douro, but had been opposed by Marshal Saldanha who preferred Napier's move to the south. Even the removal of the French general did not end the prevarication; army headquarters held up the embarkation of the troops, prompting Napier to signal ashore that he would resign if the embarkation did not resume with immediate effect. He had to repeat himself the following day to get the fleet watered. Napier was particularly anxious to move because he had intelligence that the enemy were about to send their fleet to sea.

Napier's arrival had an almost immediate impact on the Absolutists, who began to shift their heavy baggage towards Lisbon on 14 June.[290] The ministers at Lisbon closed the Tagus to all ships at night the same evening.[291] As Napier had observed, seapower, in the right hands, was a powerful force. In Lisbon Lord William Russell, the British envoy-in-waiting, saw in the arrival of Napier the resignation of Solignac and the impending movement of the Absolutist fleet, evidence that the crisis of the war had arrived.[292]

The majority of British officials and individuals resident in Portugal, diplomats, merchants and naval officers, were opposed to the Miguelite regime. Consequently, Napier received priceless intelligence from at least two sources. As Britain had not recognised the Miguelite regime, the Acting Consul General, Richard Belgrave Hoppner, was effectively the British diplomatic representative in Lisbon.[293] Known to be an ardent supporter of the Constitutional cause, Hoppner served from early 1831 until mid-August 1833, when Russell, who had been resident for some months, presented his dormant credentials as Special Envoy.[294] Hoppner's hatred of Miguel reflected a liberal revulsion at his overthrowing the constitution, his infamous personal conduct and arbitrary tyranny.[295]

Before leaving England, Napier had requested Hoppner provide him with detailed information on the sea defences on the Tagus, with a view to a naval attack. Hoppner was pleased to further 'the cause of Right and Justice', providing a very full description of the defences. He had witnessed the French attack in 1831, and reported trifling losses on both sides. He was also aware of a strong feeling in favour of the Constitutionalists among the troops manning the forts, while the Miguelite ships were miserably manned and would, he expected, simply be filled up with pressed watermen and other unfortunates when they had to go to sea.[296]

Hoppner's blatantly partisan behaviour had proved to be a thorn in the side of the altogether more discreet naval commander at Lisbon, Rear Admiral Sir William Parker. Parker's small but powerful force had been sent to protect British commercial interests, and deter other powers from intervening, notably Spain. Although a Whig and disgusted by the conduct of the Absolutists, Parker was too professional to exceed his orders in public. Consequently, while his private feelings were all on the Constitutional side,[297] he was criticised by Hoppner and the Pedroites. This criticism was wholly unwarranted. Parker was secretly supplying his fellow countrymen in Dom Pedro's fleet with intelligence. Parker had admired Sartorius's conviction and commitment, but he recognised that Napier was his superior: 'as courageous as he was shrewd', Napier understood 'more of the strategy of war' than any man he had ever met.[298] Parker provided Napier with details of the state and movements of the Absolutist fleet, whose arsenal was in clear view of his flagship.[299] Nor was this his only intelligence source. He was also able to read most of the Miguelite telegraph messages coming into Lisbon. 'We are masters of many of the secret keys,' he told Graham, 'and feel confidence, therefore, in the greater part of these communications.'[300] As Lord William Russell explained, the telegraph cypher was constantly changed, 'but always bought for a few crowns'.[301]

Throughout the tortuous business of bringing Pedro to take the risk of an expedition, Napier kept Admiral Dundas informed of every step, and enjoined that his letters should be sent on to Lord Palmerston.[302] The Admiralty building was, after all, only 100 yards from the Foreign Office. The overriding issue, as he constantly reminded Dundas, was to secure British recognition of Donna Maria.[303]

Even with the troops on board, Napier had further problems: 100 of the British seamen who had been serving under Sartorius insisted on going home. Consequently, he had to rely on Portuguese seamen to man some of his squadron, concentrating the British hands on the key ships, under his best officers. Further punishment was necessary before he could instil any order and energy into his crews.

The squadron comprised:
*Don Pedro*: ex-Indiaman 50 guns (short 18-pounders & 32-pounder carronades), 317 men

*Rainha* frigate: Flagship (ex-Argentine, ex-Swedish *af Chapman* of 1803) 42 guns (18-pounders), 300 men 'including Portuguese'
*Donna Maria:* 40 guns (short 18-pounders), 254 men
*Villa Flor:* 18 guns (18-pounders)
*Portuense:* 20 guns (32-pounder carronades), 126 men, 'half Portuguese'[304]
Three or four hired steam ships: *City of Waterford, William IV, Birmingham* (Names uncertain)[305]
A transport/hospital ship
Total manpower on the sailing warships was no more than 1,000.[306]
The first three ships were largely manned with British seamen.

Against this force, the intelligence Napier had received suggested the Miguelites would send two battleships, two frigates and a number of smaller craft. He knew one battleship was a rotten old tub, hardly fit to go to sea, and that many of the men had been pressed.

On 20 June the expedition set off, with so few troops Napier decided that an attack on Lisbon was not possible. This was fortunate, for his plans had been widely discussed in the English newspapers.[307] He would have been pleased to hear that his actual destination, the Algarve, was still a secret, to the best of Parker's knowledge.[308] It may be that the open discussion of a direct attack on Lisbon was a ruse. If so, it was highly effective. On the night of 22 June, the entire garrison of Lisbon was kept in arms, ready to respond to a landing, while the key position of Fort St Julian's was reinforced.[309] Risings at St Thomar and elsewhere on the Tagus added to the worries of the Lisbon ministers.[310] Once at sea, the army was hidden from the Absolutists, and could land anywhere. They could not hope to be strong enough everywhere, and elected to reinforce the centre. In fact they had chosen the wrong place.

Reaching the Algarve, the troops landed at Cacellas, close to the Guadiana River, late on 24 June, meeting hardly any resistance. The Constitutionalists occupied Faro on 27 June, and Lagos on 30 June, where they paused to establish local administration, recruit volunteers, add to their stores and prepare for the next move. Napier hurriedly wrote to inform Parker that he planned to sail to the Tagus, lash his steamships alongside and enter Lisbon at night: 'I wish you would give me your opinion of what I might expect from such an attempt.'[311]

The Absolutist Fleet:
*Dom Joao* (74) Flagship Commodore Aboim
*Rainha* (74)
*Princessa Real* (52) frigate
*Martim de Freitas* (49) ex-east Indiaman
*Cybele* (26) large corvette

*Princessa Real* (24) large corvette
*Isabel Maria* (22) large corvette
*Tejo* (20) brig
*Audaz* (20) brig
One xebec
Total: 3,400 men[312]

When the Absolutist ships left the Tagus, Parker recognised the crisis was at hand. He knew Napier's force was much weaker than the Absolutist squadron, not least from the wreck of a schooner at Peniche with 80 priceless British seamen on board, who were now prisoners at Peniche and in Lisbon. However, he was confident Napier would 'achieve everything that is practicable'.[313] His main concern was to be ready to respond to the result of the battle that he and Russell agreed was 'inevitable'.[314] For the next fortnight, the British representatives in Lisbon followed the progress of the Constitutional forces from the Absolutist telegraph.[315] When the Constitutional force landed in the Algarve, the Absolutist ministers finally roused themselves to act, sending their squadron to sea. However, Hoppner for one doubted that the squadron meant business:

'It is not supposed to be Commodore Aboim's intention to engage the ships from Oporto, but merely to cruise and interrupt any other troops that may be sent from thence to reinforce and support the expedition of the Duke of Terceira; nor is it improbable that the object of the Government in sending him to the Southward was only to keep their enemies in check by his appearance off the coast, and prevent their advance into the interior, until they could assemble a sufficient force to oppose their march upon the capital.'[316]

Napier put to sea on 2 July with the six sailing ships, which now included a 6-gun schooner that had joined the squadron at Faro, but she would play no part in the battle. He left the steamers to complete their fuel and follow them to Lisbon. At 8 am the following morning he caught sight of the Miguelite fleet off Cape St Vincent, and sent the *Villa Flor* back to Lagos for the steamers. He spent the rest of the day keeping between the enemy and Lagos Bay, to ensure the junction of his forces, which occurred at 5 pm. The Absolutist fleet was sailing in a tight formation, with the two battleships and two frigates in one line, the three corvettes and two brigs in line behind them. Such evidence of seamanship demonstrated that the enemy was not incompetent. The two squadrons remained within a few hundred yards of each other throughout the night, Napier looking for a favourable opportunity for battle, preferably under the land, where the sea would be calm. This manoeuvring for position continued throughout the day, to the growing impatience of the British sailors, used to simpler tactics, and simpler officers to conduct them. Napier explained to the men that he was looking for a favourable opportunity, and used the intervening hours to improve gun drill, especially fighting both broadsides at once. Throughout the two days in contact the enemy:

> 'shewed no disposition to bring us to action: we dared risk nothing till the weather became sufficiently fine to make one desperate effort to save Portugal or lose the cause.'[317]

Recognising he could not win an artillery duel, and would not obtain the necessary political impact even if he did, Napier had always planned on boarding the enemy ships, either at anchor in the Tagus or on the open ocean. He was playing for the highest stakes; he had to capture the enemy fleet, not win a tactical victory. He recognised Sartorius had achieved nothing with his battles. On the morning of 5 July, Napier's experience led him to anticipate that the weather, which had hitherto been too boisterous for a boarding action, would improve. He called the steamship captains to confer on board the flagship at 10 am, planning to use their ships to tow his warships into action. His plans were ruined by the refusal of the engineers to go under fire without a bonus of £2,000 a man. Before he had time to lament the lost opportunity, he was saved by the timely intervention of nature. The beginnings of a breeze were stirring from the north, and Napier, who was to windward, immediately shifted his plan to attack under sail. He then mustered his men on the upper deck, and gave them one of his characteristic fighting speeches, full of prize money, home and sweethearts. The men were also fed, for Napier knew that British seamen cared more for a full stomach than anything else.

The tactics of the battle were predetermined, and reflected Napier's experience. He knew that his smaller and weaker ships would be able to close more safely from astern, as long as they were sufficiently well handled to avoid the broadsides of their opponents. He had intended to attack the enemy flagship, *Dom Joao*, with his own ship, but she was ahead of the other 74, the *Rainha*, which he now elected to attack with his own ship and the *Dom Pedro*. This left the *Dom Joao* without an opponent, although he hoped to capture her with his own ship once the first 74 had been taken. As they went into action he instructed Captain Peake of the frigate *Donna Maria* to employ the same tactics against the *Princessa Real*. The *Portuense* and *Villa Flor* would attack the *Martim de Freitas*. Napier left his two small Portuguese-manned ships to do what they could with other Absolutist vessels. He knew the key to success would be the British officers, and the experienced seamen who followed them, aboard his three largest units. He took care to explain his plans to his officers.

When the anticipated breeze arose, around 2 pm, Napier led his fleet into action, heading directly for the 74-gun *Rainha de Portugal*. The Absolutists held their fire until the range came down to musket shot, about 100 yards, and then opened a heavy and rapid, but largely inaccurate, barrage. Outstripping the rest of his force, Napier's *Rainha* closed on the enemy stern, where few guns bore, and manoeuvred to yaw across her quarters, firing effective broadsides into her flimsy stern galleries. The skilful direction of the ship under heavy fire was no accident; Napier had done much the same in April 1809, working across the stern of a flying French battleship off Guadeloupe. His skill helped to minimise casualties, as did his ordering the men to lie down to avoid return fire. Even so, three gun crews and a Marine Lieutenant were cut down.

Relying on his final raking broadside to confuse the enemy, Napier ran his ship alongside her higher opponent to board. As he did so, two men standing beside him were killed. The smart seamanship required to secure the ship along-side, and board a battleship from the decks of a frigate, was only to be expected from the hand-picked officers and men involved. Almost the entire crew of the *Rainha* had been assigned to the three divisions of boarders; the first, led by Napier, went over the gangway; the second, under his stepson and Commander Wilkinson, went up and through the fore chains, while Captain MacDonough, a volunteer, led the third into the aftermost gun port of the enemy main deck. All three groups met stiff resistance. MacDonough cleared the way for his men to board, but was killed in the process. His division quickly drove the enemy up onto the quarter deck, where they met the other two divisions. The second division was held up by spirited opposition, with both officers badly wounded, but after a brief setback when the two ships drifted apart, Napier led his division over the gangway and stormed aft. He sought a quick victory by overpower-ing the enemy officers on the poop. With most of his men on board, Napier quickly secured the upper deck of the Miguelite vessel; her Captain was killed and the remaining members of the crew were driven below deck, where they surrendered. Although five British officers and six seamen had been killed, and his stepson and his friend Wilkinson were severely wounded, Napier quickly restrained his men. Every British officer who boarded the *Rainha* had been wounded; three would die, while two more were badly hurt. This was hardly surprising, for as Napier observed, the men did well at the guns, but rather hung back in boarding, needing to be lead from the front. In view of their mutinous state only weeks before, it was a testament to his leadership and training that they did so well.

From the poop Napier hailed Captain Goble on the *Dom Pedro*, directing him to make all sail after the *Dom Joao* but, just as he did so, Goble was fatally wounded by a musket ball from the lower deck of the ship Napier had just captured. Despite this, the *Dom Pedro* pressed on, engaging the enemy flag-ship from the leeward. Napier, leaving a small party to secure his prize, hast-ily reboarded his flagship, shifted the tattered remnants of two sails, patched up the rigging and joined the pursuit of the *Don Joao*. When Napier's flagship ranged up towards his windward side, the Absolutist commander surrendered. Two frigates were also taken before the end of the day, the *Princessa Real* by the *Donna Maria* in a near copy of Napier's attack on the *Rainha*, in which she suffered several casualties before luffing up across the enemy stern, raking and boarding from the fore chains, led by five British officers. The Absolutists went below, but fired at anyone trying to follow them, until a pair of 18-pounder guns were shifted from the gunports, loaded with grape, and directed down the main hatch. At this point the Absolutist officers surrendered. The speed and efficiency of the action demonstrated the value of Napier's pre-battle tactical conference.[318] The American captain of the *Martim de Freitas*, his ship crippled aloft by her smaller opponents, finally surrendered to the *Rainha*, which had left the *Dom Pedro* to secure the second 74. The corvette *Princessa Real* surrendered the following morning.[319]

The battle, fought seven miles SW of Cape St Vincent, was a triumph of skill, planning and determination over weight of metal and numbers of men. Napier recognised that his advantage lay in the professional core of his fleet, and would be most useful in dynamic circumstances. Throughout the battle he remained absolutely calm, responding to the shifting opportunities of the moment, and exploiting the weakness and errors of the enemy.

For a man credited with such an excitable temperament when ashore, Napier was astonishingly 'cool' under fire. This was the secret of his success in battle: he was not a simple fighting man, but a complex, calculating leader who could control, as far as contemporary technology permitted, the direction and pace of the battle. Despite being under heavy fire, and then in the thick of the hand-to-hand fighting, seeing his beloved stepson covered in wounds, Napier was always the Admiral, never abandoning his command responsibility to take up the simple task of individual combat. Nor did he allow the battle to end until he had no chance of taking the last enemy vessels.

That night Napier secured his prizes and made sail for Lagos, where he cast anchor the following morning. Once the fleet was secure, he wrote to tell his wife he was safe. He concluded, with characteristic brio: 'I think the prize money will be something handsome. You must give a dance on the green and think of me.'[320] He provided Parker with two accounts, the first a breathless résumé, the second a more 'professional' appreciation. Napier reported 25 killed and 92 wounded, with enemy casualties of 77 killed and 105 wounded.[321] These were severe losses, which had occurred on only four ships. Later critics would carp at Napier's triumph, claiming the enemy had been bought, or did not fight. Such slurs were unwarranted: Napier and his officers won the battle by a combination of skill, resolve and leadership. They also paid a high price for leading from the front: hardly a man among them was not wounded, while eight of the 25 killed were officers.[322] Their blood secured the Constitutional victory.

In the hour of triumph, Napier did not forget the political purpose of battle. Nor did Russell:

'The morning after we heard of it Admiral Parker and myself called Viscount Santarem, and told him that, in our opinion the issue of the contest was decided by this blow.'

The two British officials then delivered the same message to the pro-Absolutist Spanish minister.[323] Russell was so excited by what Parker termed a 'brilliant achievement' that, just for once, he forgot the proper decorum, referring to 'Admiral Napier' in an official letter.[324]

Napier's letter to Admiral Dundas, intended for Palmerston's eyes, also urged that the opportunity was now right for the ministers to recognise Donna Maria.[325] The same day, the Admiralty removed his name from the Navy List, and cancelled his Greenwich pension following Lord Londonderry's attack in the House of Lords, because he was 'absent without leave'.[326] They could do no less, under existing rules, but took care to do no more.

In the interval between the battle and the arrival of news in London, Palmerston reflected on the importance of the Portuguese crisis:

'We really ought to take some line upon this business. The failure of Pedro would be a great blow to our Power both at home and abroad, but more especially would it affect us in all our foreign relations.'[327]

On 14 July his mood changed when Chevalier de Lima showed him Napier's letter of the 6th. Palmerston hurried to inform the Prime Minister and pass the news to the First Lord of the Admiralty.[328] Political problems at home and abroad would be greatly simplified by this timely triumph. Recognising that Napier had won a great victory in the struggle between the autocratic eastern powers and the western liberals, Palmerston quickly sent the news to his ambassador in Vienna, to ensure that the reactionary leader Prince Metternich, who had long sponsored Miguel, was made aware of his defeat. 'Carlos de Ponza forever! Was there ever a more gallant exploit in the annals of seamanship?' he declared.[329] Even so, hesitation in the cabinet, and Earl Grey's continuing hostility to Pedro, delayed British recognition of Donna Maria.

Napier's success was particularly welcome at the Admiralty, which was under severe pressure to find the ships to support British foreign policy, without having to go back to Parliament for more money. Graham was delighted:

'I have just seen Lima's account of the success of de Ponza: the moral effect of the victory will be great, I should think almost decisive and I sincerely & warmly congratulate you.'[330]

The Absolutists evacuated Lisbon on 24 July, after Terceira had marched to the Tagus and defeated the Miguelite army in a battle that was decided when their general was killed.

Napier had sent the *Donna Maria* to blockade the Tagus as soon as she was ready, prompting some concern in Britain, and began beating his way north with Palmella and the bulk of the combined squadrons. However, the fleet was delayed by an outbreak of cholera, and then becalmed in Cascaes Bay on 22 July.

Nevertheless, his impending arrival and a liberal rising in the city completed the collapse of Miguelite morale. Parker, by now able to show his true feelings rather more openly, signalled the news that the city had declared for the Queen to Napier as he was trying to beat his way up river.[331] The fleet arrived off Black Horse Square on 25 July.

For Palmerston, and William IV, the occupation of Lisbon by the Queen's forces, and the fact that 'the whole of the naval force of Portugal is now serving under her flag', were the key reasons for renewing diplomatic relations, suspended by the usurpation of Dom Miguel. As long as nothing unexpected had occurred in the interval, Russell was to activate his dormant commission, and recognise the Queen. He was then to read the Constitutional ministers a lecture on the need for conciliation of the defeated, and the avoidance of problems with Spain. In exchange, he could inform them that a powerful force of British troops and ships had been assembled at Cork, to be despatched to Lisbon if any foreign power attempted to support the usurper.[332] In the hour of triumph Palmerston had not forgotten the commercial purpose of British policy, the particular relationship that existed between the two countries, or his fear that Dom Pedro's ministers were either corrupt or pro-French, or more likely both. He still favoured a government led by Palmella, which was exactly what Pedro did not desire. As soon as he had reached Lisbon, Pedro had dismissed Palmella.

With the Constitutional Party occupying the city, Russell consulted Parker, who agreed the time was right to extend British recognition.[333] Once Spain changed sides, removing all support from Miguel, the war in Portugal was effectively over.[334]

With Lisbon in Constitutional hands and Napier dominant at sea, Parker's force of three battleships would be perfectly adequate.[335] The British government would not need to ask Parliament for additional naval estimates. The Belgian crisis was already settled, so the resolution of Portugal essentially settled the liberal character of western Europe, and would place Britain 'in a condition to talk boldly to Russia' over her treatment of Poland.[336] Napier, having contributed so much to this result, was now a name to be reckoned with. He would be used to frighten the reactionaries for the next two decades.

Two months later, Sir James Graham had occasion to reflect on this new reality, and on the man behind the triumph:

'The whole letter breathes the character of the man, daring, intelligent and dauntless; but he is not to be trusted implicitly, except in the hour of danger, and then he performs prodigies far beyond all calculation.'[337]

One of his fellow mercenaries showed a deeper insight into this most complex of warriors.

'Napier was a slovenly-looking man; his trousers, for instance, had evidently once been white, but were now the worse for wear, and had become a brown yellow. He was fond of saying eccentric things, and of pretending to be in a great passion; while it was evident he was merely affecting it in words and manner, and had all his wits about him. Although he wished to be thought impelled by romantic feelings to help a young Queen to her throne, still it was not difficult to see that no man ever entered on an enterprise with more cool calculation than he did before agreeing to lead this expedition, or more resolved to be well paid, alive or dead, by prize money or insurance.'[338]

Another eyewitness at Oporto recorded:

'Napier was the most egotistical, selfish man I ever knew, but clever and brave. He never wrote or spoke well of any one with whom he served.'[339]

For all that these criticisms contained more than a grain of truth, it is doubtful if anyone else could have achieved so much in such a short space of time. The seamless manner in which Napier had dovetailed the needs of his new masters with the wider ambitions of the British ministers was a work of genius. That he discussed the whole process with ministerial, diplomatic and naval confidantes throughout demonstrates a strategic vision of the highest order. Sir William Parker was right; he really did understand more of war than any man alive. In the space of a single month Napier had transformed the course of a war that had been running for years.

Napier was careful to secure the prize money for the ships taken in his battle, reckoned at £130,000, for himself and his followers. In addition, he was given two Portuguese titles, an estate, a pension and back pay. The Portuguese war transformed his prospects: he began it as one of any number of penniless naval captains; when he returned home he was the most famous naval officer alive, and had the money to buy a fine estate. These were the tangible rewards of a job well done. His success captured the imagination of a nation, and the attention of key statesmen, most notably Lord Palmerston. He was returned to the Navy List in 1837, and went on to gather further glory. Nor had he finished with Portugal, but that, as they say, is another story.

# Afterword

## Richard Harding

The 150 years between 1700 and 1850 saw a remarkable transformation in global history. The impact of European maritime activity on the rest of the world, which had been steadily growing since the 1480s, took an enormous leap forward. In 1700 European maritime commerce and power was firmly established along the Atlantic coasts of the Americas, but elsewhere neither was particularly influential. Even in Europe, the impact of oceanic commerce and naval power was limited. Exotic luxury goods from east and west were becoming more commonplace and the legendary silver mines of Spanish America had long attracted the ambitions of statesmen, entrepreneurs and brigands. Yet almost the whole of Europe remained traditional (even feudal), agrarian and insular in its social and economic relationships. European diplomacy, while influenced by maritime events, was seldom decisively affected by them. In 1850 the prospects looked very different. Industrial and technological revolution dramatically affected supply and demand in societies serviced by maritime commerce. Intellectual and political revolution, fed by the wealth, the knowledge and the fears generated in global exchange, had reshaped Europe and its

**How to cite this book chapter:**
Harding, R. 2017. Afterword. In: Harding, R and Guimerá, A (eds.). *Naval Leadership in the Atlantic World*. Pp. 157–164. London: University of Westminster Press. DOI: https://doi.org/10.16997/book2.o. License: CC-BY-NC-ND 4.0

relationships with the rest of the world. Europe, and by then the United States, stood on the verge of an imperialist explosion of energy that started ebbing away only in the middle decades of the twentieth century. The 'Age of Vasco da Gama' may have started in the 1480s and reached its apogee in the early twentieth century, but that last great imperial surge was possible only because of the maturing of the maritime infrastructure that occurred largely between 1700 and 1850.[340]

The period was one of intense and almost constant naval conflict between European powers that extended across the globe. During this time, the broad expectation of what it meant to be a professional naval officer was honed in conflicts that covered the whole range of duties from escort and blockade work to control of piracy and large-scale fleet action. By 1700 squadrons were ranging widely from their metropolitan heartlands. Individual captains and squadron commanders were finding more autonomy and responsibility as they operated far beyond the control of their political masters.[341] The wars of the eighteenth century developed both capability and confidence in this independence. The papers in this collection suggest that this phenomenon requires far more examination. This degree of independence of action probably occurred earlier in Britain, stemming from experiences in the 1670s and validated by the general level of success that the Royal Navy achieved between 1688 and 1714. The British system, with its more diffuse and interdependent organisational power networks created a very different relationship between navy and crown than existed in the Bourbon monarchies. It may also have created a political context in which senior naval officers were able (even compelled) to use their initiative to ensure naval success, as they could not be protected from public condemnation by royal favour or instructions. The execution of Vice-Admiral John Byng in March 1757 was only the most dramatic case of how domestic political conditions interacted with operational events at sea. Throughout the eighteenth century British admirals had to be prepared to be as combative in the political arena at home as they were at sea. In France and Spain it was very different. The disappointment over the failure of d'Orvilliers's invasion attempt in 1779 inevitably had repercussions for the unfortunate admiral, but, as Olivier Chaline has shown, his fate was determined far more by relations at court than with any other element in French society. The result was that d'Orvilliers was compelled to retreat from command without public debate over the effectiveness of his performance and the responsibility of others. Napoleon tolerated public scrutiny of military or naval decisions even less than the Bourbons. His judgement was final and an appeal to other parts of society for a different or more sympathetic view was pointless. In 1805 the result was Villeneuve's tragic attempt to salvage his reputation that led to the disaster at Trafalgar and, ultimately, his suicide the following year.

Clearly, the relative absence of public scrutiny did not give French and Spanish naval leaders immunity from disgrace if they transgressed expectations, but those expectations were different. As Michael Duffy has pointed out, from the very beginning of an aspirant officer's career, both the content and process of their training or education differed from their British counterparts. The structure of the French navy, with its formal geographical division between the three major arsenals, and social division between *les rouges* and *les bleus* (not to mention the earlier division between the galley squadrons and the sailing squadrons), created significant internal political and professional barriers, which could not fail to have operational consequences. The contempt for the *gros manoeuvres* of practical seamanship within the French naval officer corps put them at a distinct disadvantage, not just because it prevented the development of an instinctive understanding of the possibilities in the heat of naval engagements, but because it created a permanent division within the officer corps and between it and the experienced seamen. Officers could impose their will in some situations, but the tense, complex and unpredictable conditions of manoeuvring a squadron into battle required a long preparation by commanders and crews to develop their understanding and commitment to what was about to happen, which could not be generated by formal signals or articles of war. Despite his other qualities, Suffren was to discover this painfully at Porto La Praya in April 1781.

Navies depend on success at sea and ashore. They had to be understood if they were to be effectively resourced by the political systems they served. Achieving this was an essential prerequisite for putting well-found and expertly trained navies to sea. It might be expected that a reputation earned at sea would be an important indicator of influence ashore, but it is remarkable how seldom this was the case in the period under review. The clearest case of these social and institutional barriers were those that prevented a fighting officer such as Antonio Barceló from reaching the very highest level of command. Of the officers in this study, perhaps only George Anson and Edward Hawke managed to bridge the wet and dry dimensions of their profession entirely successfully. Why success at sea did not translate into success at the highest political level is a phenomenon that still needs to be more fully investigated. Undoubtedly, the social structures were part of the situation. Also, the skills necessary for the successful negotiation of naval interests at the highest level were not naturally learned by spending years on a heaving deck in foul weather. In Britain, as in France, there was ingrained a disdain for those officers whose career took them down a path of engagement with the administration and politics of naval power. Interestingly, this juxtaposed with a grudging regard for the few, like Sir Charles Middleton, Lord Barham (1726–1813), who played a central role in the American War of Independence and the French Wars.[342] Naval history is most often written with a view to impressing on the reader how events at sea influenced events ashore. Far less is written to explain or explore how events ashore translated into power at sea. Without doing both, we will not understand seapower in its whole context.

An important question that arises from this is how far these social and profes-sional barriers played a role in shaping the expectations of the officers corps? Simon Surreaux has shown that in reaching the highest ranks of the French navy under Louis XV, a citation for successful, sustained and aggressive fighting was not pre-eminent. It was, of course, there, expressed in many different ways, but it did not stand out from among all the other qualities that were considered appropriate for a senior naval commander. We should be careful not to presume too great a distinction between these apparent criteria for senior leadership in France and those that were employed in other nations. In the eighteenth cen-tury, patronage and promotion were complex social processes, not driven by a nineteenth-century utilitarian rationalism that was itself never applied as con-sistently as its theorists desired. Throughout the eighteenth century, the relative importance of criteria shifted in all countries. These need to be examined in detail for a fuller understanding of how the social expectations and consequently the ambition of officers worked in different navies. For example, long periods of peace, such as between 1714 and 1739 (and for Spain between 1748 and 1779), limited the amount and type of combat experience that could be drawn upon to justify promotion. Patrons rose and fell; state policy shifted; practical experience gleaned in the heat of battle, in hard weather and even in the administrative functions of the navy, decayed as the years passed. What filled the gaps when combat experience was limited needs exploration. It was a phenomenon that repeated itself between 1870 and 1914 and has again since 1945.

In sum, we still need to know far more about what states and societies expected of their officers. Surreaux and Duffy have shown that differences clearly existed between states. This can also be deduced from other aspects of naval activity. The design of warships which emphasised different characteris-tics suggests the naval intentions of states were not identical. In the first half of the eighteenth century there was a clear difference between the heavily armed, weatherly British warships, intended for long cruises and battle, and the faster, more lightly-armed French ships whose principal purpose was not to seek bat-tle but to carry out specific missions and return to port. This was reflected in the instructions given to officers. The readiness of the political leadership of the state to dictate the operational behaviour of the fleet was evident in France and Spain. D'Orvilliers's instructions hindered his tactical options. Napoleon's plan of the naval campaign gave Villeneuve very little room for initiative and manoeuvre. Catherine Scheybeler has shown that Ferdinand VI's policy of armed neutrality imposed a restraint in action that had a distinctly detrimental impact on officer behaviour and performance, but that restraint was effectively demanded by the state. Agustín Guimerá's explanation of the tactics adopted by Mazarredo between 1797 and 1802 shows how firmly his behaviour was driven by the defensive nature of Spanish naval policy.

The social and political conditions within European states permit some broad generalisations. For example, on the whole, the Royal Navy had an offensive ideology consistently endorsed by the main political actors within the British system. They demanded success, and thus the development of skills and competence within the officer corps was honed by time at sea that its European counterparts did not experience. However, no state in Western Europe thought in terms of investment for the long-term capability of senior naval officers. Who got to command, what they brought to the situation, how they exercised their command and how they related to their political masters were the product of unique circumstances. Ultimately, therefore, understanding the role of command in campaigns is a matter of understanding detail not generalisations.

However, changes in expectations that did occur over the period are also evident from these essays. Carlos Alfaro Zaforteza shows that the task facing Salazar during his second term as minister of the navy between 1823 and 1832 was so different from his eighteenth-century predecessors that a metropolitan 'fleet in being' defensive strategy was no longer credible. Salazar had to give operational autonomy to his commander on the spot in Cuba, Ángel Laborde y Navarro. With Salazar giving support from Spain and Navarro left to make his own decisions in the West Indies, Spain's position in the Americas finally stabilised after two decades of chaos and disaster.

Navarro was not alone in the independence of action he enjoyed. By 1815 a generation of naval officers had become used to the freedom, responsibility and challenges of distant stations. They had also become used to a degree of public recognition that had very seldom been enjoyed by previous generations. However, outside of Spain, even as the French Wars ended, governments were taking advantage of the dramatic reduction in the size of the fleet to claw back control of these officers. It was a long and disjointed process that was never completed. It continues to the present day as technology and operational conditions put new demands on commanders and the political authorities.[343] Naval officers lost to the fleet through retrenchment and paying off were not necessarily lost to the state. Andrew Lambert's study of Captain Charles Napier shows the value of allowing capable, independent officers to use (and continue to hone) their skills in the service of other powers. The Constitutional Party in Portugal was provided with an officer who brought a decisive edge to the naval war, leading to the occupation of Lisbon and the ending of the civil war in 1833. Britain found its foreign policy objectives cheaply and effectively served as well as having an improved officer return to her own naval service in 1837.[344]

What impact did all this change have on the naval officer? Perhaps the most significant was the emergence of a popular ideal of a naval officer, understood not just within the profession but by the wider public. Britain was undoubtedly one of the great winners in the wars of 1793–1815. She was richer; her empire was more extensive and her economy demonstrably moving beyond that of her neighbours. Much of this could be attributed to the great industrial changes that were going on, but behind them it was clear to contemporaries that this depended on national independence and the free flow of raw materials and finished products across the world. In turn, this depended on the Royal Navy. The sea power that the Royal Navy wielded was deep and complex, but it was easily comprehended by the public by the simple fact of victory in battle. The Royal Navy won battles and it did so because its men and materiel were superior to that of its enemies. Naval leaders were an essential part of this. Nelson has a place of his own in public and professional recognition of his qualities, but by 1815 the pantheon of naval heroes was full and their names were to endure in the public mind in histories, monuments, art works and literature.

There is no doubt that the period between 1700 and 1850 saw major social, political and economic changes. There is equally no doubt that naval leadership penetrated far more deeply into the public consciousness by the end of the period, principally as a result of the wars of 1793–1815. However, what is far less clear is how far the practice of officership actually changed in the period. Compared to the dramatic tactical and operational changes in land warfare brought about by the 'levée en masse' and Napoleonic organisation, the war at sea seems to have retained its essential character from the *ancien régime*.[345] The totality of land warfare, with societies engaged more fully in all aspects of conflict from large-scale conventional armies to guerrilla wars and intense economic engagement, seemed to be of a different character from the wars that had dominated the previous 100 years. From it there seemed to emerge a more professional approach to war and a desire to establish a universal theory of war which developed during the nineteenth century.[346] Social background and courage in the field were still vital attributes, but there were the faltering first steps towards a more professionally educated army officer and a more 'scientifically' organised military force; the latter eventually being exemplified by the Prussian Great General Staff.[347]

Navies appear to have been untouched by this military revolution. The technologies remained largely unchanged. The organisation of navies, their operational imperatives and tactical concepts were very similar to those that had been inherited from previous generations. The idea of a universal theory of naval warfare only really attracted interest in the last decade of the nineteenth century. This needs far more investigation across a range of navies, and it is probably wise to be cautious at this stage about drawing too large a distinction between the higher education of naval and army officers in this period. Progress in military education was slow and varied greatly between states. Officers in both armies and navies had to master the essentials of their professions. Surviving at sea required a far more demanding and formally tested initial education than that required on land. This understanding applied to both naval officers and the common seaman. Both services relied on the ability of officers to command a disciplined performance from soldiers and sailors. Both services were strongly influenced by a geometric approach to movement and manoeuvre. There was always a fundamental difference in the demands placed upon army and naval officers, however. Armies are essentially people who have weapons, and in the chaos of combat people have options. Maintaining control in a crisis was an important role for an army officer. Conversely, ships are weapons that have people. The weapon only works when the people are carrying out their function exactly as demanded. Individual options in combat are very limited and the nature of control in a crisis consequently differed. While this is a highly simplistic distinction, it points to the fact that from daily routines of existence to the ultimate crisis of battle, armies and navies were different. How important this was in the way they and their officer corps performed has yet to be examined in any detail. Add to this the different contracts for service in an army and a navy, and the different social milieux from which they recruited, and the current lack of clarity in our understanding of officership in the period 1700–1850 becomes more obvious.

Clearly these essays leave many questions unanswered and, indeed, raise more questions. There are also other areas of study that need to be added. For example, the United States navy is missing from this collection. This was the formative period for a new navy and a new republic. America had plenty of skilled seamen employed along the Atlantic seaboard, but improvising a navy was even more challenging than creating an army. The Americans had at least a well-established militia system and experience of raising provincial expeditionary forces. They had little to guide them in raising naval forces. A new weapon had to be forged and the role of the officers chosen for this task was going to be critical. In 1776 Congress found itself with many more applicants than commands to fill. A navy had to emerge from competing demands for ships, for funding and for political authority.[348] Victory in that war did not resolve some fundamental tensions within American society about the role of a navy. A navy was revived in 1794, largely to protect trade from North African corsairs, but also to protect United States interests under threat from the belligerents in the great war that had broken out in Europe.[349] The years that followed, with a quasi-war against France (1798–1801), continued action against the Barbary states and increasing conflict with Great Britain, which led to war in 1812, forged the United States navy as an instrument of policy.[350] The naval successes against Britain and the North Africans created a founding legend that became important in the development of the US navy, but did not resolve the debate in Congress about how the navy should be structured and led. American scholars have taken a great interest in the emergence of a distinctive officer corps, reflecting republican values that were debated in Congress.[351] The experience of the United States naval officer corps is an important feature of the period 1794–1850 that needs to be explored in far greater depth in relation to its distinctiveness from the European norm.

Finally, there are the other naval powers that were developing in this period. Russia became a naval power in the Baltic as a result of the Great Northern War (1700–21) and was an expanding naval power in the Black Sea in the 1770s and 1780s. Throughout, Russia turned to foreign expertise to help build her naval power. While some important work has been done on the foreign officers who influenced the Russian fleet, there is a great deal more that is needed to fully understand how the Russian and foreign officers worked together in establishing Russian naval power in the Baltic and Black Sea.[352] Another state whose naval power was undergoing major change at the end of the eighteenth century was the Ottoman Empire. After the devastating defeat of the Turkish fleet by a Russian squadron at Çeşme in July 1770, the Ottomans began a major technological and design shift in their naval construction. With the help of foreign expertise, principally from France, the Turks created a new fleet that successfully constrained Russian ambitions in the Black Sea between 1787 and 1791.[353] How far Ottoman naval leadership changed in this period, and how much it was linked to foreign navies in this process, is still something that needs to be discovered. Less dramatic, but equally important if a full picture of professional development in this period is to be understood, are the navies of the United Provinces, Denmark-Norway, Sweden and Venice.

Collectively, the authors of these essays have tried to create a focus on the performance of various officers or officer corps at a critical period in European and world history. They have highlighted contrasts and comparisons that can help explain the differential performances of navies during a period of intense naval competition. What they have also done is emphasise that despite the masses of work carried out upon navies in this period, and the equally vast energy that has been put into understanding the concept of leadership over the past four decades, important questions about naval leadership still remain to be answered.

# Notes

1 Goldrick, J., 'The Problems of Modern Naval History', in *Doing Naval History: Essays towards Improvement*, ed. Hattendorf, J.B. (Newport: Naval War College Press, 1995), 11–23, quotations on 11.
2 For a short and informative overview of the approaches of recent scholarship on leadership, see Jackson, B. and Parry, K., *A Very Short, Fairly Interesting and Reasonably Cheap Book about Studying Leadership*, 2nd edition (London: Sage, 2011).
3 See a similar discussion in relation to diplomacy in Sharp, Paul, *Diplomatic Theory of International Relations* (Cambridge: Cambridge University Press, 2009), 1–7. DOI: https://doi.org/10.1017/cbo9780511805196
4 For the modern and post-modern nature of naval problems, see Till, Geoffrey, *Seapower: A Guide for the Twenty-First Century*, 3rd edition (London: Routledge, 2013), 32–44. DOI: https://doi.org/10.4324/9780203105917
5 White, Colin, *Nelson the Admiral* (Stroud: Sutton, 2005); White, Colin, *Nelson: The New Letters* (Woodbridge: Boydell Press, 2007).
6 The history of this process is beginning to emerge. See for example, Hayes, G., 'Science and the Magic Eye: Innovations in the Selection of Canadian Army Officers, 1939–1945,' *Armed Forces and Society* 22 (1995/6): 275–295. Similarly, research on the contemporary Royal Navy is appearing. See Young, M. and Dulewicz, V., 'Leadership Style, Change Context and Leader Performance in the Royal Navy,' *Journal of Change Management* 6 (2006): 383–396. DOI: https://doi.org/10.1080/14697010601081860

[7] Examples include Rodger, N.A.M., 'Commissioned Officers' Careers in the Royal Navy, 1690–1815,' *Journal for Maritime Research* 3 (2001).) DOI: https://doi.org/10.1080/21533369.2001.9668314; Jones, D.M., *The Making of the Royal Naval Officer Corps, 1860–1914* (unpublished PhD, University of Exeter, 2000); Verge-Franceschi, M., 'Les officiers généraux de la marine royale,' *Revue Historique* 564 (1987): 335–361; McKee, C., *A Gentlemanly and Honorable Profession: The Creation of the U.S. Naval Officer Corps, 1794–1815* (Annapolis: Naval Institute Press, 1991).

[8] A major exception to this was Charles Middleton, Lord Barham. He served very little at sea, but his contribution to the administrative development of the Royal Navy whilst Comptroller of the navy from 1778 to 1790 and as First Lord of the Admiralty in the crisis of 1805, was publicly acknowledged by contemporaries. See, Talbot, J.E., *The Pen and Ink Sailor: Charles Middleton and the King's Navy, 1778–1813* (London: Cass, 1998). DOI: https://doi.org/10.4324/9781315037080

[9] Ronald, D.A.B., *The Symbolic Power of Youth as Represented in The Naval Chronicle (1799–1818)* (unpublished PhD., University of Exeter, 2011); McNairn, A., *Behold the Hero: General Wolfe and the Arts in the Eighteenth Century* (Liverpool: Liverpool University Press, 1997); Jenks, T., *Naval Engagements: Patriotism, Cultural Politics and the Royal Navy, 1793–1815* (Oxford: Oxford University Press, 2006).

[10] This conception of the evolutionary nature of leadership, essentially a constant negotiation and trial and error, sits well with the work of scholars interested in the development of eighteenth-century criminal law. See Hay, D., Linebaugh, P., Rule, J., Thompson, E.P. and Winslow, C., *Albion's Fatal Tree: Crime and Society in Eighteenth-Century England* (Harmondsworth: Peregrine, 1977), 51–55. However, leadership in the Royal Navy has not been systematically examined from this perspective, and older histories of the officer corps focused on the structure of the corps rather than its performance. See, for example, Lewis, M., *England's Sea Officers: The Story of the Naval Profession* (London: Allen and Unwin, 1939).

[11] Gordon, A., *The Rules of the Game: Jutland and British Naval Command* (London: Murray, 1996), 350–353.

[12] Moretz, Joseph, *Thinking Wisely, Planning Boldly: The Higher Education and Training of Royal Navy Officers, 1919–1939* (Birmingham: Helion, 2015); Farquharson-Roberts, Mike, *Royal Naval Officers from War to War, 1918–1939* (London: Palgrave-Macmillan, 2015), 149–156. DOI: https://doi.org/10.1057/9781137481962.

[13] The revisionist literature on the army command of the First World War, started in the early 1960s, is now substantial and is the new orthodoxy. One of the first works of this genre was Terraine, J., *Douglas Haig: The Educated Soldier* (London: Hutchinson, 1963). The debate over Haig's leadership continued for the next three decades. Meanwhile, detailed examinations of army

command structures began to yield significant results. See Gardner, N., *Trial by Fire: Command and the British Expeditionary Force in 1914* (Westport: Praeger, 2003); Simpson, A., *Directing Operations: British Corps Command on the Western Front, 1914–1918* (Stroud: Spellmount, 2006); Prior, R. and Wilson, T., *Command on the Western Front: The Military Career of Sir Henry Rawlinson, 1914–1918* (Oxford: Blackwell, 1992). For a wider selection of essays, see also Sheffield, G., ed., *Leadership and Command: The Anglo-American Military Experience since 1861* (London: Brassey's, 1997); Sheffield, G. and Todman, D., *Command and Control on the Western Front: The British Army's Experience, 1914–18* (Staplehurst: Spellmount, 2004). For the revision to Haig's reputation in particular, see Sheffield, G., *Forgotten Victory: The First World War: Myths and Realities* (London: Headline Books, 2001); Philpott, W., *Bloody Victory: The Sacrifice on the Somme* (London: Little Brown, 2009). Studies of individual commanders are regularly appearing, all far more sympathetic to their subjects than would have been common fifty years ago. The first generation of studies of the army commanders of the Second World War has ranged from uncritical, authorised biographies to the continuation of wartime hostilities between officers. More recent studies are beginning to put these officers more fully into their organisational contexts. For example, see Hart, S.A., *Colossal Cracks: Montgomery's 21st Army Group in Northwest Europe, 1944–45* (Mechanicsburg: Stackpole, 2007).

[14] I have tried to provide an answer to this question in 'Naval Leadership: Les amiraux anglais' (paper presented at Les marines de la guerre d'indépendance américaine, 1763–1783: Leurs mise en oeuvre opérationnelle, École Militaire-Univérsité Paris-Sorbonne Paris IV, 8 February 2013).

[15] Clark, J.C.D., 'Providence, Predestination and Progress: Or Did the Enlightenment Fail?,' in *Ordering the World in the Eighteenth Century*, eds. Donald, D. and O'Gorman, F. (Basingstoke: Palgrave Macmillan, 2006), 27–62. DOI: https://doi.org/10.1057/9780230518889_2

[16] Rodger, N.A.M., 'Navies and the Enlightenment', in *Science and the French and British Navies, 1700–1850*, ed. van der Merwe, P. (London: National Maritime Museum, 2003), 5–23.

[17] Ryder, A.P., 'The Higher Education of Naval Officers', *Journal of the Royal United Services Institution* 15 (1872): 734–808. Lambert, A., '"History is the Sole Foundation of Construction of a Sound and Living Common Doctrine": The Royal Naval College, Greenwich and Doctrine Development down to BR1806,' in *The Changing Face of Maritime Power*, eds. Dorman, A. and Smith, M.R.H. (Basingstoke: Macmillan, 1999), 33–56; Lambert, A., 'The Development of Education in the Royal Navy 1854–1914,' in *The Development of British Naval Thinking: Essays in Memory of Bryan Ranft*, ed. Till, G. (London: Cass, 2006), 34–59.

[18] Lambert, A., 'The Principle Source of Understanding: Navies and the Educational Role of the Past,' *Hudson Papers* 1 (2001): 35–72.

[19] Roskill, S.W., *The Art of Leadership* (London: Collins, 1964); Warner, O., *Command at Sea: Great Fighting Admirals from Hawke to Nimitz* (New York: St Martin's Press, 1976), 206–209. This raises important questions for current leadership development. Without the opportunity of sustained leadership in combat situations at any level, how is the leadership capability of the officer corps to be maintained?

[20] An interesting tension this created occurred in relation to historical interpretations of Nelson. Nelson's unconventional personal life caused problems for his reputation during his lifetime. The moral dimension of leadership had been growing in Romantic approaches to the hero. Nelson's execution of the Neapolitan republican leader Francesco Caracciolo in 1799 smacked to some of a further moral weakness and has caused disputes between historians into the twentieth century. See Gutteridge, H.G., ed., *Nelson and the Neapolitan Jacobins; Documents Relating to the Suppression of the Jacobin Revolution at Naples, June 1799* (London: Navy Records Society, 1903); Lambert, A., *The Foundations of Naval History: John Knox Laughton, the Royal Navy and the Historical Profession* (London: Chatham Publishing, 1998), 173–183; Coleman, T., *Nelson* (London: Bloomsbury, 2001), 206–213.

[21] For example, Admiral Kimmel has traditionally borne responsibility for the failure of the USN to respond to the Japanese attack on Pearl Harbor on 7 December 1941. For a modern study that takes a more systematic analysis of the operation, see Zimm, Alan D., *Attack on Pearl Harbor: Strategy, Combat, Myths, Deception* (Philadelphia: Casemate, 2011).

[22] Allen, D.W., 'The British Navy Rules: Monitoring and Incompatible Incentives in the Age of Fighting Sail,' *Explorations in Economic History* 39 (2002): 204–231. DOI: https://doi.org/10.1006/exeh.2002.0783

[23] The best exploration of this is Scott J., *When the Waves Ruled Britannia: Geography and Political Identity, 1500–1800* (Cambridge: Cambridge University Press, 2011). DOI: https://doi.org/10.1017/cbo9780511921780. See also Claydon, T., *Europe and the Making of England, 1660–1760* (Cambridge: Cambridge University Press, 2007).

[24] For example, Callender, G., *The Naval Side of British History* (London: Christophers, 1924), 19–23; Mathew, D., *The Naval Heritage* (London: Collins, 1945), 12–15.

[25] Richmond, H.W., *The Navy in the War of 1739–1748*, 3 vols (Cambridge: Cambridge University Press, 1920). For Richmond's leadership ideas, see the collection of quotations, Richmond, H.W., *Command and Discipline* (London: Stanford, 1927).

[26] The early popular representation and appeal of the navy can be traced in Lincoln, M., *Representing the Navy: British Sea Power, 1750–1815* (London: National Maritime Museum, 2002). The late nineteenth-century recasting of the image of the navy is examined in Conley, M.A., *From Jack Tar to Union Jack: Representing Naval Manhood in the British Empire, 1870–1918*

(Manchester: Manchester University Press, 2009). The wider propaganda role is traced in MacKenzie, J.M., *Propaganda and Empire: The Manipulation of British Public Opinion, 1880–1960* (Manchester: Manchester University Press, 1984). The impact this had on the naval officer corps can be found in Davison, R.L., *The Challenges of Command: The Royal Navy's Executive Branch Officers, 1880–1919* (Aldershot: Ashgate, 2011), 38–48. DOI: https://doi.org/10.4324/9781315614397.

27 Lambert, N., *Sir John Fisher's Naval Revolution* (Columbia: University of South Carolina, Press, 1999); Sumida J.T., *In Defence of Naval Supremacy: Finance, Technology and British Naval Policy, 1889–1914* (Boston: Unwin Hyman, 1989); Brookes, J., *Dreadnought Gunnery and the Battle of Jutland: The Question of Fire Control* (London: Routledge, 2005); Till, G., *Air Power and the Royal Navy, 1914–1945: A Historical Survey* (London: Jane's, 1979).

28 Hamer, W.S., *The British Army: Civil-Military Relations, 1885–1905* (Oxford: Clarendon Press, 1970); Bond, B., *The Victorian Army and the Staff College, 1854–1914* (London: Eyre Methuen, 1972); Spiers, E.M., *The Army and Society, 1815–1914* (London: Longman, 1980); French, D. and Holden Reid, B., eds., *The British General Staff: Reform and Innovation, 1890–1939* (London: Cass, 2002).

29 Searle, G.R., *The Quest for National Efficiency: A Study in British Politics and British Political Thought, 1899–1914* (Oxford: Blackwell, 1971); Thomas, R., *The British Philosophy of Administration: A Comparison of British and American Ideas, 1900–1939* (London: Longman, 1978).

30 Morriss, R., *Naval Power and British Culture, 1760–1850: Public Trust and Government Ideology* (Aldershot: Ashgate, 2004); Macleod, R., ed., *Government and Expertise: Specialists, Administrators and Professionals, 1860–1919* (Cambridge: Cambridge University Press, 1988), 1–26.

31 Although the concept of enlightenment is problematic and its impact on leadership or leaders can only be inferred as one among a number of possible stimuli, see Gruber, I.A., *Books and the British Army in the Age of the American Revolution* (Chapel Hill: University of North Carolina Press, 2010). DOI: https://doi.org/10.5149/9780807899403_gruber; Darnely, M.H., *Military Writings and the Theory and Practice of Strategy in the Eighteenth-Century British Army* (unpublished PhD, University of Kansas, 1991); Starkey, A., *War in the Age of Enlightenment, 1700–1789* (Westport: Praeger, 2003); Speelman, P.J., *Henry Lloyd and the Military Enlightenment of Eighteenth Century Europe* (Westport: Greenwood Press, 2002). See also Shanahan, W.O., 'Enlightenment and War: Austro-Prussian Military Practice, 1760–1790,' in *East Central European Society and War in the Pre-Revolutionary Era*, eds. Rothenberg, G.E., Király, B.K. and Sugar, P.F. (New York: Columbia University Press, 1982), 83–111.

32 Twiss,T., ed., *The Black Book of the Admiralty* (London: Longman, 1914); Wood, A.B., 'The Law of Oleron,' *The Mariner's Mirror* 4 (1914): 195–9.

[33] Lewis, M., *England's Sea Officers: The Story of the Naval Profession* (London: Allen and Unwin, 1939).

[34] For a fuller discussion of this issue, see Doe, H. and Harding, R., eds., *Naval Leadership and Management 1650–1950* (Woodbridge: Boydell and Brewer, 2011), 11–25.

[35] For example, see Spinadi, G., *From Polaris to Trident: The Development of the US Fleet Ballistic Missile Technology* (Cambridge: Cambridge University Press, 1994). DOI: https://doi.org/10.1017/cbo9780511559136, especially 9–18, 164–94; Bijker, W.E., Hughes, T.P. and Pinch, T.J., *The Social Construction of Technological Systems: New Directions in the Sociology and History of Technology* (Cambridge, Mass: MIT Press, 1987). For a recent review of network theory, see Moliterno, T.P. and Mahony, D.M., 'Network Theory of Organization: A Multilevel Approach,' *Journal of Management* 37 (2010): 443–67. DOI: https://doi.org/10.1177/0149206310371692; Collins, H.M., 'The TEA Set: Tacit Knowledge and Scientific Networks,' *Science Studies* 4 (1974): 165–184.

[36] For an introduction to social network theory, see Scott, J.P., *Social Network Analysis: A Handbook*, 2nd edition (Thousand Oaks: Sage Publications, 2000).

[37] Corbett, J.S., *The Campaign of Trafalgar* 2 vols (London: Longmans Green, 1919), vol. 1, 270–271.

[38] For a full examination of the war, see Harding, R., *The Emergence of Britain's Global Naval Supremacy: The War of 1739–1748* (Woodbridge: Boydell and Brewer, 2010).

[39] The Earl of Toulouse was admiral from the age of 5 until his death, then replaced by his son.

[40] See Meyer, J., 'Amiral,' in *Dictionnaire de l'Ancien Régime*, ed. Bély L. (Paris: PUF, 1996).

[41] In 1777, a third post was established for India's and America's seas. Charles Henri d'Estaing (1729–94) got it. In 1784, the 'bailli de Suffren' (1728–88) was provided with a vice-admiralty of India's seas. See Monaque, R., *Suffren. Un destin inachevé* (Paris: Tallandier, 2004). DOI: https://doi.org/10.3917/talla.monaq.2009.01.

[42] Vergé-Franceschi, M., *Les officiers généraux de la marine royale (1715–1774). Origines, conditions, services*, 7 vols (Paris: Librairie de l'Inde, 1990); Taillemite, E., *Dictionnaire des marins français* (Paris: Tallandier, 2002).

[43] Furetière, A., *Dictionnaire universel contenant généralement tous les mots français tant vieux que modernes, et les termes de toutes les sciences et des arts...* (La Haye & Rotterdam: Leers, 1690).

[44] *Dictionnaire de l'Académie française* (1694), 398, accessed 25 February 2016, http://portail.atilf.fr/cgi-bin/dico1look.pl?strippedhw=reputation&dicoid=ACAD1694&headword=reputation&dicoid=ACAD1694

[45] Littré, P.E., *Dictionnaire de la langue française* (Chicago: Encyclopaedia Britannica, 1982).

46 Archives nationales [AN], Minutier central des notaires parisiens [now MC], RE LXXXVI, 8 and LXXXVI, 459, probate inventory of Jean-André de Barrailh (1671-1762), vice-admiral of the Levant (1753-62), part 'Papiers', document 12: 'item the original on parchment manuscript of the letters confirming the appointments of the office of vice-admiral within the scope of the Mediterranean sea, *accordées en grande chancellerie* to the aforementioned deceased Mr de Barrailh, signed on the fold by the King, earl of Provence, Rouillé'.

47 AN. P 2460, Memorial from June to December 1750, fol. 26-29, 'Lettres patentes de provisions de la charge de vice-amiral des Mers du Levant et lettres de délai au Sieur de Salaberry pour prêter serment de ladite charge, avec jouissance des gages et appointements y attribués (fol. 29-32)'.

48 AN, Z¹, Amirauté de France.

49 The eight letters of provisions to the French vice-admiralty are those issued to Victor-Marie d'Estrées (1660-1737) in 1684: AN, Marine, C⁷ 101 bis, 'Lettres de provisions de survivance de la charge de vice-amiral de France en Ponant pour M. le comte d'Estrées, à Versailles, le 1ᵉʳ décembre 1684 ' to François Rousselet de Château-Renault (1637-1716) in 1707: AN, Marine, C⁷ 62, piece 6, extracts from the letters of provisions of the vice-admiralty for the marchioness of Château-Renault; to Antoine François de Pardaillan de Gondrin (1709-41), marquess of Antin in 1731: AN, Marine, C⁷ 6, file of the vice-admiral d'Antin, letters of provisions of vice-admiralty of France, 21 April 1731 ; to Vincent de Salaberry de Benneville (1663-1750) and to Claude-Élisée de Court la Bruyère (1666-1752) in 1750: AN, Marine, C⁷ 76, n° 11, letters of provisions to the vice-admiralty of France, 7 February 1750, to Charles Félix de Poilvilain (1693-1756), count of Cresnay in 1755: AN, Marine, C⁷ 77, piece 42, 25 September 1755 in Fontainebleau, to Hubert de Brienne de Conflans (1690-1777), [AN, Marine, C⁷ 71, piece 34, copy of the letters of provisions to the vice-admiralty in Levant seas dated 14 November 1756] and to Jean-Baptiste Macnémara (1690-1756) in 1756: AN, Marine, C⁷ 191, letters of provisions to the vice-admiralty. Letters of provisions to the marshalship of France issued to d'Estrées and Château-Renault (in 1703), to Coëtlogon (in 1730) and to Conflans (in 1758) enable us to complement or emphasise the previous letters.

50 They all start with the subscription (name and title of the author of the Act), the addresses (name of the person(s) it is addressed to), the preamble (which restates the origins of the decision), the pronouncement (statement of the decision, causes, injunctive clause enjoining royal officers to have the decision executed 'if mandated'), the intentional clause (which emphasises the royal will by the term 'car tel est notre plaisir'), the corroboration clause, ,including the announcement of the seal and potentially that of the royal signature 'en témoin de quoi'), the date (introduced by the word 'donné') followed by the place, date and sometimes the day, the year of incarnation

and year of reign, and then the signatures. Those were sealed with yellow wax via a simple queue as the addressee was a particular person see Barbiche, B., *Les institutions de la monarchie française à l'Époque Moderne* (Paris: PUF, 1999), 166–169.

51 The eight patent letters which were found for the vice-admirals are those of Victor Marie d'Estrées in 1684, François Rousselet de Château-Renault in 1701, Antoine François de Pardaillan de Gondrin, marquess d'Antin, in 1731, Vincent de Salaberry de Benneville and Claude-Élisée de Court de La Bruyère, in 1750, de Charles Félix de Poilvilain, Comte de Cresnay, in 1755, Hubert de Brienne de Conflans and Jean-Baptiste de Macnémara in 1756. The patent letters for the Marshal of France of d'Estrées and Château-Renault (1703), Coëtlogon (1730) and Conflans (1758) allow us to complete the former letters.

52 Rey, A., 'Mérite' in *Dictionnaire historique de la langue française* (Paris: Le Robert, 2004)

53 Furetière, *Dictionnaire universel*, 'Mérite'.

54 Furetière, *Dictionnaire universel*, 'Mérite'.

55 Rey, *Dictionnaire historique* , 'Récompenser'.

56 Furetière, *Dictionnaire universel*, 'Récompense'.

57 Rey, *Dictionnaire historique*, 'Génie'.

58 Furetière, *Dictionnaire universel*, 'Prudence'.

59 Furetière, *Dictionnaire universel*, 'Prudence'.

60 Furetière, *Dictionnaire universel*, 'Zèle'.

61 Vergé-Franceschi, *Les officiers généraux*, vol. 4, 1598.

62 Vergé-Franceschi, *Les officiers généraux*, vol. 4, 1599.

63 Vergé-Franceschi, *Les officiers généraux*, vol. 4, 1603.

64 Vergé-Franceschi, *Les officiers généraux*, vol. 4, 1770.

65 Vergé-Franceschi, *Les officiers généraux*, vol. 3, 1058. This battle took place in Bavaria between the French army under the Duc do Noailles, who was supporting the Bavarian claimant to the Habsburg lands and the throne of the Holy Roman Empire, and an army under King George II of Britain that was supporting the Habsburg claims.

66 Vergé-Franceschi, *Les officiers généraux*, vol. 3, 1073–75.

67 Soubise commanded a Franco-Imperialist army supporting the Austrians against Prussia at the beginning of the Seven Years' War. The Battle of Rossbach was fought in Saxony and the defeat of the Franco-Imperialist army gave Frederick II of Prussia his first great victory of the war, securing his western flank and enabling him to turn on the Austrians and defeat them a month later at Leuthen. See Duffy, C., *Frederick the Great: A Military Life* (London: Routledge and Kegan Paul, 1985), 141–45. DOI: https://doi.org/10.4324/9781315684215. Contades's defeat at Minden in Prussian Westphalia by an allied army under Prince Ferdinand of Brunswick-Luneburg forced the withdrawal of French forces and reduced the pressure

on Prussia from the west. See Savory, R., *His Britannic Majesty's Army in Germany during the Seven Years War* (Oxford: Clarendon Press, 1966), 173–186.

68   Vergé-Franceschi, *Les officiers généraux*, vol. 5, 2311.

69   Vergé-Franceschi, *Les officiers généraux*, vol. 5, 2328.

70   Vergé-Franceschi, *Les officiers généraux*, vol. 5, 2318.

71   Vergé-Franceschi, *Les officiers généraux*, vol. 2, 552. In 1758, Barrailh did not agree with the Marshal's promotion for Conflans. Il 'se plaignit de cette injustice auprès de Berryer qui transmit au roi ses doléances'.

72   Barbier, E., *Chronique de la Régence et du règne de Louis XV ou journal de Barbier 1718-1763*, (Paris: Charpentier, 1857–1863), vol. 7, 28.

73   D'Albert duke of Luynes, C.P., *Mémoires du duc de Luynes sur la cour de Louis XV (1735-1758)*, (Paris: Firmin Didot Frères, 1860–65), vol. 15, 387–88.

74   AN, B⁴, 74, fol. 101 and 104, quoted by Vergé-Franceschi, *Les officiers généraux*, vol. 5, 2325.

75   Vergé-Franceschi, *Les officiers généraux*, vol. 5, 2325.

76   Taillemite, 2002, 'Conflans', pp. 107–108.

77   Taillemite, 2002, 'Conflans', pp. 107–108.

78   About Quiberon Bay, see Le Moing, G., *La bataille navale des 'Cardinaux' (20 novembre 1759)* (Paris: Economica, 2003), particularly the bibliography, 163–165; de La Condamine, P., *Le combat des Cardinaux: 20 novembre 1759, baie de Quiberon et rade du Croisic* (La Turballe: Editions Alizes L'esprit large, 2000); Raffin-Caboisse, P., *La bataille des Cardinaux 1759, cinquante vaisseaux de ligne dans la baie de Quiberon* (Coudray-Macouard: Cheminements, 2008); Marcus, G.J., *Quiberon Bay: The Campaign in Home Waters, 1759* (London: Hollis and Carter, 1960).

79   Marshal of Rochambeau, *Mémoires militaires, historiques et politiques de Rochambeau, ancien maréchal de France*, (Paris: Fain, 1809), vol. 1 190: 'Les Anglais, maîtres de la mer depuis la défaite de la flotte de Brest, aux ordres de M. de Conflans, multiplièrent leurs expéditions sur nos possessions maritimes.'

80   Barbier was mistaken because Conflans was an earl.

81   Barbier, *Chronique de la Régence*, vol. 7, 213.

82   Le Moing, *La bataille navale*, note 2, 99, and quoted by Marcus, *Quiberon Bay*, 171.

83   Barbier, *Chronique de la Régence*, vol. 7, 219.

84   On the contrary, many 'lieutenants généraux des armées du roi' were defeated on the battlefield. Yet they could still become Marshals of France. Soubise is the most famous. He was defeated at Rossbach on 5 November 1757. He was successful in the next year at Lützenberg with Mon. Chevert. He was promoted to Marshal of France after this battle, in October 1758. The Prince of Beauvau did not succeed in Portugal in 1760-1, but he became Marshal

of France in 1783. Du Muy was defeated at the Battle of Marburg in 1761 but he became a Marshal and Secretary of War in 1775. Louis XVI did not forget Du Muy had been the 'menin' of his father since 1745. The menin was one of the six gentlemen who were particularly attached to the person of the Dauphin, the first King's son.

85   Vergé-Franceschi, *Les officiers généraux*, vol. 5, 2327.

86   Vergé-Franceschi, *Les officiers généraux*, vol. 6, 2514: the Marine's budget was 33.4 billion livres in 1691, and 8–9 billion livres for years after1728.

87   Monaque, R., *Suffren*, 13.

88   Rodger, N.A.M., 'Form and Function in European Navies, 1660–1815,' in *Essays in Naval History, from Medieval to Modern* (Farnham: Ashgate, 2009).

89   Pritchard, J., *Louis XV's Navy 1748–1762. A Study of Organisation and Administration* (Montreal: McGill-Queen's University Press, 1987), 55–70.

90   Sullivan, F.B., 'The Royal Academy at Portsmouth 1789–1806,' in *The Mariner's Mirror* 63 (1977): 311–326; Rodger, N.A.M., *The Command of the Ocean. A Naval History of Britain, 1649–1815* (London: Allen Lane, 2004), 386–89, 508–12.

91   Gwyn, J., *An Admiral for America: Sir Peter Warren, Vice Admiral of the Red 1703–1752* (Gainsville: University Press of Florida, 2004), 172; Mackay, R.F., ed., *The Hawke Papers: A Selection 1743–1771* (Navy Records Society, Aldershot: Ashgate, 1990), vol. 129, 168; Berkley, G., *The Naval History of Britain from the Earliest Periods … Compiled from the Papers of the Late Honourable Captain George Berkley*, ed. Hill, J. (London, 1756), v.

92   Ralfe, J., *The Naval Biography of Britain Consisting of Historical Memoirs of Those Officers of the British Navy Who Distinguished Themselves during the Reign of George III*, 4 vols. (London: Whitmore & Fenn, 1828), iii–iv.

93   Falconer, W., *Universal Dictionary of the Marine* (London: Cadell, 1780 edition), 3.

94   Anderson, R. (1805), National Maritime Museum, MS 80/201 Log entry; Van Creveld, M.L., *Command in War* (Cambridge, Mass.: Harvard University Press, 1985), 12–13.

95   Pritchard, *Louis XV's Navy 1748–1762*, 66.

96   Willis, S., *Fighting at Sea in the Eighteenth Century. The Art of Sailing Warfare* (Woodbridge: Boydell, 2008), 53–6. DOI: https://doi.org/10.1017/upo9781846156373.

97   Dull, J.R., *The French Navy and American Independence* (Princeton: Princeton University Press, 1975), 44–45, 278–79, 316.

98   Trew, P., *Rodney and the Breaking of the Line* (Barnsley: Pen & Sword, 2006), 155–155; quotation cited in Willis, *Fighting at Sea in the Eighteenth Century*, 66.

99   Wareham, T., ed., *Frigate Commander* (Barnsley: Pen & Sword, 2004), 214.

100  Mahan, A.T., *Types of Naval Officers, Drawn from the History of the British Navy* (London: Sampson Low, 1902), 151–152.

[101] Syrett, D., *The Rodney Papers II* (Navy Records Society, Aldershot: Ashgate, 2007), vol. 151., 514.

[102] Corbett, J.S., ed., *Signals and Instructions 1776-1794* (London: Navy Records Society, London, 1908), vol.35, 48-49; Willis, S. *The Glorious First of June*,(London: Quercus, 2011), 268.

[103] Nicolas, N.H., ed., *The Dispatches and Letters of Vice Admiral Viscount Lord Nelson* (London: Colborn, 1846), vol.7 89-91.

[104] Mackay, R.F. and Duffy, M., *Hawke, Nelson and British Naval Leadership 1747-1805* (Woodbridge: Boydell, 2009), 93-98.

[105] Mackay and Duffy, *Hawke, Nelson and British Naval Leadership*, 112-15 (Saunders), 106-8 (Pocock).

[106] Richmond, H.W., ed. Papers Relating to the Loss of Minorca in 1756 (London: Navy Records Society, 1913) 94

[107] Rodger, N.A.M., *The Command of the Ocean. A Naval History of Britain, 1649-1815* (London: Allen Lane, 2004), 283; Mackay and Duffy, *Hawke, Nelson and British Naval Leadership*, 477-88.

[108] Taillemite, E., *L'Histoire ignorée de la marine française* (Paris: Perrin, 1988), 172-73.

[109] Dull, J.R., *The French Navy and American Independence*, 248.

[110] Duffy, M. and Morriss, R., eds., *The Glorious First of June 1794. A Naval Battle and Its Aftermath* (Exeter: Exeter University Press, 2001); Johnson, K.G., 'Louis-Thomas Villaret de Joyeuse. Admiral and Colonial Administrator (1747-1812)' (unpublished PhD thesis, Florida State University, 2006), 71-102; Willis, *The Glorious First of June*.

[111] The three leading admirals of the Napoleonic navy, Decrès, Ganteaume and Villeneuve, were all at the Nile.

[112] Ferdinand's minister for war, finance and the joint department of the navy and the Indies from 1746 to 1754. 'Armed neutrality' was introduced alongside a 'diplomatic neutrality' policy advocated by Ensenada's rival and Foreign Affairs minister, José de Carvajal y Lancáster (1698-1754); see Delgado Barredo, J.and Gómez Urdañéz., J. eds., *Ministros de Fernando VI* (Córdoba: Universidad de Córdoba, 2002) for various viewpoints on this subject.

[113] Transcribed in full in Rodríguez Villa, A., *Don Cenón de Somodevilla. Marqués de la Ensenada* (Madrid: M. Murillo, 1878), 31-42, 62-4, 80-1, 109-111, 113-41.

[114] The description of the Spanish navy at this time as 'a fleet in being' differs slightly from the interpretation of the term given by Corbett, J.S., *Some Principles of Maritime Strategy* (London: Longmans, Green & Co., 1911), 211-228, and Hattendorf, J. B. 'The Idea of a "Fleet in Being" in Historical Perspective,' *Naval War College Review* 67:1 (2014): 43-60, yet it still seems apt since it encapsulates so many of the perceived functions of the Spanish fleet. It was a deterrent; its existence alone was intended to occupy British naval resources, and it was expected to achieve its ends actively at sea.

[115] Rodríguez Villa, *Don Cenón de Somodevilla*, 118.

[116] Except for Cartagena, which until 1748 was primarily a galley base before being transformed to cater to ships of the line and a xebec squadron during the 1750s, at which point the first dry docks in Spain were built there.

[117] Archivo General de Simancas (AGS) Marina 438, Francisco López to Ensenada, *San Felipe*, 16 June 1750.

[118] Ibid., Victoria to Ensenada, Cádiz, 13 July 1750; Victoria to Ensenada, Cádiz, 20 July 1750; and Cerda to Ensenada, Cartagena, 29 July 1750.

[119] Ibid., Cerda to Ensenada, Barcelona, 15 August 1750.

[120] Ibid., Francisco Barrero to Ensenada, Cartagena, 19 August 1750.

[121] Ibid., Barrero to Ensenada, Cartagena, 30 September 1750; and Pedro de Hordeñana to Ensenada, Cádiz, 5 October 1750.

[122] Ibid., Joseph de Contamina to Ensenada, Barcelona, 19 December 1750.

[123] Ibid., Ensenada to Cerda, 7 August 1751. Provincial money was gold and silver deliberately issued lighter and baser to prevent its exportation and intended for circulation as subsidiary coin in peninsular Spain.

[124] Ibid., Cerda to Ensenada, Barcelona, 13 October 1751; and Contamina to Ensenada, Barcelona, 14 October 1751.

[125] See Gómez Urdáñez, J.L., *El proyecto reformista de Ensenada* (Lleida: Editorial Milenio, 1996) for Ensenada's political career and reformist programme and Baudot Monroy, M., *La defensa del imperio* (Madrid: Ministerio de Defensa and Universidad de Murcia, 2012) for Arriaga's naval career before 1754.

[126] AGS Marina 439, Ensenada to Juan Benito Erasun, Madrid, 6 October 1753.

[127] See *Ordenanzas de Su Magestad para el Govierno Militar, Político y Económico de su Armada Naval* (Madrid: Imprenta de Juan de Zuñiga, 1748), vol. I, 15–28, for a description of their responsibilities. Matters relating to arsenals, arsenal personnel and ship construction and maintenance were the responsibility of the Departments' Intendentes de Marina.

[128] AGS Marina 438, 'Resolución' taken on 14 April 1752, signed by Ensenada.

[129] Ibid., 'Horden y instrucción de lo que deven observar el paquebot el *Marte* y fragata la *Galga*,' Ferrol, 14 April 1752, signed by Cosme Alvarez: 'la buena conducta, prudencia, celo y valor de los comandantes'.

[130] Ferdinand VI had prohibited Spanish trade with Hamburg and instructed for all its ships to be searched for warlike materials following Hamburg's signature of a treaty with Algiers; AGS Marina 769, Royal Decree, San Lorenzo, 19 October 1751. Similar measures were already in place against Sweden and, from 1753, Denmark too. Spain considered any neutrality agreements signed with the Barbary states as hostile acts.

[131] *Ordenanzas*, vol. I, 1–2: 'he resuelto, que sin interpretación alguna se observe inviolablemente lo que expressan los Tratados, y Articulos siguientes'.

[132] *Ordenanzas*, vol. I, 46–65, 65–90.

[133] AGS Marina 439, Victoria to Ensenada, Cádiz, 5 February 1754.

134 AGS Marina 438, Alvarez to Ensenada, Ferrol, 20 February 1753: 'Me hice presentar los diarios de todos los officiales y pilotos, y concuerdan en un todo, sin diferencia la menor circunstancia con el de el capitan comandante de el navio cuya copia passo a las manos de VE no hallando en la conducta de este capitán y officiales la menor maneobra digna de reprehensión.'

135 Ibid., Rojas to Ensenada, *San Felipe*, at Ferrol, 20 February 1753: 'es el primero que en mi dilatado y frecuente navegar he visto, y me ha quebrantado la salud'.

136 Ibid., Ensenada to Victoria, Madrid, 18 September 1753: 'con los leves motivos de componer sus baos'.

137 Ibid., Vegaflorida to Ensenada, Puntales, 15 October 1753. The Conde de Vegaflorida, being from a well-established noble family, had the political weight to counter Ensenada's accusation as he did but this sort of interaction between naval minister and naval officers was not unusual.

138 See Baudot Monroy, *La defensa del imperio*, 237–71.

139 *Relación de los Principales Acaecimientos ocurridos al Capitán de Navío Don Pedro Stuart y Portugal, Comandante de los Navíos de S. Mag. el Dragon, y la America, con el nombrado el Dancik, Capitana de Argèl, el dia 28 de Noviembre de 1751* (Cádiz: Imprenta Real de Marina, [1751]).

140 AGS Marina 440, Garcia de Postigo to Arriaga, *Soberano*, 15 June 1758.

141 AGS Marina 439, Flon to Arriaga, Alicante, 17 April 1755: Arriaga to Flon, Madrid, 23 April 1755: Flon to Spínola, Cartagena, 22 April 1755: Arriaga to Spínola, Madrid, 26 April 1755: Flon to Arriaga, Cartagena, 28 April 1755: Arriaga to Flon, Madrid, 3 May 1755.

142 'quando por noticias probables se prometa mejor éxito'.

143 'que toda evolución de fuga a vista de los enemigos augmenta su osadía y desdora á él que manda'.

144 'Y que no menos fía S. M. del valor de Us. que de su conducta … no se dexa de navegar en tiempo de guerra con dos, quatro y seis navíos aún sabiendo que ay en la mar esquadras de ocho, diez y doze'.

145 See Scheybeler, C., 'A Study of Spanish Naval Policy during the Reign of Ferdinand VI' (unpublished PhD, King's College, London, 2014), 217–26, for the difficulties with 'armed neutrality' as a naval strategy, and Kuethe, A.J. and Andrien, K.J., *The Spanish Atlantic World in the Eighteenth Century* (Cambridge: Cambridge University Press, 2014), 219–23. DOI: https://doi.org/10.1017/cbo9781107338661 for issues with it as a foreign policy.

146 See, for example, AGS Marina 439, Arriaga to Stuart, Madrid, 21 August 1756, and a further order of the same date.

147 Ibid., Idiázquez to Arriaga, *Palas*, 23 November 1756: 'regla a fin de que con su literal observación se evite por los comandantes todo desacierto y se consiga el honor del pabellon'.

148 Ibid., Arriaga to Wall, Madrid, 10 December 1756: 'esta conforme a el presente sistema', 'regla fija'. Wall came to be Ferdinand's chief minister

following Carvajal's death and Ensenada's banishment from court following a political coup in 1754.

[149] Ibid., Orozco to Arriaga, Ferrol, 7 December 1756: Arriaga to Wall, Madrid, 10 December 1756,:and Arriaga to Orozco, Madrid, 14 December 1756.

[150] AGS Marina 440, Arriaga to Victoria, Aranjuez, 25 May 1758: 'hacer respetar el pavellón del Rey y sus costas como es devido'.

[151] Ibid., Vegaflorida to Victoria, *Aquiles*, 24 June 1758; and Victoria to Arriaga, Cádiz, 28 June 1758.

[152] AGS Marina 438, 'Relación', signed Ortega, *Garzota*, 4 October 1753; 'Relación', signed Vera, *Aventurero*, 3 October 1753; and 'Relación', signed Lastarria, *Gávilan*, 3 October 1753.

[153] See *Ordenanzas*, vol. II, 51–72, and Lafuente, A. and Sellés, M., *El Observatorio de Cádiz (1753–1831)* (Madrid: Ministerio de Defensa, 1988), 78–9 for the academic curriculum, and *Ordenanzas*, vol. II, trat. 7, tit. 8, art. 2, 12, 34, 39–40, pp. 86, 95–6, 97–8 for their service at sea.

[154] In May 1752, for example, the *Asia* and *Fernando* sailed with seven and six Guardias Marinas respectively, AGS Marina 438, 'Estado' dated 30 May 1752, enclosed in Antonio de Perea to Ensenada, Esteiro, 30 May 1752. Among those mentioned here who had begun their naval careers in Malta were Pedro Mesía de la Cerda and Andrés Reggio y Brachiforte.

[155] See AGS Marina 725, 'Propiedades de Vaxeles, 1733–1771'.

[156] See Scheybeler, 'A Study of Spanish Naval Policy', 161–198.

[157] AGS Marina 438, Rojas to Ensenada, *San Felipe*, 20 Ferrol 1753: 'inútil, por ser toda la más juventud criada en las rías, en el exercicio de la pesca, sin saver pisar navío, hazer travajo, ní suvir sobre una berga'.

[158] Newton, L.W., 'The Spanish Naval Officer Corps in the Eighteenth Century', *Revista de Historia de América* 103 (1987): 31–73, has already made a valuable contribution towards this.

[159] Fernández de Moratín, Nicolás., *Egloga a Velasco, y Gonzalez, famosos españoles* (Madrid: Imprenta Miguel Escrivano, [1763]): 'barata la Victoria'.

[160] See Archivo General de Indias (AGI) Santo Domingo 1579 for Real Transporte's trial, 1763–5, and Morón García, J.J., 'El Juicio por la Pérdida de La Habana en 1762', *Baluarte* 1 (1994): 19–48, for a general analysis of the trials resulting from the loss of Havana.

[161] AGS Marina 406, Real Transporte to Arriaga, *Tigre*, Havana, 6 March 1762.

[162] Recent works include Doe, H. and Harding, R., eds., *Naval Leadership and Management 1650–1750* (Woodbridge: The Boydell Press, 2012); Lambert, A., *Admirals* (London: Faber and Faber, 2008): and Mackay, R. and Duffy, M., eds., *Hawke and British Naval Leadership 1747–1805*(Woodbridge: The Boydell Press, 2009).

[163] Rodger N.A.M., 'Image and Reality in Eighteenth Century Naval Tactics', *The Mariner's Mirror* 89 (2003), 292. DOI: https://doi.org/10.1080/0025335 9.2003.10659294

[164] Two exceptions worth noting: Caron, F., *La Victoire volée: La bataille de la Chesapeake – 1781* (Paris: Service historique de la Marine, 1981), 289–307; and Villiers, P., 'La tentative franco-espagnole de débarquement en Angleterre en 1779,' in Villiers, P. and Pfister-Langanay, C., eds., *Le Transmanche et les liaisons maritimes XVIIIe–XXe siècle*, Revue du Nord, hors série 9 (1995), 13–28.

[165] Taillemite E., 'L'amiral d'Orvilliers et la marine de son temps,' *Études bourbonnaises* 264 (2ᵉ tr. 1993): 305–319. It's my duty to express my deep gratitude to M. le comte Henri de Chantemerle de Villette, descendant of the admiral d'Orvilliers, for allowing me to consult his familial archives. The admiral's military file is kept by the Archives Nationales (now AN), Marine, C¹ 167.

[166] About family links, see the genealogical studies written by general Henry d'Esclaibes in the *Mélanges généalogiques (Nord et Centre de la France)* (Paris: Peyronnet, 1965), chapter V, 57–71 and the *Mélanges généalogiques* 2ᵉ série (Paris, 1971), chapter XXVI, 242–257. The fief of Orvilliers (or Les Sacrots) was situated inside the parish of Agonges, near Bourbon-l'Archambault, in the province of Bourbonnais (nowadays the department de l'Allier) in central France.

[167] AN Marine B⁴ 118. Chaline, O., 'Les escadres d'évolution à la veille de la guerre d'Indépendance américaine,' in Chaline, O. Bonnichon, Ph. and Vergennes, Ch.–Ph. de, eds., *Les Marines de la guerre d'Indépendance américaine 1763–1783* (Paris: PUPS, 2012), 365–80.

[168] AN Marine B⁴ 118, f° 96–97, 9 September 1772.

[169] See the study about d'Orvilliers's flagship: Forrer, C., and Roussel, C.-Y., *La Bretagne, vaisseau de 100 canons, pour le roi et la république 1762–1796* (Spézet: Coop-Breiz, 2005).

[170] Cheyron du Pavillon, T. du, *Un maître de la tactique navale au XVIIIe siècle. Le chevalier du Pavillon (1730–1782)* (Paris: Guénégaud, 2010), 373–428.

[171] Lever, E., *Philippe-Egalité* (Paris: Fayard, 1996).

[172] AN Marine B⁴ 136.

[173] About Ushant, see Villiers, P., 'La stratégie de la marine française de l'arrivée de Sartine à la victoire de la Chesapeake,' in Acerra, M., Merino, J. and Meyer, J., eds., *Les Marines de guerre européennes XVIIᵉ-XVIIIᵉ siècles* (Paris: Presses Université Paris-Sorbonne, rééd. 1998), 211–247.

[174] Claude Forrer and Claude-Youenn Roussel concluded (*La Bretagne*, 163) that without further direct evidence about what happened on board the *Saint-Esprit* when the general's signal was seen, it remains impossible to settle.

[175] See AN Marine B⁴ 155.

[176] AN Marine, B⁴ 155, 1779. His instructions were published in extenso in Villiers, 'La stratégie,' 224–227.

[177] Dull, *The French Navy and American Independence*, 120–126. Two monographs about the landing attempt are Perugia, P. del, *La tentative d'invasion*

*de l'Angleterre de 1779* (Paris: Alcan-PUF, 1939) and Patterson, A.T., *The Other Armada: The Franco-Spanish Attempt to Invade Britain in 1779* (Manchester: Manchester University Press, 1960). Attacking the Isle of Wight was proposed by Vergennes when Floridablanca had refused a landing attempt in Ireland: Dull, J.R., *The French Navy and American Independence*, 138; Murphy, O.T., *Charles Gravier Comte de Vergennes. French Diplomacy in the Age of Revolution, 1719-1787* (Albany: State University of New York Press, 1982), 268; Coquelle, P., 'Les projets de descente en Angleterre,' *Revue d'histoire diplomatique* XV (1901): 433–452 and 591–624; XVI (1902): 134–157.

178  AN Marine B⁴ 155, 4 July 1779.

179  AN Marine B⁴ 155, 14 July 1779.

180  The Chevalier du Pavillon wrote to Sartine, 6 August 1779 (AN Marine B⁴ 155) in a less diplomatical tone: ' J'ai l'honneur de vous envoyer la dernière lettre de monsieur de Cordova par laquelle vous verrez qu'il est inutile de résister plus longtemps aux opinions très fausses mais germées depuis plus de 80 ans dans la tête de ce respectable officier. La crainte de finir par l'indisposer a dicté la réponse que je lui ai faite par ordre de mon général qui m'a dit avoir reçu une lettre de monsieur de Montmorin pour lui faire part de l'extrême délicatesse de monsieur de Cordova et des ménagements qu'elle exigeait.'

181  See the account made by Vergennes for the ambassador Montmorin in Madrid, Archives du Ministère des Affaires Etrangères, Espagne, t. 593. Quoted by Perugia, *La tentative d'invasion de l'Angleterre*, 76–77.

182  AN Marine B⁴ 155, 2 August 1779.

183  His last will, dated 8 August 1779, on board *La Bretagne*, was published by general (then colonel) Henry d'Esclaibes in his *Notes sur les familles Hugon de Givry et Guillouet d'Orvilliers* (n.p., 1958), 18–19.

184  See the letter of the Chevalier du Pavillon to Sartine, 15 September 1779, Marine B⁴ 154.

185  Scipion de Castries in *Souvenirs maritimes*, ed. Colbert-Turgis, G. de (Paris: Mercure de France, 1997, 2ⁿᵈ edition. 2005), 243.

186  Voltaire, referring to this event, writes in *Candide*: 'In this country, it seems good to kill from time to time an admiral to encourage the others.'

187  Griffith, P., *The Art of War of Revolutionary France, 1789–1802* (London: Greenhill Books, 1998), 24.

188  Gat, A., *A History of Military Thought from the Enlightenment to the Cold War* (Oxford: Oxford University Press, 2001), 97–137.

189  Craig, G.A., 'Delbrück: The Military Historian,' in *Makers of Modern Strategy: Military Thought from Machiavelli to the Nuclear Age*, ed. Peter Paret (Princeton: Princeton University Press, 1986), 341–343.

190  Goerlitz, W., *History of the German General Staff* (Boulder: Westview Press, 1985), 85–99; Bucholz, A., *Moltke and the German Wars, 1864–1871* (Basingstoke: Palgrave Macmillan, 2001).

191 Levêque, P., *Histoire de la Marine du Consulat et de l'Empire*, 2 vols., (Paris: Libraire Historique Tesseidre, 2014).

192 Knight, R., *Britain Against Napoleon: The Organization of Victory, 1793–1815* (London: Allen Lane, 2013).

193 Duffy, C., *The Fortress in the Age of Vauban and Frederick the Great, 1660–1789: Siege Warfare Volume II* (London: Routledge and Kegan Paul, 1985), 291–295.

194 Lambert, A., 'William, Lord Hotham, 1736–1813,' in *British Admirals of the Napoleonic Wars: The Contemporaries of Nelson*, Le Fevre, P. and Harding, R., eds. (London: Chatham Publishing, 2005), 23–43; Tracy, Nicholas, 'Sir Robert Calder, 1745–1810,' in Le Fevre and Harding, *British Admirals*, 197–217.

195 De la Graviére, J., *Souvenir d'un amiral* (Paris, 1860–72).

196 Several sources testify to the rapid collapse of the squadron's morale. See especially, Des Touches G., 'Souvenirs d'un marin de la République,' *Revue des Deux Mondes* 28 (juillet-août 1905).

197 Villeneuve was nevertheless successful in the reconquest of the Diamant, a strong position on the south coast of Martinique.

198 Newnham Collingwood, G.L., *Correspondence and Memoirs of Vice Admiral Lord Collingwood* (London, 1828).

199 Ferrari Billoch, F., *Barceló* (Madrid-Barcelona, 1942); Janer Mansilla, G., *El general Barceló* (Palma de Mallorca, 1984); Rodríguez González, A.R., *Barceló* (Barcelona, 1990); and Codina Bonet, R., *D. Antonio Barceló, almirante de la Real Armada y corsario del Rey* (Madrid: Ministerio de Defensa, Centro de Publicaciones, 2010). See also the magnificent articles of J. Llabrés Bernal, in numerous issues of *Revista General de Marina*.

200 Archivo General de Marina (hereafter AGM), 'D. Álvaro de Bazán,' Expedientes Personales, Cuerpo General, Antonio Barceló i Pont de la Terra.

201 Rodríguez González, *Barceló*, 32.

202 AGM, 'D. Álvaro de Bazán,' Expedientes Personales, Cuerpo General, José Mazarredo Salazar y Cortázar.

203 Archivo Municipal de Palma de Mallorca (hereafter AMPM), Fondo Barceló, caja 13.1, quoted in Codina Bonet, *D. Antonio Barceló*, 114.

204 Llabrés Bernal, J., 'Un combate naval infortunado en 1765,' *Apuntes para la historia marítima de Ibiza* (Palma de Mallorca, 1958), 28–43.

205 AMPM, Fondo Barceló, caja 16, quoted in Codina Bonet, *D. Antonio Barcelo*, 241–243.

206 AGM, Arsenales, Mahón, I.

207 AGM, 'D. Álvaro de Bazán,' *Libros de Registro de Arsenales, Cartagena*, acerca de las cantidades adelantadas por Barceló para que no se paralizasen las obras en los arsenales, de otros rasgos de desprendimiento, en Codina Bonet, *D. Antonio Barceló*, 269–271.

208 White, C., *Nelson, the Admiral* (Stroud: The History Press, 2005).

209 Lambert, *Admirals: The Naval Commanders who Made Britain Great* (London, 2008), especially 'Pursuit and Professionalism. Samuel Hood (1724–1816) and John Jervis (1735–1823),' 157–200.

210 The modern bibliography on leadership is huge. See, for instance, Heifetez, R.A., *Liderazgo sin respuestas fáciles. Propuestas para un nuevo diálogo social en tiempos difíciles* (Barcelona, 1997); Heifetez, R.A. and Linsky, M., *Leadership on the Line. Staying Alive through the Dangers of Leading* (Boston, 2002); Boyatzis, R. and Mckee, A., *Liderazgo emocional* (Barcelona, 2006); and Heider, J., *El Tao de los líderes: El Tao Te-Ching de Lao Tse adaptado a la nueva era* (Barcelona, 2007). See also the humanist view of a war leader in Sun-Tzu and Lawson, J., *El Arte de la Guerra para ejecutivos y directivos*, 6th edition (Barcelona, 2006).

211 Barbudo Duarte, E., *Don José de Mazarredo, Teniente General de la Real Armada* (Madrid, 1945); Bernaola Martín, I., 'Guerra naval y diplomacia: José de Mazarredo, un marino ilustrado embajador en París,' *Revista de Historia Naval* 131: 9–38 (Madrid, 2015); Guimerá, A., 'Trafalgar y la marinería Española,' in Guimerá, A. and Peralta, V., eds., *El equilibrio de los imperios. De Utrecht a Trafalgar* (Madrid, 2005), vol. 2, 821–838; Guimerá Ravina, A. and García Fernández, N., 'Un consenso estratégico: Las Ordenanzas Navales de 1793,' *Anuario de Estudios Atlánticos* 54-II (2008): 43–81; Rodríguez González, A.R., 'Las innovaciones artilleras y tácticas españolas en la campaña de Trafalgar,' in *XXXI Congreso Internacional de Historia Militar (Madrid, 21–27 Agosto 2005)* (Madrid, 2006), 539–552.

212 Morriss, Roger, 'St Vincent and Reform,' *The Mariner's Mirror* 69:3 (1983): 269–290.

213 Crimmin, P.K., 'John Jervis, Earl of St Vincent', in Le Freve, P. and Harding, R., eds., *Precursors of Nelson. British Admirals of the Eighteenth Century* (London: Chatham, 2000), 324–355; Crimmin, P.K., 'Jervis, John, Earl of St Vincent (1735–1823), Naval Officer,' in *Oxford Dictionary of National Biography* (Oxford, accessed January 2006), electronic edition; Davidson, J.D., *Admiral Lord St Vincent, Saint or Tyrant? The Life of Sir John Jervis, Nelson's Patron* (Barnsley, 2006); Horsfield, J., *The Art of Leadership in War: The Royal Navy from the Age of Nelson to the End of World War II* (Westport, Conn., 1980); Moriconi, E. and Wilkinson, C., 'Sir John Jervis: The Man for the Occasion,' in Howarth, S., ed., *Battle of Cape St Vincent. 200 Years. The Bicentennial International Naval Conference. Portsmouth-England, 15 February 1997* (Shelton, 1998), 8–21; Palmer, M.A.J., 'Sir John's Victory: The Battle of Cape St Vincent Reconsidered,' *The Mariner's Mirror* 77, 31-46 (1991); Mackay, R.F., 'Lord St Vincent's Early Years (1735–55),' *The Mariner's Mirror* 76, 51-65 (1996); and White, C., *The Battle of Cape St Vincent. 14 February 1797* (Shelton, 1997).

214 López-Cordón, M.V. 'Entre Francia e Inglaterra. Intereses estratégicos y acuerdos políticos como antecedentes de Trafalgar,' in Guimerá, A.,

Ramos, A. and Butrón, A., eds., *Trafalgar y el mundo atlántico* (Madrid, 2004), 19–60; and Seco Serrano, C., 'La política exterior de Carlos IV', in *Historia de España fundada por Ramón Menéndez Pidal y dirigida por José María Jover Zamora. Tomo XXXI. La época de la Ilustración. Volumen 2. Las Indias y la política exterior* (Madrid, 1988), 449–732.

[215] Marqués de Santa Cruz de Marcenado, *Reflexiones Militares* [1742] (Madrid, 1984), chapters I, II and XIII; especially Díez Alegría, M., 'La milicia en el siglo de las Luces', 15–31 and García Escudero, J.M., 'Sobre el Derecho de la Guerra', 80–106.

[216] Von Clausewitz, K., *De la guerra* (Barcelona, 1984); Heuser, B., *Reading Clausewitz* (London: Pimlico, 2002); Strachan, H., *Clausewitz's 'On War'* (Atlantic Monthly Press, 2006); Bell, D.A., *La primera guerra total. La Europa de Napoléon y el nacimiento de la guerra moderna* (Madrid, 2007); and Broers, M., 'The Concept of "Total War" in the Revolutionary–Napoleonic Period', *War in History* 15 (July 2008): 247–268. DOI: https://doi.org/10.1177/0968344508091323

[217] Guimerá, A., 'Métodos de liderazgo naval', in *El mar en los siglos modernos*, eds., García-Hurtado, M.R., González-Lopo, D L. and Martínez-Rodríguez, eds. (Santiago de Compostela: Xunta de Galicia, 2009), vol. 2, 221–233.

[218] Table VII: Exports from Cádiz to Spanish America, 1796–1811; Guimerá, A., 'Commerce and Shipping in Spain during the Napoleonic Wars', in Howarth, S., ed., *Battle of Cape St Vincent 200 Years* (Shelton, 1998), 22–37.

[219] For the Spanish gunboats, see Rodriguez González, A.R., 'Admiral Antonio Barceló, 1716–97: A Self-Made Naval Leader', in this volume, 114–5.

[220] The Spanish sources are 'Correspondencia, Bloqueo de Cádiz, 1797–1799', in *Archivo del Museo Naval*, Madrid (AMN), Colección Mazarredo, legajos 2385–2386; and 'Extracto de los Diarios de la Mayoría General de la Armada del Océano, sobre lo ocurrido en la misma desde 1797 a 1802, formado por el Mayor General Escaño para su gobierno', 1 June 1802, in Quadrado y De-Roo, F.P. *Elogio histórico del Excelentísimo Señor Don Antonio de Escaño, Teniente General de Marina... por Don..... ministro plenipotenciario, etc. etc.* (Madrid, 1852), 85–130, appendix 8 (hereafter Quadrado).

[221] Nelson to Dixon Hoste, 25 Nov. 1796: 'I should be sorry to have a Peace before we make the Dons pay for meddling.'; Nelson to William Suckling, 29 Nov. 1796: 'I hope yet to assist him in beating the Dons, which we shall do if we have a proper force to seek them out.'; Nelson to the Reverend Edmund Nelson, 13 Jan. 1797: 'its very probable you will soon hear of another Action, for I am very much inclined to make the Dons repent of this war.' All letters quoted are from Nicolas, N.H., *The Dispatches and Letters of Vice Admiral Lord Viscount Nelson with notes by... The Second Volume, 1797 to 1797* (London: Chatham, 1997) [1845] Unless otherwise stated, quotations from Nelson's correspondence are from Nicolas.

222    The frigate *La Sabina*, Jacobo Stuart commander, 40 guns and 286 men, was captured on Cartagena road, after heavy fighting. The Spanish casualties were 164. Nelson to Edmund Nelson, 1 Jan. 1797: 'My late prisoner, a descendant from the Duke of Berwick, son of James II, was my brave opponent; for which I have returned him his sword, and sent him in a Flag of truce to Spain. I felt it consonant to the dignity of my Country, and I always act as I feel right, without regard to custom; he was reputed the best Officer in Spain, and his men were worthy of such a Commander; he was the only surviving Officer'; Nelson to Edmund Nelson, 13 Jan 1797. In the famous action of 3 July in Cádiz, the barge commanded by Tyrason had 30 men, all of whom were killed or wounded; Nelson to Jervis, 4 July 1797: 'I must also beg to be permitted to express my admiration of Don Miguel Tyrason, the Commander of the Gun-boats. In his Barge, he laid my Boat alongside, and his resistance was such as did honour to a brave Officer.'

223    Jervis to Nelson, 6 May 1797: '...for it appears by the letter [Rear-Admiral Parker] that Moreno covered Cordova in the evening; and the Rear-Admiral shall go to [la Isla de] Leon, and prove the letter, if Moreno requires it; this is due to a brave man under persecution.': Nelson to Moreno, 8 June 1797, sending him Jervis's praise of the good performance of Moreno's flagship, *Príncipe de Asturias*, during the battle; Nelson to Jervis, 9 June 1797.

224    *Archivo Histórico Nacional*, Estado, leg. 4039, núm. 1, Mazarredo to Antonio Valdés, 27 Aug. 1795. In 1797 Mazarredo accepted the fleet command for various reasons. One was 'to challenge the English navy and compensate its power and ambition'; Mazarredo to José de Lángara, 15 March 1797, quoted in Barbudo Duarte, *Don José de Mazarredo*, 169.

225    On 25 May 1797, the British fleet captured a merchant brig, using Spanish colours (Quadrado, 89). This ruse was common to all European naval powers: Willis, S., *Fighting at Sea in the Eighteenth Century. The Art of Sailing Warfare* (Woodbridge: Boydell and Brewer, 2008), 23–26.

226    AMN, legajo 2385, Saumarez to Mazarredo, 9 May 1797; Mazarredo to Saumarez, 12 May 1797

227    Guimerá, A., "From Cádiz to Tenerife: The Account of Captain Ralph W. Miller," *The Trafalgar Chronicle* 23 (2013): 45–72.

228    Nelson to Jervis, 7 July 1797.

229    Mazarredo to Obispo de Cádiz, 29 May 1797, quoted in Barbudo Duarte, *Don José de Mazarredo*, 176–178.

230    Nelson to Miguel Gastón, 21 Dec. 1796: 'It becomes great Nations to act with generosity to each other, and to soften the horrors of war.'; Nelson to Gastón, 29 Dec. 1796: 'I shall not urge the humanity attending the frequent Exchange of unfortunate people.'

231    AMN, 2385, Mazarredo to Jervis, 18 April 1797.

[232] AMN, 2385, Mazarredo to Jervis, 18 April 1797; Jervis to Cádiz foreign consuls, 19 April 1797; Cádiz foreign consuls to Mazarredo, 21 April 1797; Mazarredo to Cádiz foreign consuls, 22 April 1797.

[233] AMN, 2385, Jervis to Mazarredo, 19 April 1797; Saumarez to Mazarredo, 12 Aug. 1797; Mazarredo to Saumarez, 13 Aug. 1797; Jervis to Mazarredo, 14 Aug. 1797; AMN, 2386, Mazarredo to Lángara, 21 Sept. 1798; Mazarredo to Jervis, 2 May 1798.

[234] AMN, 2386, Mazarredo to Lángara, 8 May and 21 Sept. 1798.

[235] AMN, 2386, Mazarredo to Lángara, 21 Sept. 1798.

[236] AMN, 2385, Mazarredo to Jervis, 18 April 1797.

[237] Nelson to Mazarredo, 30 June 1797: '… numbers of the Spanish fishing-boats are found at such a distance from the land as plainly to evince that they have something farther in view that catching fish; and, therefore, that orders are given, that no Fishing-vessel be in future permitted to go farther from the shore than their usual fishing-ground; which, we understand, is in about thirty five fathoms water… For the information of the fishermen, that their boats will be sunk…'

[238] AMN, 2385, Saumarez to Mazarredo, 12 Aug. and 13 Aug. 1797.

[239] Jervis to Mazarredo, 14 Aug. 1797, returned him a fishing boat with oysters: 'I have a high respect for your Excellency's judgment and penetration'.; Mazarredo to Jervis, 15 Aug. 1797, praised the humanity and the honorable expressions of Jervis: 'I would be happy to show my respectful consideration to Your Excellence in every chance.'

[240] AMN, 2385, Saumarez to Mazarredo, 9 May 1797.

[241] AMN, 2386, Mazarredo to Lángara, 21 Sept 1798.

[242] AMN, 2392, Mazarredo to Jervis, 5 July 1798. Jervis's answer was the following: 'The Count of St Vincent is highly pleased with the magnificent present of Don Joseph de Mazarredo, and the fineness of His Excellence for introducing the name of Lady St Vincent in his note, which is making that more acceptable. *Ville de Paris*, off Cádiz, 5 July 1798.'

[243] AMN, 2385, Nelson to Mazarredo, 30 May 1797; Mazarredo to Nelson, 1 June 1797.

[244] AMN, 2385, Saumarez to Mazarredo, 13 June 1797; Mazarredo to Saumarez, 14 June 1797.

[245] Jervis to Mazarredo, 24 Aug. 1797; *Revista de Historia Naval*, 74 (2002), 103–106.

[246] Lambert, *Admirals*, 197–98.

[247] Santovenia, E., *Bolívar y las Antillas hispanas* (Madrid: Espasa-Calpe, 1935), 124–26.

[248] Restrepo Tirado, E. et al, ed., *Archivo Santander* (Bogotá: Academia de la Historia/Aguila Negra Editorial, 1913–32), vol. 13, 191–92.

[249] Archivo General de Indias, Seville, Estado, 17, N130, War Minister to State Minister, 21 July 1825; Archivo General de Marina, Álvaro de Bazán, El

Viso del Marqués, Ciudad Real (AGMAB), Expediciones 75, State Minister to Navy Minister, 16 Aug. 1825.

250  Ibid., Salazar to State Minister, minute, 20 Aug. 1825.

251  *Actas del Consejo de Ministros* (Madrid: Ministerio de la Presidencia, 1989–1996), vol. 1, 429 (21 Dec. 1825 session).

252  Mendoza, D., 'Estudios de historia diplomática. Relaciones entre Colombia y México,' *Boletín de Historia y Antigüedades* 11 (1904): 341–44.

253  AGMAB, Expediciones 75, No. 10, Memorandum by Miguel Gastón, 15 Mar. 1825.

254  Ibid., Oficiales 620, s.v. Luis María de Salazar.

255  Ibid., Expediciones 78, Laborde to Salazar, confidential, 8 Nov. 1828.

256  Ibid., Expediciones 77, Finance Minister to Salazar, 21 Feb. 1826; Director General de la Armada to Salazar, 1 Mar. 1827; Salazar to Laborde, 28 Mar. 1827.

257  *Actas del Consejo de Ministros*, vol. 1, 222 (12 May 1825 session), Archivo Histórico Nacional, Madrid (AHN); Estado 6367/75/2, Vives to State Minister, private, 9 Aug. 1824; AGMAB, Expediciones 76, War Minister to Salazar, 24 Apr. 1825.

258  *Estado General de la Armada*, 1828, 30–32.

259  AGMAB, Expediciones 75, No. 16, Minute of 25 Mar. 1825 meeting between the Captain General, the naval commander and the Intendant.

260  Luis María de Salazar, *Manifiesto del Conde de Salazar, a cuenta de la Exposición leida a las Córtes generales del Reino por el Excelentísimo señor Secretario de Estado y del Despacho de Marina en los dias 11 y 13 de agosto de 1834* (Madrid: Imprenta de D. Miguel de Burgos, 1834), 13.

261  Ibid., 17–18.

262  *Actas del Consejo de Ministros*, vol. 1, 170 (26 Mar. 1825 session). Luís López Ballesteros (Finance Minister), 'Memoria ministerial sobre el estado de la Real Hacienda de España en los años de 1822, 1824 y 1825,' in Canga Argüelles, José, ed., *Diccionario de Hacienda con aplicación a España* (Madrid: Imprenta de D. Marcelino Calero y Portocarrero, 1834), vol. 2, 724–725.

263  AGMAB, Consignaciones 7414, Salazar to Cádiz Intendant, minute, 26 July 1825; Salazar to Navy Paymaster, 26 July 1825.

264  Ibid., Navy Intendant to Salazar, 30 Jan. 1826.

265  Ibid., Expediciones 75, Laborde to Salazar, confidential, 1 Apr. 1826.

266  Ibid., Deputy Commander of *Apostadero de la Habana* to Navy Minister, 22 May 1825, appended confidential intelligence report.

267  AHN, Estado 6369–1, Vives to State Minister, 22 and 30 Sep. 1826; AGMAB, Expediciones 77, Vives to War Minister, 30 Sep. 1826.

268  For the American view, see Flaccus, Elmer W., 'Commodore David Porter and the Mexican Navy,' *The Hispanic American Historical Review* 34 (1954): 365–73. For the Spanish view, see Delgado, Jaime, *España y México en el*

*siglo XIX* (Madrid: Consejo Superior de Investigaciones Científicas, 1950), vol. 1, 309–36.

269  Mario Lavalle Argudín, ed., *Memorias de Marina, buques de la Armada de México, acaecimientos notables, 1821–1991* (México: Secretaría de Marina, 1991–2), vol. 1, 47, 49–50.

270  Livermore, H.V., *A New History of Portugal* (Cambridge: Cambridge University Press, 1966), 268–79.

271  See Macaulay, N., *Dom Pedro; 1798–1834: The Struggle for Liberty in Brazil and Portugal* (Durham NC.: Duke University Press, 1986), 254–305, for Pedro's role in the war.

272  Schroeder, P.W., *The Transformation of European Politics, 1763–1848* (Oxford: Oxford University Press, 1994), 720–1; Bourne, K., *Palmerston: The Early Years, 1784–1841* (London: The Free Press, 1982), 387–96; Williams, J.B., *British Commercial Policy and Trade Expansion, 1750–1850* (Oxford: Oxford University Press, 1972), 152–55.

273  The National Archives (hereafter TNA), FO 63/398, Palmerston to Russell, 5 July 1833, no. 2; ADM 1/4252, Foreign Office to Admiralty, 5 July 1833; FO 63/399, Russell to Palmerston, 16 July 1833, no. 59: by this time news had reached Russell of Napier's victory.

274  Bollaert, W., *The Wars of Succession of Portugal and Spain. Vol. 1 Portugal* (London: Edward Stanford, 1870), 251. Bollaert was an officer in the garrison of Oporto, and met Napier more than once. He also consulted the memoirs and memories of his fellow officers before compiling his own account.

275  TNA, ADM 1/2239, Napier to Sir James Graham, 26 Aug. 1832: no. 23, requesting a Greenwich Out Pension.

276  British Library (hereafter BL), Napier MSS, BL Add. 40,018 f.192–4, Palmella to Napier, 29 Aug. and 4 Sept. 1832: quote from 4 Sept. 1832.

277  Lima to Napier, 1 Feb. 1833; Napier, C., *An Account of the War in Portugal between Don Pedro and Don Miguel* (London, 1836), 2 vols; vol. 1, 321–22, original in National Maritime Museum (hereafter NMM), Napier Papers, NAP/11 f. 6; Palmella to Napier, 1 Feb. 1833, NAP/14, Napier to wife, 5 Feb. 1833; Elers-Napier, C., *Admiral Sir Charles Napier, KCB: From Personal Recollections, Letters and Official Documents*, 2 vols.(London: Hurst and Blackett, 1862), vol. 1, 169.

278  Napier to Lima, undated, replying to the offer of 1 Feb. 1833: Napier, *An Account of the War*, 326–8 (NAP/11 f.7).

279  Graham, MS, MS 50, Graham to Dundas, 30 Nov. 1833.

280  Torrens, W. Mc., *Life and Times of Sir James Graham* (London, 1863), 78.

281  TNA, ADM1/3478, Graham, minute 12 Sept. 1832, granting the Pension. The Napier MSS contains several such letters.

282  Elers-Napier, *Admiral Sir Charles Napier*, vol. 1, 173–4, 14 Sept. 1833.

283  Ibid., 171, 8 April 1833.

284  NMM, NAP/16, Sartorius to Napier, 14 March 1833.

285  NMM, NAP/16, Sartorius to Napier, 24 April 1833.

286  Elers-Napier, *Admiral Sir Charles Napier, KCB*, 176–7.

287  Bollaert, W., *The Wars of Succession of Portugal and Spain*, footnote, 256.

288  Napier's temper deserves an essay of its own. He clearly deployed it pretty much to order, although there were occasions when his anger was genuine. It seems unlikely that a man who remained so cool under fire was incapable of governing his rage.

289  Elers-Napier, *Admiral Sir Charles Napier, KCB*, 186; Pedro to Napier, 11 June 1833.

290  Bollaert, *The Wars of Succession of Portugal and Spain*, 255.

291  TNA, ADM 1/360, Admiral Parker to Admiralty 14, rec'd 27 June 1833, no. 183.

292  TNA, FO63/399, Russell to Palmerston, 17 June 1833, no. 54.

293  Buckland, C.S.B., 'Richard Belgrave Hoppner', *English Historical Review* (1924): 373–85.

294  Bindoff, S.T., Smith, E.F.M. and Webster, C.K., eds., *British Diplomatic Representatives, 1789–1852* (London: Camden Society, 1934), 94.

295  Webster, C.K., *The Foreign Policy of Palmerston* (London: Bell and Sons, 1951), vol. 1., 240–1.

296  Hoppner–Napier, R.B., 10 May 1833: 40.019 f.9–17. This report is endorsed 'I do not think you have any right to make this report public, Papa did not'. The comment was written by Fanny Napier-Jodrell to her step-brother Edward Elers-Napier, who was then compiling the two-volume biography.

297  Phillimore's second volume is an exhaustive record of Parker's service at Lisbon, a case study in the conduct of armed diplomacy.

298  Phillimore, Sir A., *The Life of Admiral Sir William Parker* (London: 1880), vol. 2, 209–10.

299  Phillimore, *The Life of Admiral Sir William Parker*, 223, Parker to Napier, 17 June 1833.

300  Phillimore, *The Life of Admiral Sir William Parker*, 237, Parker to Graham, 3 July 1833. For the Portuguese telegraph system, see Wilson, G., *The Old Telegraphs* (London: Philimore, 1976), 183–4.

301  TNA, FO 63/399, Russell to Palmerston, 25 June 1833, no. 55.

302  Elers-Napier, *Admiral Sir Charles Napier, KCB*, 187–8, Napier to wife, 15 June 1833.

303  BL, BL Add. 40.019, ff.54–60, Napier to Dundas, 19/20 June 1833. See also letters of 10 June, 27 June and 6 July 1833.

304  BL, BL Add. 40.019, f. 79, details from Napier to Dundas, 6 July 1833.

305  Hired from the City of Dublin Steam Packet Company.

306  This squadron was equivalent to a single British battleship in manpower, but far less impressive in firepower.

307  Phillimore, *The Life of Admiral Sir William Parker*, 212, Parker to Graham, 5 June 1833.

[308] Phillimore, *The Life of Admiral Sir William Parker*, 228–9, Parker to Napier, 23 June 1833.

[309] TNA, FO 63/405, Hoppner to Sir George Shee (Parliamentary Under Secretary at the FO), 22 June 1833. no. 116: FO 63/399, Russell to Palmerston, 25 June 1833, no. 55.

[310] TNA, FO 63/399, Russell to Palmerston, 3 July 1833, no. 56.

[311] Phillimore, *The Life of Admiral Sir William Parker*, 232–233, Napier to Parker, 30 June 1833.

[312] BL, BL Add. 40.019, f. 79, details from Napier to Dundas, 6 July 1833.

[313] Phillimore, *The Life of Admiral Sir William Parker*, 237–9, Parker to Graham, 3 July 1833.

[314] TNA, FO 63/399, Russell to Palmerston, 3 July 1833, no. 56.

[315] TNA, FO 63/405, Hoppner to Shee, 25 June 1833, no. 117.

[316] TNA, FO 63/405, Hoppner to Shee, 9 July 1833, no. 125.

[317] Napier, C., *Civil War*, vol. 1, 195.

[318] For Napier's own account, which is persuasive, and accords with his contemporary writings, see Napier, *An Account of the War in Portugal*, vol. 1 191–206 (see note 277). Bollaert provides a very interesting eyewitness account written by one of *Donna Maria*'s petty officers on pages 295–301.

[319] Bollaert, *The Wars of Succession of Portugal and Spain*, 291–2, Napier, 6 May 1833, Dispatch.

[320] Elers-Napier, *Admiral Sir Charles Napier, KCB*, 215–6, Napier to wife, 10 July 1833.

[321] Phillimore, *The Life of Admiral Sir William Parker*, 243–5, Napier to Parker, 7 and 10 July 1833.

[322] Napier, *Civil War.*, vol. 1, 363, Napier 'List of Killed and Wounded'.

[323] TNA, FO 63/399, Russell to Palmerston, 15 July 1833, no. 58.

[324] TNA, ADM 1/360, Parker to Admiralty, 15 July, rec. 31 July 1833.

[325] BL, BL Add. 40.019, f.84, Napier to Dundas, 10 July 1833.

[326] TNA, ADM 1/3480, Admiralty minute, 10 July 1833.

[327] Graham MS MS 57, Palmerston to Graham, 12 July 1833.

[328] Graham MS MS 57, Palmerston to Grey, 14 July 1833.

[329] Bourne, *Palmerston: The Early Years*, 397, Palmerston to Frederick Lamb, 16 July 1833.

[330] Broadlands MSS, GC/GR 39, Graham to Palmerston, 14 July 1833, endorsed 'Sunday Night'.

[331] TNA, FO 63/399, Russell to Palmerston, 25 July 1833, no. 61; ADM 1/360, Parker to Admiralty, 25 July 1833, rec. 3 Aug. 1833, no. 252.

[332] TNA, FO 63/398, Palmerston to Russell, 7 Aug. 1833, endorsed by William IV, no. 9.

[333] TNA, FO 63/399, Russell to Palmerston, 16 Aug. 1833, no. 67; Bourne, *Palmerston: The Early Years*, 397–8.

[334] Schroeder, *The Transformation of European Politics*, 722–3.

335   Broadlands, GC/GR 42, Graham to Palmerston: 5 Aug. 1833.

336   Graham, MS 28, Graham to Grey, 2 Aug. 1833.

337   Broadlands, GC/GR 44, Graham to Palmerston, 1 Sept. 1833.

338   Shaw, T.G., *Wine and the Wine Cellar* (London: 1863) cited in Bollaert, *The Wars of Succession*, 249.

339   Sir C. Shaw. Letter of December 1865 cited in Bollaert, *The Wars of Succession*, 256.

340   A narrative of this expansion and consolidation, which is still valuable, can be found in Parry, J.H., *The Age of Reconnaissance: Discovery, Exploration and Settlement, 1450–1650* (London: Weidenfeld and Nicholson, 1963); Parry, J.H., *Trade and Dominion: European Overseas Empires in the Eighteenth Century* (London: Weidenfeld and Nicholson, 1971). For the unravelling of this historical age, which commenced with the 'European Civil War' of 1914–18, see Panikkar, K.M., *Asia and Western Dominance: A Survey of the Vasco Da Gama Epoch of Asian History, 1498–1945* (London: Allen and Unwin, 1953), particularly 259–371. For a recent study of this continuing process, see Yoshihara, T. and Holmes, James R., *Red Star over the Pacific: China's Rise and the Challenge to U.S. Maritime Strategy* (Annapolis: Naval Institute Press, 2013).

341   For a study that shows how English naval commanders grew into more autonomous commanding roles in the Mediterranean, see Hornstein, S.R., *The Restoration Navy and English Foreign Trade, 1674–1688: A Study in the Peacetime Use of Sea Power* (Aldershot: Scholar Press, 1991).

342   Talbot, John E., *The Pen and Ink Sailor: Charles Middleton and the King's Navy, 1778–1813* (London: Frank Cass, 1998).

343   Nicholas Rodger identifies the beginnings of the recovery of centralised control of the officer corps as early as 1794, occurring contemporaneously with the breakdown of other traditional power-trust relationships within the British bureaucratic system. However, the full impact of this process would not be realised until the exigencies of the war were finally over in 1815. See, Rodger, N.A.M., 'The Inner Life of the Navy, 1750–1800: Change or Decay?' in *Guerres et Paix*, ed. by Anon. (Vincennes: Service Historique de la Marine, 1987), 171–79; Rodger, N.A.M., 'Officers, Gentlemen and Their Education, 1793–1860,' in *Les Empires en Guerre et Paix, 1793–1860*, ed. Freeman, E. (Vincennes: Service Historique de la Marine, 1990), 139–54. For the broader picture of reform and centralisation, see the works of Roger Morriss, especially, *Naval Power and British Culture, 1760–1850: Public Trust and Government Ideology* (Aldershot: Ashgate, 2004).

344   Napier was not alone in serving in foreign fleets. The navies raised during the campaigns for independence in South America and which served those new states in regional conflicts were manned and officered by significant numbers of British seamen. See Vale, Brian, *A War Betwixt Englishmen:*

*Brazil against Argentina on the River Plate, 1825–1830* (London: I.B. Tauris, 2000).

345  Griffiths, P., *The Art of War in Revolutionary France, 1789–1802* (London: Greenhill Books, 1998); Rotenberg, G.E., *The Art of War in the Age of Napoleon* (Staplehurst: Spellmount, 1997); Chandler, David, *The Campaigns of Napoleon* (London: Weidenfeld and Nicholson, 1990), especially 133–201.

346  Gat, Azar, *A History of Military Thought from the Enlightenment to the Cold War* (Oxford: Oxford University Press, 2001), 170–265.

347  Bucholz, A., *Moltke and the German Wars, 1864–1871* (Basingstoke: Palgrave Macmillan, 2001).

348  Fowler, William M., *Rebels Under Sail: The American Navy During the Revolution* (New York: Charles Scribener's, 1976).

349  Symonds, C.L., *Navalists and Antinavalists: The Naval Policy Debate in the United States, 1785–1827* (Newark: University of Delaware Press, 1980), 27.

350  Hagan, Kenneth J., *This People's Navy: The Making of American Sea Power* (New York: Free Press, 1991), 21–90.

351  Bradford, James C., ed., *Command under Sail: Makers of the American Naval Tradition, 1775–1850* (Annapolis: Naval Institute Press, 1985); McKee, Christopher, *A Gentlemanly and Honorable Profession: The Creation of the US Naval Officer Corps, 1794–1815* (Annapolis: Naval Institute Press, 1991).

352  Morriss, Roger, *Science, Utility and Maritime Power: Samuel Bentham in Russia, 1779–91* (Abingdon: Ashgate, 2015); Kipp, Jacob W., 'The Russian Navy and the Problem of Technology Transfer: Technological Backwardness and Military-Industrial Development, 1853–1876,' in *Russia's Great Reform, 1855–1881*, ed. Eklol, B., Bushnell, J. and Zakharova, L. (Bloomington: Indiana University Press, 1994): 115–38; Morda Evans, R.J., 'Recruitment of British Personnel for the Russian Service 1734–1738,' *The Mariner's Mirror* 47:2 (1961): 126–37; Anderson, M.S., 'Great Britain and the Growth of the Russian Navy in the Eighteenth Century,' *The Mariner's Mirror* 42:2 (1956): 132–46: Anderson, M.S., 'Great Britain and the Russian Fleet, 1769–1770,' *Slavonic and East European Studies Review*, December (1952): 148–64; Clendenning, Philip H., 'Admiral Sir Charles Knowles and Russia, 1771–1774,' *The Mariner's Mirror* 61:1 (1975): 39–49.

353  Zorlu, Tuncay, *Innovation and Empire in Turkey: Sultan Selim III and the Modernisation of the Ottoman Navy* (London: I.B. Tauris, 2011).

# Index